∞

Classic Catholic Meditations

Bede Jarrett, O.P.

Classic Catholic Meditations
To Enrich Your Faith and Help You Pray

SOPHIA INSTITUTE PRESS®
Manchester, New Hampshire

Sophia Institute Press®
Box 5284, Manchester, NH 03108
1-800-888-9344
www.sophiainstitute.com

Nihil obstat: Hugh Pope, O.P., S.T.M., D.S.
Wulstan McCuskern, O.P.
Imprimatur: Humbert Everest, O.P., S.T.B.
Provincial of English Dominicans
Nihil obstat: F. Thomas Bergh, O.S.B.
Imprimatur: Petrus Epus Southwarc
May 5, 1915

Library of Congress Cataloging-in-Publication Data

Jarrett, Bede, 1881-1934.
    [Meditations for layfolk]
    Classic Catholic meditations : to enrich your faith and help you pray / Bede Jarrett.
        p. cm.
    1. Meditations. I. Title.
BX2182.3 .J37 2004
242 — dc22   2003024729

∞

Contents

Part 1: The Holy Trinity

Part 2: The Blessed Mother

Part 3: The unity of God's creatures

Part 4: Human life and its reward

Part 5: The Christian life

Part 6: The ages of man

Part 7: Dealing with others

Part 8: Faith

Part 9: The Church

Part 10: Prayer

Part 11: Studying your Faith

Part 12: Self-discipline

Part 13: Forming yourself

Part 14: The sacraments

Part 15: Daily virtues

∞

∽

Preface

For a great many of the laity, Catholic life consists simply in the Sunday Mass, the occasional sacraments, and daily prayers; and this narrow practice they would defend as though it were all that they were, in virtue of their state, called upon to show. Now, it is surely to be regretted that the whole treasury of the Church, which is most needed just by those whose busy lives are crammed with material interests, should be left to the hands of so small a proportion of her children. Is it any wonder that prayers become listless and uninteresting, that Mass itself develops into routine, that the sacraments become badges of respectability, or, at the most, professions of faith? The real inner life, which Christ came to endow with fuller life, shrivels up. The very idea of loving God seems to many of our generation an ideal too lofty for serious attempt.

Now, surely one great remedy for this is the use of meditation. To confront ourselves every morning with some deep truth of revelation is to realize our dignity as Christians. The high doctrine that St. Paul taught to his converts, men indeed just rescued from a rather degraded paganism, insisted always on the lofty position to which each had been called. He dealt with the sinner by making him realize that he was intended to be a saint. All of us need this inspiriting view of our vocation. Our lives are cast in "mean streets," and we therefore count them without honor or value. Conscious simply of their pettiness, we make no attempt to see their true grandeur. We see but dimly if we see only the vision of the glory of the world. Taking, then, day by day a glimpse at one or other of the mysteries of God, we shall surely be led to understand ever more and more the worth of those souls of ours for which Christ did not disdain to die.

There will, of course, be no need to worry ourselves if, through some cause or other, we are not able each day to fit in our meditation. So long as we can make it a general rule, we can well afford to allow some exceptions.

Meditation consists in contemplating some fact of Faith or some attitude of my soul, and then addressing on that account fervent prayer to God. I put myself in the presence of God, implore His aid, then read a little — one point or even one sentence (should that suffice for me) — and consider how far it affects me, how far it is a message that should have a distinct meaning for my soul. Thinking it over, I find reason for addressing myself to God, asking for guidance, asking for strength, then quietly speaking to Him out of the fullness of my heart. For it must not be forgotten that meditation is mental prayer, a prayer of mind and heart; hence its extreme importance for all those whose lives are crowded with incident, interests, or business.

For the layman, meditation is really of far more importance than it is for the religious or priest. After all, the general arrangement of day, the choral or private office, and the religious cloister are all in themselves very great helps to an attitude of mind that looks at all things from the heavenly standpoint; whereas the layman, with his own responsibilities, as binding on him as vows are binding on the religious, has almost everything against him. His need is the greater and his calling, in that sense, more heroic.

Meditation, therefore, has now become a great necessity for layfolk, and, as has been noted, it is for this reason that this book has been written. The actual form that the meditation should take must, of course, be left to the particular fashion of each individual. There is no general method that has not to be considerably adapted to the particular temperament of the user, but at the front and back of the book, one is suggested that has been found of very great service by a layman of much experience. It will, however, be to the interests of each to form for himself such a scheme as he may find congenial.

In the actual meditations are enshrined ideas that have come from many quarters. Some have been worked from a single phrase let fall by a great thinker; some bear a much nearer relation to the writings of others. In this latter case, due acknowledgment has been made, but in many places, there must be sources that have completely escaped the memory of the writer. As far as possible, he has set down references, yet had that been done completely, he is aware that the footnotes would assume an undue prominence. Who, however, can give in any detail the full pedigree of his opinions?

Within the meditations themselves, much has been left undeveloped; but it is hoped that enough has been said to encourage the individual to work out his own ideas. Above all, it must be remembered that the personal application must be made by each reader for himself.

Bede Jarrett, O.P.
St. Dominic's Priory
Haverstock Hill, London
Whitsuntide, 1915

∞

Classic Catholic Meditations

Part 1

∞

The Holy Trinity

∞

God is near to you

The foundation of all religion and all life is belief in God. To feel His help and taste His sweetness is the purpose of all spiritual ambition, for He is not merely the beginning, but also the end of all things; from Him we come, and to Him we go. It is this overwhelming thought of God that is generally our primary view of Him, this intimate relationship between Him and creation, between Him and all the intricate complications that make up the sum of human life.

The Old Testament is full of this nearness of all things to Him. The holy men of Israel are all marked with this sign of their appreciation of the divine presence. It would indeed be difficult to express the difference that exists between this and other sacred books merely in the high moral teaching, for it is very evident that in the Scriptures we find that God in early times was content to reveal a very rudimentary form of moral doctrine. But all the time, despite the repeated failure of the Hebrews to live up to their high prerogatives among the nations of the ancient world, there is in them a wonderful and unique perception of the unceasing nearness of God. "Enoch walked with God, and God took him"[1] is the

[1] Cf. Gen. 5:22, 24.

most perfect description of holiness, and it occurs quite early in the record of the Jewish religion. So, again, in the book of Deuteronomy (which may well in parts bear the stamp of later editing) we find this characteristic phrase: "Beneath us are the everlasting arms."[2] The peculiar spiritual tone of the Scriptures comes from this recognition of the nearness of God.

Now, this consciousness of God's all-pervading power is based on real doctrine, for in any analysis of what we mean by *God* we must notice that from the necessity of His being, He can never be idle. It is true that Scripture suggests that on the seventh day of creation God rested, but His sabbath, or rest, is interpreted by St. Augustine[3] to mean that thereafter He created no new matter (except the human soul), but left all things to evolve according to the laws that He gave to each; that is, He ordained the increase and multiplication of creation and ordained it to be performed by creation itself.

Yet within the perfect circle of the divine life, within the intimate relation of the Father, the Son, and the Holy Spirit, is perpetual activity, the highest pitch of life, since in that sacred mystery, knowledge and love constitute the work of the Three Persons. The Father knows Himself in the Son, and from Them both proceeds the Holy Spirit — namely, the love that is consequent on knowledge.

Now, it is obvious that the life of God could not be interrupted by creation, since eternity means nothing more than an unceasing present. There can be neither past nor future. Consequently, as far as God Himself was concerned, there can have been no time, if this expression be allowed, when He was not the Creator, nor when that fullness of life was in any way slackened. Therefore, it is clear that God, in the full activity of His existence, has, since the

---

[2] Cf. Deut. 33:27.
[3] St. Augustine (354-430), Bishop of Hippo.

dawn of human destiny, been unceasing in the exercise of His power, wisdom, and love.

But since this incessant life of power, wisdom, and love constitutes the divine nature, and since the extent of them affects, not only God Himself, but the things that He has made, it is obvious that all creation itself must be steeped in God. Not merely has He called them into existence, but they could not continue in that existence without His support. Unless beneath them were the everlasting arms, they would slip back into that nothingness from which they sprang at the divine command.

Again, to an all-seeing mind and providence the whole universe must be open and naked, lie outstretched before His gaze. Even His very being must be intimate with all creation. Nothing could be itself without God's essence making it what it is. His power, His presence, His being enter into all creatures. Hence, we have to realize this consciousness of God. No practice spiritualizes us more easily than the perception of His presence. Grace comes readily to those in whose minds this nearness of God is the customary thought. Communion, frequent and devout, makes it a living truth.

"Behold, I stand at the door and knock; if any man open the door to me, I will come in and sup with him and he with me."[4] This saying becomes intelligible when we understand that the divine life is unceasing from all eternity; that this life must affect not merely God Himself, but (because He is a creator of things that are distinct from Him) also intimately the nature of everything that He has made, and, finally, because they are affected by Him, He must be Himself close to every one of us.

---

[4] Cf. Apoc. 3:20 (RSV = Rev. 3:20).

∞

God governs every event
at every moment

The mysteries of Faith are revealed as truths, but the purpose of their revelation is life. They are received by the intelligence, but they perfect their work in the will. They enlighten the mind, but they inflame the heart. Nothing has been told us by God as a mere matter for remembrance, but it is committed to us to become a means to achieve the higher life. Even the doctrine of the Trinity comes as an aid in the struggle of my soul to its perfect develop- ment, not as a mere puzzle that I have with difficulty to remember in some examination by God or man.

Let me, then, consider the meaning of this mystery as far as the halting and inadequate language of human thought allows me to do so. All the while I must be conscious that I am using human ex- pressions and therefore merely endeavoring to state infinite things in finite categories, to pack divinity into human pigeon-holes. But there can be no harm in my making use of such a method (namely, the attempt to grasp the meaning of mysteries), so long as I realize that any such attempt must be frankly inadequate. The use of this must be fairly admitted, since it is something (for which I should be eternally grateful) to have even an incomplete view of God, so long as it is the best view that at the moment is possible to me. The

Church has never suggested that, with the advance of time, she does not obtain a clearer comprehension of the truths of Faith; indeed, she has frequently proclaimed by repeated decisions and definitions the gradual unfolding of her sacred deposit.

The Blessed Trinity is, then, the name we give to that mystery of the divine Persons, who are three yet one, Father and Son and Holy Spirit, constituting in Themselves one single God. Of these, the Father represents power, for I begin my Creed by professing belief in "God, the Father Almighty, Creator of Heaven and earth." To God in the person of the Father, therefore, I attribute omnipotence.

Of the Son, I learn that He is the Word (the *Logos* as the Greek of the Gospel terms it, making use of the very phrase current among the philosophers of the time) of the Father, that He is the figure of the Father's substance, the brightness of the Father's glory. By all of this, I see that the Son is represented as the reflected image of the Father, the idea that the Father has of Himself, the knowledge of Himself in the mind of the Father, the exact reproduction of Himself begotten of His own intelligence. To the Son, therefore, I attribute wisdom.

Now, God knowing Himself must love Himself. His perfections are so lovable that once (if these expressions of time may be used of that which is outside all time) God is known even to Himself, He must be loved. Hence, the love of the saints toward Him is not free, but follows necessarily from the sight of Him. Hence also, God's knowledge of Himself must be followed by a second or final act, His love. That love, then, which proceeds from the Father and the Son (for in love, there are always two) is the Holy Spirit. It must not be forgotten that we are trying to put into human language what is above language, but we can in this way obtain some glimpse of the truth.

By my belief in the Holy Trinity, then, I acknowledge, in one single God, Power, Wisdom, and Love, and I repeat that these three are one. Therefore are these three inseparable. I cannot suppose that one can operate without the other two, since it is part of my belief that they constitute a Trinity.

Now surely I do see what an immense effect such a doctrine must have upon life. It is no mere question for theologians, but one that concerns every living soul. Whatever is allowed by God's power must be guided by His wisdom and urged on by His love.

All that happens to me in life, the little worries and the great anxieties, the crises and the daily annoyances, the sorrows and the joys, the harms that reach me through the sins of others, the great crimes of history, the huge and devastating wars, the partings and loves and the whole cycle of human experience are permitted by Power, which is itself wise and loving. These three Persons determine my life, and, since I walk by faith, I must surely grow very patient in my attitude toward life. For how can I complain or criticize God's Providence, since it all comes under that triple influence of Power, Wisdom, and Love?

Under the guidance, then, of this mystery, I can walk through the valley of death or the more perilous borders of sin without loss of courage or hopefulness. Nothing can make me afraid. How these are separate, yet one, I do not know, nor can I reconcile in my concrete experience the claims of each. It is always a mystery, but a mystery in which I believe. Whatever Power allows on earth is designed in Wisdom and attuned by Love.

∞

God made you

God made me. How many men have desired to hear the things that we hear and have not heard them! To think that for thousands of years before the coming of Christ and for all the hundreds of years since He came, there have been unnumbered souls who were anxiously longing to hear that answer with assurance.

The problem has always troubled the children of men. As the human race began its uphill climb to the full story of revelation, which it has felt for unceasingly in its heart, it has gradually grown more interested in the problem of its origin, whence it took its rise, and for what purpose, if even for any purpose, it is here. Reason has always faced life with the question on its lips as to what is the business of its existence. The traditions that the race had gathered from its primitive revelation were soon obscured by many myths, so that we are expressly told that, when God chose Abraham, He called him out from his family who worshiped many gods; but at any rate, they worshiped. Somehow, although the truth had become overgrown with the strange growths of time, the light still glimmered beneath all this obstruction. Falsely, inhumanly, distorted into fantastic shapes, the remembrance of the Divine Master lingered as a memory. Man, despite his primitive knowledge, gradually lapsed from the sure doctrine of a Creator; then, also gradually, he began again to piece together the scraps of truth that yet remained, and out of them he formed for himself a faulty and variable gospel.

Then God broke through the silence. Gradually in shafts of illumination, in growing glory from prophet to prophet, the light began to break upon the horizon and to herald the perfect day. In the Old Testament may be followed the unfolding of successive revelation; then, when the fullness of time arrived, Christ our Lord, the bright light, appeared; no longer in broken gleams, but in the full splendor of the sun came His revelation. He made known to us the divine life and the mysterious working of the Three-in-One, and brought to the human race knowledge of many things that helped it to understand some of the problems that had for so long perplexed it. What had seemed to the wise and devout beyond all human power to know — what still appears so to many of our own generation who are seeking after God in perfect faith and hope and love — can now be understood by a Catholic child.

From my earliest years, I have been familiar with the thought of God, my Creator, Redeemer, and Sanctifier. No doubt the very simplicity of my belief, the very fact of its familiarity, the clear way in which it does at once help to the understanding of life, the complete answer it affords to so much that perplexes others may blind me to the fact of the greatness of the revelation. I cannot conceive myself as without the truth of God's personal creation of me and, consequently, do not value as I should the preciousness of that knowledge. Yet the remembrance that it was the death of Christ that purchased it for me should convince me of the divine compassion, whereby I was made conscious in my infancy that God had made me.

That acknowledgment of my dependence upon God for the first beginnings of life, as well as for my continuance in this present existence, is the keystone of my faith. The Infinite Mind that can, because of its very infinity, attend as industriously to each single member as to the whole race, called me into being, purposed my end for His own greater glory, and arranged my life to achieve its decreed destiny. I find myself handicapped by this and that: my passions, my circumstances, the tendency of the environment in which I find myself, the evil effect, perhaps, of my hereditary weakness — all seem to prejudice my freedom.

Ah, well, He made me! I did not choose the surroundings of my life, but He did; therefore, He knows more clearly even than do I the difficulties of that life. He is to be my judge, yes, but He made me and will understand. The very fact, then, that I am His creature is itself of great consolation. Just as I ease my anxieties about others by my consciousness that they are in His keeping, and that if I, with all my inherent selfishness, can feel disquieted about them, His care and solicitude can be no less, His love being greater; so also is the same thought to steady me, too, in life's perplexities. At my Communions, the nearness of that Presence should force the prayer from my heart: "Cast all your care on Him, for He hath care of you."[5] Surely St. Peter, when he wrote that phrase, had his mind full of the mystery of the death he had watched from afar off, with eyes that wept bitterly. But no less does the text tell me of God's tender care for me, since I am His own handiwork. I shall walk, then, in perfect trust, for God made me.

---

[5] Cf. 1 Pet. 5:7.

∞

Trust in God's omnipotence, even when evil baffles you

In his *Summa Theologica*, St. Thomas Aquinas[6] allows only two possible objections to the existence of God, and one of these is the existence of evil. How can we, he suggests, suppose God to be omnipotent if we find things in the world that spoil His plan? And if God is not omnipotent, how can he be God at all?

Now, this objection made by St. Thomas from the writers of his time, taken by them from the first questionings of the human spirit, or learned, it well may be, from the spontaneous askings of their own hearts, is common even in our day. We are not to consider it here from the controversial standpoint; the whole problem is only mentioned in order that, from its mystical appreciation, we may the more hopefully face life. However our beliefs run, we all find that the trouble in the world is something that staggers us; nor is it the sad sight of war, but the unceasing miseries of peace that are more likely to affect us, since they seem so much more clearly to be allowed by God. The difference is no doubt one of imagination; but through convention we are wont to look upon war as

---

[6]   St. Thomas Aquinas (c. 1225-1274), Dominican philosopher, theologian, and Doctor.

definitely the work of man, while the miseries of daily existence, the wear and tear of it, appear the sole effect of God.

The answer of St. Thomas can be very briefly given. It is really nothing else than a quotation from the works of St. Augustine, which can be thus stated: "If evil and sin spoiled the plan of God, He would clearly not be omnipotent, would not be God. But if He is so powerful that He can make even sin fit into the working out of His design, then the whole objection falls. Out of evil He brings forth good."

To see what this means, we must first of all remember the old truth that the mysteries of God are above reason, can never find really any solution, and must continue to perplex every thinking being who faces frankly the riddle of the universe. Therefore, it is good to begin by insisting that there is no answer, and the religion that would suppose that it had at last discovered the way through would stand itself condemned.

But granting all this, there is still much that a Catholic can see to help him to bear patiently the evils of this present life. Of course, he cannot admit that the power to sin is an essential accompaniment of free will; he cannot say, as many outside the Church say, that God could not create a human free will without permitting it to fall into sin. In the case of our Lady, we believe that God did, compatibly with her freedom, prevent her from ever sinning; and what He did for her He could have done for each. Why did He not? We do not know, and it is simpler to say so at once. We cannot tell why He has allowed sin to enter in. We know only and have to confess that He has done so, and that He could have prevented it.

Nor is it of much satisfaction to say that courage demands evil, patience requires it, and unselfishness cannot be exercised without it. These do, indeed, depend for their exercise on the presence of evil in the world, but not for their existence. That is to say, it is quite possible for me to have virtue that I have never used, but came infused into my soul by the grace of God. Thus, the very poorest may have the virtue of liberality without even an opportunity for its practice.

Have I any comfort in this perplexing puzzle? Just this much: that I am on the wrong side to be able to judge whether evil works havoc in my life. For the lives of others I am unfit to say anything, and I am too much part of my own life to understand what is happening to me. I stand on the wrong side of the loom. I see only the blotches of color, the broken ends of thread, the chaos of line, and the tumult of fantastic shapes. To me it is all a medley without meaning. But if it were possible, as one day it will be possible, to get around to the other side and view the whole embroidery from the throne of Him for whom the whole is being worked, then I would see that patient fingers were weaving a design that had depth of color, firmness of line — a masterpiece of the machinery of God.

This is indeed no answer to the problem, for we began by seeing that answer was impossible; but it is at least the direction in which one day the answer will ultimately come to us. Here I cannot see. Let me be patient; God is omnipotent. He can, with the failing tools of human life, build to Himself palaces of delight; with the worn-out implements of our saddened life, gather a harvest of souls; with the arts and crafts of man, effect something priceless to God. There is comfort, then, and reason for courage in the phrase of St. Augustine that St. Thomas repeats. It suggests to us never to despair, to trust that out of evil He can bring forth good, to live so perfectly in patience as to have faith in the hope that we may one day contemplate the plan of God.

∞

Life is a gift from God

We have two principles of action: duty and love. The first follows the law of being, the second the lure of love. To do one's duty is really nothing else than to fulfill the purpose of existence. It is the natural development of being itself. The duty of the soul or the duty of the body signifies just that: the soul using to the fullest its every power, the body putting to the highest exercise, all the wonderful capacities given it and using them for the purposes for which they were intended. That is the law of duty, the law that bids us put into practice the latent faculties of our nature.

But love is the attraction that beauty sets to the will under the impulse of discerning reason; that is to say, when we love, it is because reason (outpacing or roughly guided by sentiment) has discovered something that calls from our heart an echo, something to which we eagerly go forward. Even to love oneself is nothing else than to discover in oneself, by a reflex act, that there are certain excellences in us that appeal strongly to us — make us, as it were, go out to ourselves all the more yearningly because it is ourselves.

Hence, we can sum up the life of man in his double activity. He does his duty; he loves what is lovely. The ideas described in the words *ought, must,* and so forth, and the feeling of a moral obligation are responsible for one-half of human actions; the other half are governed by the appeal made to us by things, people, and actions that draw us to them. Doing my duty, loving the lovable, is the sum total of my life.

Now, we can say, with obvious modifications, that these two laws can be found also in God Himself. The forces whereby God the Father, in our human language, begot the Son, and whereby from the Father and the Son proceeded the Holy Spirit, are termed not free but natural. That is the precise phrase of the theologian, by which he endeavors to say, in language that is of scientific construction, that the Father, in knowing Himself in the Son and loving Himself in the Holy Spirit, could not have done otherwise, could not have chosen otherwise. He was not free to have acted differently. Not, of course, that He was compelled to this by some higher power, for there can be no higher power than God; but it is out of the very essence of His own being that this act of life comes.

Again, too, it should be noted that when we say of God that He loves anything that He has made, we cannot suppose that His love is caught by something outside of Himself. He cannot be affected by anything that is outside of Him, or else would He not be sole, independent God. What He sees in us worthy of love is not us, but His own reflection: He is enamored of the loveliness of Himself. That is, we must not look upon Him as at all influenced by any higher power, for He is Himself the highest power that is. We repeat, then, that it is in a more excellent way that God is affected by these two laws. He fulfills the law of duty and the law of love. He is affected by His being, which is self-existing, and by His Beauty, which is uncreated, for His being and His beauty and He are one.

Yet there is also a third law, which is goodness. It consults no interest, awaits no command, and solicits no attraction of beauty. In a sense, it includes in itself the law of being insofar as it is a spontaneous movement of its nature, and the law of beauty insofar as goodness is beauty's highest perfection. Yet in a sense, too, it seems nobler than both; for it was divine beauty and divine being that were led by Divine Goodness to create the world. There was certainly no obligation on God's part to call the world into existence. We are compelled by our belief in God to say that He had no need for us. He could have been perfectly happy without us; hence, we cannot say that His nature forced Him to have us. Neither, as we have explained above, could we pretend that God could see in us any beauty that attracted Him and was not already part of Himself. We did not even influence Him to create us. Consequently, we have to suppose some sort of divine generosity that, apart from the movement of His nature, led Him to make the world. It was as though "He heard the cry of worlds that were not, the cry of unmeasured misery calling to unbounded goodness."

My attitude toward God, therefore, must be one of intense thankfulness that I have had the gift of life, that with His own perfect generosity, without any advantage to Him (although indeed finding pleasure in it), He began the world. And all the subsequent kindnesses lavished on me are, again, not demanded from Him by Himself, but are the spontaneous gift of His goodness.

∞

God is all-powerful

The power of God is beyond the conception of man. Just as the being of God and the life of the Blessed Trinity are known to us only through the light vouchsafed us by revelation, so also are His actions equally impenetrable to our gaze, except for His condescension in telling us about Himself. We would really be unable to follow the progress of His power had He not Himself assured us of His intervention and His design in the history of the race. Indeed, the unity of God is so straight and close that it is absolutely and logically necessary to admit that in God there is no distinction between His acts and Him. His very being and His acts are one; hence, His power is as infinite, as limitless, as is His nature.

For the same reason, too, I can never look for the cause or motive of His action outside of Himself. If it were possible for Him to find the reason of His actions in what I do, then He could not be all-powerful. It is essential that He should do all things for Himself alone, for a God who was directed by this or that, by what He saw in His creatures, would be changeable and no longer independent.

When, then, I say that God is all-powerful, I mean quite simply that His power is commensurate with every possibility; and I am assured that this is true, because I realize that His power is identical with His being and, in consequence, as the one is infinite, the other must be infinite also.

Yet it might seem as though there were things that He could not do, limits that might be set to His power. He could not, it is obvious, make something that would be at once and, from the same point of view, both round and square. He could not make Himself or any other thing three in exactly the same sense as He is one, for that would be a sheer impossibility. He is, indeed, three and one, but one in nature and three in personality; that is, He is not, in the meaning of the word, three and one from the same standpoint.

Still, even in cases like these that could be multiplied indefinitely, St. Augustine tells us that it is true to say that God can do everything, for he points out that really it would be more correct to express the apparent contradiction in this way: not that God cannot do the thing, but that the thing itself cannot be done. And the reason that he brings forward for this is most interesting. In all these things, he tells us, God is moved by His intelligence and not by His will: that is to say, there are truths in ethics, in faith, in science, and so forth, that are true, not because God wants them to be true, but because He knows them to be true.

We may put this more clearly perhaps, but less accurately, by saying that some things are wrong, not because God has forbidden them, but He has forbidden them because they are wrong. Thus, polygamy is wrong, not in itself, but because it has been forbidden; whereas injustice is wrong in itself and is for that reason forbidden by God. Just then, as in these moral cases, certain things cannot be allowed, so in those other instances that seem to limit God's power, we see really that it is the contradiction which is opposed by the intelligence of God.

God, then, in a certain sense can be said to at the mercy of truth. And this is truly so, for God is Truth. He is at the mercy of Himself. He is almighty, but he is also Truth, Mercy, and Justice; therefore truth, mercy, and justice must prevail. The interplay of these great forces is beyond my reason to discover; I cannot find limits of each. Humanly speaking, it is difficult to reconcile justice and mercy, truth and charity, wisdom and love; but with Him, all these things are one, for they are all Himself. He, in the height of His Godhead, includes all these attributes, and with Him they are in perfect order. So, too, His power is compatible with truth. Let me take this to a personal point. The whole series of commandments and the articles of Faith are not the choosing of God, but spring from God's own nature. They are all true because God is truth. The faith that, if you will, tyrannizes over me, tyrannizes also over God. I submit to it; and so, if you will, does He, for it is Himself. No doubt my ideas of His power are often at fault. I want this done and that, forgetting, it may be, that God cannot act contrary to His own nature. There are, in that inaccurate sense, limits to the power of God — namely, the limits set by His own being. I have grumbled because I did not see that the very truth of His nature forbade what seemed to me to be necessary for myself or another.

Let me then, as always, put myself passively into His hands. He is almighty, but there is also the full domain of truth. With Him, although not with man, might is right.

∞

Creation reveals God's serene wisdom

We profess faith in God as the Creator; it is the opening phrase of our Creed. But surely this conflicts with the prevalent scientific theory that the world grew gradually by means of some mysterious and spontaneous power from forms simpler than the complicated species that exist today. It is abundantly evident that, among older generations, the opinion was common that the whole world sprang straight into being, ready-made, with all the various divisions of earth and water, and the life that clothed its nakedness with myriad forms of beauty in color and plumage. Not the long persistent war of ages, such as Darwin postulated and such as science now generally demands, but the swift saber-cut of God's own word, would have been put forward as Christ's own teaching.

Can we say, therefore, that the idea of creation as taught us by the Church depends wholly upon scientific suppositions that are now declared on all hands to be faulty? If so, then surely it is time to set aside all these worn-out methods of explanation and adjust our false science to more perfect knowledge.

This is indeed the attitude taken up by a great number of people outside the Church; the examination of the points they raise will be of help to me in getting a true view of what is meant by *creation* and, in consequence, in obtaining a deeper knowledge of the part that God unceasingly plays in the story of the world. It is clear that the more I understand the essential relation that creation bears to the Creator, the more shall I be able to repose in the consciousness of His presence.

Let us admit, then, the principle of evolution. Let us suppose that from nebulous matter or from some cell of simple structure there gradually grew up the still-evolving and complicated universe that we know. There are obvious difficulties against certain presentations of this theory. Schools have arisen that dispute vehemently as to positions that were at one time considered vital to the Darwinian hypothesis; but it is fair to add that these do not really affect the main principle: that out of what was at one time largely undetermined eventually appeared something that apparently, by the law of its own growth, was widely different from its original parent seed.

However, let us suppose that it has been demonstrated that the world, as we know it, has evolved in its material aspect out of some primitive cell. What, then, do we claim for God? Just this: that the first cell came into being at His command. We may vary the scientific facts, and alter our theories, and restate them afresh in the light of the most recent research; and when we have done all this, the Church simply insists that in whatever form it began, it came into that form at the express word of the Almighty. Whether as a single cell or as a fully perfected earth makes little difference to the theological concept; for at least it began, not through any inherent vitality (for certainly that did not as yet exist), but through the external interference of God. The decree of the Biblical Commission (June 30, 1909) insists on the acceptance of two points: the particular creation of man, and the formation of the first woman out of the first man. Science need not teach creation, but it cannot deny it.

Yet does not this modern scientific explanation of the world give me greater matter for wonder at the wisdom of the Creator?

His supreme power must be invoked to bridge the gap between nothingness and being; yet to realize the slow course by which the cell in patient action blossomed at length into the fair world that we know, and by its inherent needs and purposes became fit habitation for the infused soul of man and climbed so high that out of the material of its womb should spring at last the human nature of God — is not this to exalt, more splendidly than did the other view of creation, the serene wisdom of the Most High? The deeper the law, the deeper the intelligence. Thus, the wonders of evolution become themselves a great gospel.

The more research reveals to us the marvels of creation and draws out for us the long series of species that culminate, after apparently endless ages of uphill struggle, in the universe of which scientific men speak, the more does the whole world show its utter dependence on the power of someone greater than itself. All these laws, as we call them — although they are rather the formulated happenings in nature that experiment records — prove to us the presence of an intelligence presiding over the birth of things. Without chance, without the fortuitous concourse of atoms (a phrase that earlier writers much affected), without the movement of purposeless hazard, life has been patiently planned. My very material body has been created in its original essence by the divine intelligence of God.

∞

Love reveals life's meaning

We learn as children that God created all things by His word, and St. John, in the tremendous preface that he puts to his Gospel, tells us who this Word of God is: "In the beginning was the Word. . . . All things were made through Him, and without Him was made nothing. . . . The Word was made flesh."[7] It is obvious, then, that God the Father created everything through the Son, who was therefore the image according to which everything was formed. Thus is the whole world stamped with a divine personality, whose traces are conspicuous in the details and laws of created nature. The old idea of a blind force working its way through all creation, trampling underfoot in its mad fashion the ineffective and inefficient wastrels, slaughtering the welter of all unselfish being, cannot readily obtain any evidence to support it. Even evil as well as good shows clear signs of an intelligence directing, controlling, and planning.

Here, too, the whole value of evolutionary research, such as has been gathered by the science of our own and past time, can be appreciated by no one more than by ourselves. I, as a Catholic, welcome the many detailed laws that are now found to govern

[7] John 1:1, 3, 14.

even the formation of a crystal. Some take shape in one figure, some in another, all in definite mathematical precision. As in the child's story of Robinson Crusoe, there are evident traces of intelligent being on the shores of nature. And the deeper our knowledge becomes, the more clearly do we see the gradual breakup of that old-fashioned materialism that supposed nothing rational in the organization of the universe.

Indeed, so full is the world of personality that it is the lover alone who discovers the full meaning of life. Unless you are in love, you will never find a purpose in the ebb and flow of existence. Thus, to love is to understand.

The lover, as he sets about his daily toil, finds in all the earth things that remind him of his beloved. Every corner of the street comes to him and tells him of some excellence or the memory of some past happiness. The whole world spells to him just one name. Hence, the object of his love, because it is a personality, does give him the meaning of life. The personality may actually, because of the very vehemence of his passion, obscure for him the divine idea; human forms may block out the radiance of the divine; but the fact remains that they alone who are in love find an answer to life's riddle.

The old pagan idea that found the gods lurking in field and wood and stream was evidence of the instinct of man's nature. Faulty were their legends, gross and carnal their interpretation, but human nature did find out the high secret of earth: that it sprang from the hands of a personal God. A mother discovers the meaning of sorrow in the heart of her child; she sees that God deals with her as she with her little ones. The lover finds the name of his beloved written across the stars. The sighing of the wind, the fragrance of the flowers and delicate hue of the rose, and the music of the birds do but repeat to the friend his friend's loveliness. For the love of a person alone can unlock the secrets of creation, and make pain almost divine, and even parting such sweet sorrow,

27

since it was through a person that the world was made. It is just, then, this personal touch that can alone explain it.

Further, it will be noticed that the nearer the person we love approaches to the Divine Ideal through whom all things were created, the truer is our understanding of life. The more clearly their souls mirror the perfections of Christ, the better is the vision they unfold to us of the inner depths of life.

One meaning of the devotion to the saints is precisely for that purpose. They are the imitators of Christ, and because they so closely followed in His footsteps, they do the better explain to us, once we have found a love for them in our hearts, the troubled perplexities of our existence. Our love for them, just because they are human and because they do reproduce in some way the life of our Master, helps our own lives along. But it is only in Him that we shall find the complete answer: the saints are at best faulty copies of a faultless original.

By taking, then, into our hands Christ's gospel and setting the crucifix before our eyes, and feeding upon His broken Body and His outpoured Blood, we shall be getting into our minds the real vision that alone will make the universe explainable. Through Him all things were made; it will be therefore in our increasing knowledge of Him and in a corresponding love of Him that we shall find our way about in the little furrows of our lives. In the perfect realization of Him alone can the meaning of all things be made clear; not indeed as though the world explains Him, although this, too, is true, but rather that He explains the world. Frequent communication with Him, frequent communion in the Blessed Sacrament, will therefore be of great help to me. It will help me to know Him better, experience His love, and find the answer to all the troubles of life in Him.

∞

Jesus Christ is true God

The foundation of the Christian name is belief in the divinity of Christ — that is, a belief that He is God equally with the Father and the Holy Spirit. Without this clear expression of faith, there can be no acceptance of the plain meaning of the gospel. For if He were not God, then He could not even have been a good man, since He certainly claimed to be divine in a sense altogether different from everyone else, and distinct from the vague conceptions that made Buddha and Mohammed the sons of God. Schlegel has crystallized this in a sentence: "If Christ was not more than a Socrates, then a Socrates He certainly was not." Lessing turns it another way: "If Christ is not truly God, then Mohammedanism was an undoubted improvement of the Christian religion. Mohammed on such a supposition would indisputably have been a greater man than Christ, as he would have been far more veracious, more circumspect, and more zealous for the honor of God, since Christ by His expressions would have given dangerous occasions for idolatry; while, on the other hand, not a single expression of the kind can be laid to the charge of Mohammed."

Our Lord proclaimed Himself unique, sinless. Now, to do this, and not to be this, is either hypocrisy or madness, for the claim of a man to be God is such an act of assurance as can come only from knowledge or from an unbalanced mind. The whole force of existence is continually teaching us our own littleness by means of the little aches, pains, and disappointments of life, so that for one habited in human flesh to claim immortality, infinity, almightiness, and responsibility for all existing beings requires full deliberation and absolute conviction. Even the Caesars who demanded to be worshiped in their lifetime looked upon themselves merely as symbols of empire and heroes, not as unique in divinity.

Now, Christ our Lord did make this absolute claim. In His parables and broken sayings, apart from the definite allusions to His Sonship of God (which might indeed be differently interpreted), He shows us the greatness of His claim. In one place, He tells us about a vineyard, to which the king (who is evidently God) sent his messengers to demand the fruit of the vines. These messengers, whose coming was received by the people with insults, injuries, and persecution, are admitted by all to represent the prophets. Then, the parable continues, the father sent at last his son. This son was of his own nature, sole heir to his possessions, whom at least, he thought, the workers would treat with respect. The prophets were God's messengers, but the new arrival was His Son. Our Lord, therefore, put Himself above the prophets as the sole Son of God. We are told expressly that the Pharisees knew that He was speaking of them.[8]

In another place, He says that the day of judgment is known neither to the angels nor to the Son, but to the Father.[9] Here He places Himself above the angels also.

Finally, He claims the privilege of a unique and mutual relation with the Father: He alone knows the Father, and the Father alone knows Him.[10] What is this but the claim of an equality of

[8] Matt. 21:33-45.
[9] Matt. 24:36.
[10] Luke 10:22.

knowledge with God? To know and be known solely by another is surely to be equal to that other — to be so penetrated with his spirit and so to dominate him with one's own spirit that nothing can in any sense separate one from the other.

Nor is there, finally, any passage in the New Testament in which our Lord ever asks for the prayers of others.

Jesus Christ, then, claims to be God, and justifies that claim by miracles and still more by a blameless life. He is not merely one who is conscious of the indwelling of the Spirit of God, not simply divine in the sense in which all are touched by the spark that is of God, but uniquely the only-begotten Son of the Father, full of grace and truth.[11] "My Lord and my God," was the confession of St. Thomas.[12]

O true and perfect God! Like the apostle, I, too, am on my knees before Him. I can see in His life signs evident and manifest that He is human. I read of Him under the terrors of life and death. Man surely I know Him to be, but He is more.

"I know men," said Napoleon, "and Jesus Christ was not a man." My eyes may see only the human form. I see the print of the nails and spear, the marks of scourging and crowning, the linen cloth lying, the very signs of death. Yet all the while, I know Him to be God as well as man. I profess my belief in His divinity precisely in the same sense in which I profess the divinity of the Father. There is no difference of nature between them, without beginning or end, eternal, yesterday and today and the same forever, the King of ages, immortal, invisible, the only God.[13] The importance of the revelation is immense. Neither flesh nor blood could reveal it, but only the Father who is in Heaven. By His grace is it that I say, "My Lord and my God."

[11] John 1:14.
[12] John 20:28.
[13] Heb. 13:8; 1 Tim. 1:17.

∞

Jesus Christ is true man

The coming of Christ was for a definite purpose: to atone for the sins of the world. Whether He would have come if the world had not fallen into sin, it is impossible to say, although Scripture implies that it was sin alone that made His coming imperative. Even the Church sings in one of her most beautiful hymns, "Happy fault of Adam that required so worthy a Savior!" But that is a point apart and needs no mention here.

We know that man sinned. Through the action of Adam the whole race was, by the decree of God, involved in the loss of original justice and suffered the privation of grace and became children of wrath. Man had sinned, yet he could not make satisfaction for his sin, for, since a fault is partly to be measured by the dignity of the person against whom it is committed, sin took on something of the infinity of God. Man himself, therefore, was not able of himself to atone. God alone could do that.

Yet how was God to suffer or make redemption? He is immortal, impassible. The Divine Wisdom discovered a way, in the person of one who would be at once God and man: man that He might suffer, God that His suffering might have infinite avail. Hence, our blessed Lord was born God and man, as we see to have been rigorously demanded by the circumstances of the case.

Before He came as man, He was already a person, the Second Person of the Blessed Trinity. His humanity, therefore, could not add a second personality to Him, or else the redemption would have been useless, being achieved by one who was only man or only God. Hence, the Church, under the impulse of the Holy Spirit, has defined that in Christ there are two natures, but one person.

Christ our Lord, therefore, is a true and perfect man. He came into the world through the same portal as all others come, formed out of the flesh and blood of His mother's womb. Slowly He grew to man's estate, increasing "in wisdom and grace before God and man";[14] adding to the fruits of His knowledge by experience, learning language from His mother, whom He had created, growing conscious of the outward fabric of the universe that His own hands upheld. Boylike He strayed away from His parents and was found at that pursuit that has always been the pleasure of all childhood: asking questions that His grown-up hearers could not answer. In the desert, after He had fasted, He was hungry; on the Cross He cried aloud that He thirsted. He was weary when He sat down at the well and spoke those revealing words to the woman of Samaria which drew her to faith in His Messiahship. As a true patriot, He whose own country was no less than all the world wept over the far sight of His own fair city when He saw it in His prophetic vision overrun and battered by the Roman arms.

Hypocrisy and cant were abhorrent to Him; He denounced them with all the scorn of which humanity is capable and, in His terrible anger, flung the tables of the money-changers down the front steps of the Temple, and scourged with cords all those who trafficked where had been built a House of Prayer. And even as He took upon Himself all the weakness of humanity, save that He did not sin, so into His soul crept that great dread of death that is so distinctive of the human heart.

[14] Luke 2:52.

33

Ah, yes, He came in the winsome garb of childhood, for He came as a brother to save. He is as truly man as I — with all a man's limitations, save that He did not sin. Tempted, He knows our weakness, for He had trial of it in Himself. "He needed not that anyone should show Him what was in man,"[15] for He was man. In life and after death, He retained His divine powers over all creation. His body had qualities not given to us or to ordinary flesh and blood; none in all the world could convince Him of sin. Yet for all that, He was truly man:

> *Our fellow in the manger lying,*
> *Our food within the supper room,*
> *Our ransom on the Cross, when dying,*
> *Our prize in His own kingly home.*

I must, therefore, always be conscious of His humanity. I must realize that my sorrows are akin to His, that my difficulties are such that He will understand; that, although His strength is divine and is upheld by all the force of his Godhead, His compassion is thereby not less human; that He is God indeed from all eternity, but man as truly from the moment of the Incarnation: man to understand by experience, God to help; man to suffer and die, God that death and suffering may have infinite avail.

Oh, the dignity of my human nature, that it, too, is clothed about the strength of God! Oh, the real union achieved in the Blessed Sacrament when I am one with Christ! No wonder Lacordaire broke out in accents of human love in his address to his Redeemer: "O Father, O Master, O Friend, O Jesus!" There is a real relationship of love between me and His humanity.

[15] Cf. John 2:25.

Christ's Passion
reveals the depths of love

The life of Christ was evidently less thought of in the early days of Christianity than His death and its preceding Passion. The authors of the Gospels devote to the three last days of His time on earth an amount of space altogether out of proportion to that given to the rest of His thirty-three years. St. John, for example, out of his twenty-one chapters allots seven, or exactly one-third, to the events of the Passion. Again, in the first and simplest of the Creeds, there is hardly any mention of Christ's life at all; attention passes on at once from the birth to the death: "He was born of the Virgin Mary, suffered under Pontius Pilate."

The same is true of the whole devotional attitude of the Church; the birth and the Passion and death absorb almost the whole of the attention of her children. In the Liturgy, in the artistic tradition, in the ascetic meditations of the Fathers, always it is to the Passion that thoughts are turned. It has, indeed, been made a taunt against the Catholic Church that she has made Christianity nothing else than the religion of the crucifix, and, in a sense, this is perfectly true, for it represents the whole attitude of the followers of the Crucified. Our thoughts move more swiftly to the Passion because, in a quite definite sense, the Passion is of more value in itself and to us than the rest of the crowded moments of Christ's life on earth.

Why do we insist that the value of the Passion outweighs the rest of our Lord's days on earth? Because it is through the Passion that we have been redeemed. But surely, we make answer, He could have redeemed us without any of that agony. He had no need to die, since every single action of His life could have made atonement for the sins of all the world. Yes, truly He had no need to suffer; we could, of course, have been saved by the simple decree of His divine will.

There is but one answer to all this questioning as to why He died. There is but one word that can explain the tenderness of the Crucified: "God so loved the world";[16] "Christ also hath loved us";[17] "Having loved His own who were in the world, He loved them to the end";[18] "Greater love than this no man hath, than that he lay down his life for his friend."[19]

Blessed Juliana of Norwich[20] says in a passage of beautiful phrasing, "Love is His token. Who told it to you? — Love. Wherefore told He it to you? — For love." Yes, love is His token. Love alone supplies the reason for His death willingly suffered, since this is the highest expression of love. Truly when He hung upon the Cross, He cried out that all was consummated, for even love almighty could go no further. Like the penitent whose sins He forgave so freely, He broke the fair, white alabaster box of His own dear body, and the whole world has been filled with the fragrance of it.

---

[16] John 3:16.

[17] Eph. 5:2.

[18] John 13:1.

[19] Cf. John 15:13.

[20] Blessed Juliana of Norwich (d. c. 1423), recluse whose book, *Revelations of Divine Love*, in which she recounts her visions, speaks of God's loving dealings with man.

Thus it is, then, that, quite rightly, the Passion and death of our blessed Lord come most powerfully into our lives, since it was by His death that we were redeemed, and because His death represents to us the highest achievement that love can offer. Love expresses itself in the broken phrase of sacrifice.

It behooves me, therefore, to keep ever fresh in mind the Passion of our Lord. How is this best to be done? By a tender devotion to the five wounds of Christ. It is true that devotions are always personal, that the whole value of them depends precisely on their being the spontaneous movement of our own hearts. If they are not of our own choosing, if they are foisted on us by someone else who has found them helpful and who would have us therefore take them up, they lose all their efficacy.

Hence, it is quite possible that this particular devotion may have to be replaced by another according to the feelings of each individual — for one, perhaps the Sacred Heart; for another, the Sorrowful Mysteries of the Rosary. But the devotion to the five wounds was so popular all over Christendom (witness its carved shield on the bosses of the roofs of our cathedrals, its appearance on the bench-head of our old parish churches, its colored glory in the ancient windows), is so full of love, yet not of sentiment or gush, is so bracing with its refining fierceness of suffering that it must find many who would welcome its reappearance in this modern world. It is an old devotion, but it is coming back, just because it does keep alive the memory of Christ's death.

The sight must steady me and give me the necessary sternness to meet life sturdily, yet it adds to all this strength the tenderness of love. At Communion or when I make a visit to the Blessed Sacrament, and words and thoughts seem to fail, let me turn to these "dumb mouths that open their ruby lips to beg the voice and utterance of my love."[21]

[21] William Shakespeare, *Julius Caesar*, Act 3, scene 1.

∞

The Sign of the Cross should be
made with reverence and attention

The Sign of the Cross, the emblem of the Christian Faith, has long been in use in the Church. Already on the rough walls of the catacombs we find it traced among the earliest representations of religion. Mention is made of the Cross so often, too, in the letters of St. Paul that it seems evident that even then it had become an actual sign of the Faith. It not only stood, that is to say, as the emblem or memorial of the Passion of the Savior, but was looked upon rather as summing up in itself the whole religion of Christ; it was symbolic of all Christian Faith. In St. Peter's writings, too, it has a deep mystical meaning.

Then we also find that in the same fashion as we use it, the early Christians traced the form of the Cross upon themselves as a constant reminder of the love and gratitude they owed to their Master, and to ask a blessing upon all their actions during day and night. From a well-known passage in the writings of Tertullian, we can be certain that as they went about their business, these early followers of Christ used it openly and frequently as a sign of fellowship and as something that summed up in itself the whole of the Creed.

Again, according to the story that has become a tradition of the Christian people, it was the Cross that Constantine saw in a vision on the eve of his great battle against Maxentius. Through it was victory promised to him; but what is of greater interest is to see that in this legend, it is assumed that the Cross already stood for the whole Faith of Christ.

Thus, too, we note that it has entered into the Liturgy of the Church. Her rites begin and end with it. Her ceremonial is spangled with its brightness. The Church seems unable to place herself in the sanctuary, or move from one office to another, or put her benediction upon things of common use, without an appeal to that saving sign. As her children put themselves to sleep or rise to their labors in the morning, as they begin the day or end it, as they pray or eat, it is under the invocation of that sign. At the baptismal font, they are welcomed by it, and when it is time for them to go from this world to the next, it is formed in blessed oil upon those several senses through which the soul has gone out to its fall, so that, by its potency, the vestiges of sin may be removed. Even in death, before all their muscles have grown stiff, their arms are crossed upon their breasts in memory of it: they can no longer form it otherwise than dumbly, unconsciously; and all through life, it continues to be part of the blessed things that the Church can offer. The absolving words are spoken by the priest in Confession while he forms upon the empty air that symbol through which all efficacy came to the sacrament in the beginning. At Confirmation it becomes itself the symbol both of the persecution life has in store and the strength through which these persecutions are to be outfaced. The touching rite of Marriage, by which the union of human hearts in love is consecrated to God, has the peace foreshown by mutual sacrifice in the unending symbol of that supreme love of Calvary.

The actual words used while we trace the sign show us, indeed, what all the various rites and customs imply — namely, that the Cross is the shortest profession of the Christian Faith, and sums up in itself all the chief mysteries that are incumbent upon the belief of every follower of Christ. We say, in truth, that we acknowledge the Trinity — the Father, Son, and Holy Spirit. To this we add, in memory of the event of which it is a sign, our acceptance of all that is included in the tragedy of the Crucifixion — namely, the divinity and humanity and redeeming power of our Master. From these truths spring the radiating glory of all the other mysteries of our Faith.

Now, we must, therefore, constantly ask ourselves whether we really make use of this sign in the way we ought, whether we really attend to the full meaning of it. Are we conscious of the words and the form when we so hurriedly begin our prayers or scurry through our grace before and after meals? Should we not be much more reverent and exact in our use of the Sign of the Cross? At meals, how often does it not become a mere hasty wave of the fingers that is in no danger of compromising us in the profession of our Faith? There is, indeed, no reason we should parade our beliefs, but neither is there any reason we should be ashamed of them.

Let the Sign of the Cross supply, then, the material of my devotions, when I have made my meditations on it, with its memories of the Trinity, the Incarnation, the whole cycle of the sacraments, and the prefiguring of my own death. Surely as truly as to Constantine the vision has been vouchsafed me, that it is in the sign of the Cross that I shall conquer, if I am to conquer at all. Let me always use it as a real prayer.

∽

The Holy Name of Jesus is itself a prayer

It is astonishing to note the power that names have over us. At the time of a parliamentary election, it would seem as though the whole purpose of the rival candidates, by posting their names over all public places, was to hypnotize us into thinking all the more of them according to the frequency with which we meet their names when on our walks abroad — the more conspicuous the name, the greater the success. Indeed, the very formation of the name may have its own consequences in the sense that there are certain names which by their very sound make an appeal. This is not a question of the names that are hallowed by venerable history or the exploits of past heroes, but the simple sound of the letters.

Again, the modern science of advertisement that struggles to combine startling effects with familiar phrases insists always on the importance of the name; it must be something that can easily be asked for. A novel will have its sale largely determined by its title. Revolving lights are brought into requisition, brilliant colors, verses — anything that can stamp a name on the memory.

Nor is this unreasonable, since, to human fancy, the name sums up the man. It awakens unconscious echoes; at the mention of a name, our imagination goes dreaming on, of faces, words, deeds, of long ago. In an age of abridgments, a name is the shortest abridgment of human life. There is something touching in the re-mark of Scripture that God knows each one of us by name. It seems to make Him more intimate with us, more familiar.

The use, therefore, of names is a custom of human nature. Now, it is noticeable that all human customs have received from God consecration, so that it is not to be wondered at that this custom should also receive from Him its hallowing. This comes through that Name which is above all other names, since at its sound every knee in Heaven and earth must bow.[22] It towers above every other because it sums up in itself the human life of One who was unique. "He shall be called Jesus," said the angel, "for He shall save His people from their sins."[23]

That work was possible to One only; consequently, that one name takes on an importance that is supreme. It is itself the record of a tremendous event, without equal in importance since the world began. The work was unique, so the name that was given to signify the work must also be unique.

Throughout Scripture there is continuously the idea that names signify the office given by God, both in the Old and in the New Testament. Here the holy Name *Jesus* does itself mean "Savior." At the sound of it, therefore, we catch the echoes of power, trust, and mercy. It is like some quickly drawn sketch that, with its bold strokes, suggests rather than defines a perfect picture. It rings the haunting memories of so many scenes, the calling of Matthew, the forgiveness of the Magdalen, the repentance of Peter, the chosen friendship of the Beloved Disciple, the wonders of the death. About it, too, is the fragrance of the parables with their repeated tale of infinite compassion, and the miracles worked as the fruit of that compassion. The sacred Name is, indeed, an epitome of the Gospels.

[22] Phil. 2:10.
[23] Cf. Matt. 1:21.

The Holy Name of Jesus is itself a prayer

The Holy Name therefore, echoed in Christ, the Anointed of God, has dominated history. By its sound we find that the first miracles were worked, and its power was put forward to the first persecutors by the first Apostles. Many were willing to lay down their lives for it. Even the crusading wars that seemed to be hostile in their fierceness to the meekness of Christ were defended and preached for the honor of it. The very beggar in the street begged for alms for the love of that sacred sound. To how many, too, in life, has it not come as a spell to be repeated softly to themselves that the mere echo might ease them in the midst of their troubles, as the lover steels himself to labor in a foreign land or in some distant place by repeating the name of his beloved? And in death's approach, it has brought a steadiness to the wayward fear that ebbs and flows in the souls of the dying. For so many of the martyrs it brought strength, for the confessors hope, for the virgins purity. In Catholic days in England, the prayer was familiar: "Jesus, be to me a Jesus." Richard Rolle[24] says of it, "It shall be in thy ear joy, in thy mouth honey, in thy heart melody." Indeed, as we grow older, we find that the simpler prayers are best. We get into the way of repeating prayers we have found to suit us, instead of venturing upon new fields or more complicated emotions.

Thus the short prayer of the Holy Name supplies the place of all others; it is the shortest, the simplest, the best. In the busy hours of daylight, let it be upon my lips as an unceasing prayer.

---

[24] Richard Rolle of Hampole (1290-1349), English hermit and mystic.

∞

Christ's Resurrection
foreshadows your own resurrection

The resurrection of our blessed Lord from the grave has been regarded as the central mystery of the Catholic Faith. Certainly from apostolic times it has been held to be the pivot around which revolved and on which depended the arguments of Christian theology. For while the death of Christ might be taken to imply that He was in no way different from other men, His triumph over death could have no other meaning than the significant challenge of His claim to unique divinity. To die in defense of one's belief is evidence, indeed, of sincerity, but it cannot demonstrate the authenticity of that conviction, since men have died for contradictory beliefs. That Christ was sincere cannot be denied; the conclusion that He was therefore divine is also itself paradoxically logical; for one who sincerely believes Himself to be God and dies to prove it, must either be hopelessly insane or really divine.

But the final touch is given to the argument, and all the proof rendered irresistible, when to it is added the reappearance of the dead Christ, clothed and habited in a human body. The argument may be put thus: Our Lord claimed to be God, died to attest the sincerity of His claim, and was raised up by His own divine power to life again in testimony of the truth of His doctrine. The author of life and death has therefore added His own witness to the witness of Christ. God has sealed by His power the declaration of His Son. If Christ were not God, God Himself would have been a party to the deceit.

St. Paul is so persuaded of the efficacy of this retort that he seems to be content to base the whole argument of Christianity upon it; for he says expressly that if it be not a fact that Christ has risen from the dead, then is our faith vain.[25] For him, it is no question of spiritual experience of a risen Master, but he is convinced of the bodily life of the man Christ. He proceeds, in fact, in the letter to the Corinthians to arrange with scientific procedure those who had been witnesses of the fact of Christ's reappearance. He puts them in some sort of chronological order. The only two whom he mentions by name, Peter and James, are the very two of whom he tells us in another place that he had personal relations with in Jerusalem.

Nor was there evidently any expectation in the minds of those who saw Him buried that Christ would break through the portals of the tomb. Looking back, they might remember the hints He had made about a three days' sojourn in the grave; but the holy women set out on the first Easter morning to anoint a body that was presumably dead, and thus preserve it from ensuing corruption. The account, too, of the disciples who were on their way to Emmaus when our Lord Himself met them, points in the same direction. They were actually going away from Jerusalem, although they had heard the report of the women that an angel had told them of the Resurrection of the Master, so unprepared were they for any vision of Him. Even when the rest had seen Him, St. Thomas could continue to doubt, confident in the unexpectedness of the event. The Resurrection, then, is to be accounted a fact, not of hysteria, but of history.

[25] 1 Cor. 15:14.

For me, therefore, the historical side of the mystery must never become obscure. Undoubtedly there is a mystical meaning that lies hid within the truth. The new birth, the rising sap of spring, and the feeling of hope that the very season of the year brings with it are all contained in the notion of Easter and its festive interpretation. But beneath all that, and giving it the value it bears for me in life, is the underlying occurrence that was witnessed to by so many: "He rose again according to the Scriptures."

No hallucination will account for it, for they felt His hands and feet, and put their fingers into the print of the nails and into the open wound of the spear. By the lakeside He ate with them. In the room He appeared when not expected, and He was seen by more than five hundred brethren at once. This shows no sense of visionary excitement, but a fact vouched for by as good evidence as any other fact in history. On this fact our Faith rests, in the sense that it testifies to the divinity of Christ. As such the Jews demanded it, the Pharisees understood it and prepared for it, our Lord promised it; and to it the Apostles confidently appealed.

For me, then, it is the earnest of my own resurrection. It tells me that, as He triumphed over death, so must I triumph. It bids me look forward to the new life, not back to the wasted and fallen years. It comes, indeed, as the basis of faith, but also as pointing the lesson of hopefulness, for the actions of Christ are not merely the examples that I must strive to copy, but they are still more importantly the very power by which I get grace to overcome and to attain my final reward.

∞

Christ intercedes for you in Heaven

After asserting our belief in the Resurrection of our Lord, we continue in the Creed to profess our belief in His Ascension. This
doctrine of the Church is clear from both Scripture and Tradition.
After the forty days during which He still lingered on the earth,
He gathered the Apostles around Him, upbraided them all with
their slowness to accept the fullness of His teaching, commissioned them to go forth to preach and to baptize, and then was
withdrawn from their midst. His sacred body, by virtue of His own
divine power, was itself transported to Heaven, where it takes pre-
cedence over all other created nature and exercises forever the
atoning purpose for which He came. In His own human species,
that is, in the outward semblance of humanity that had been visible to the Apostles and the people of Palestine, He has dwelt at
the right hand of the Father, in the possession of His unlimited
power over all creation. To Him is also committed the judgment of
the world. He is present, indeed, on the altars of the Church, body
and soul alike — not, as is evident, in the visible form of His manhood, but under the appearance of bread and wine. As man, He is
in the highest place in Heaven.

This bodily presence must be insisted on as part of the Christian
Faith. There, alone, is the material body still, no mere phantom,

but the true and proper figure of life indeed. He is perfectly human, and humanity requires the double existence of soul and body. The Church has always frankly professed this and never allowed the idea that things of corporeal matter are unfitted for the majesty of God. With all her intense asceticism, she has unswervingly taught the doctrine of the "human form divine."

His continual work, therefore, of interceding for the children of men goes on unabated, since the marks of the wounds appeal unceasingly to the Father. His power is a power, not of destruction, but of salvation.

The older painters with their high contemplative talent expressed this in their own picturesque way. Florentine or Fleming or Venetian, they made no effort to suppose that the Crucifixion and all that it entailed was some past event. For them, it was an eternal act that was as true and as present to their own day as it ever had been; hence, you find that the soldiers of the Passion are dressed in the garments of the artist's own fashion. The towns and architecture that are at the back of the picture are nearly always the familiar scenes of their life.

Nor is it to be thought that the appearance of contemporary modes was due to an ignorance of Palestinian custom; they had, indeed, the unchanging East ready at hand, and with the extensive commercial connection that Venice and the other cities of Italy kept up with the Byzantine Empire, there was plenty of opportunity for them to find out how things were done. They knew the dress and architecture of the Holy Land as well as we, and better. But it was a deliberate attempt to make the life and death of Christ an ever-living event of eternity rather than of time. Hence, too, in the frescoes of Fra Angelico one sees in the corner a saint contemplating some scene of the Gospels, present in spirit at that far-off tragedy. Nor are these things mere whimsical fancies; they are the sober truths of the Faith. Christ is always being born, always dying, always at the right hand of the Father.

Let me realize what this means. It forces me to view the life of Christ as unending and unended. It means that Christ our Lord is now in Heaven at His Father's side "always living to make intercession for us," as St. Paul expressly notes it.[26] The promise of divine assistance until the end of time, the never-failing springs of grace that the sacraments continually conduct to the soul, and the abiding presence of Christ in the hearts of those who love Him show, indeed, that these events are not far off, but continuous. Just as Mass can never be a repetition, but only a continuation of Calvary, so Calvary itself can never cease, since the risen Savior, wounded and glorified, is forever before the majesty of the Father. The Redemption becomes a fact that is linked, not to a date, but to a person who is our sole Mediator, since no other can be needed. This mediation was not the work of a time, but of eternity. Christ is risen indeed and is at the right hand of the Father.

Now, it cannot be too often repeated that the main safeguard to the spiritual life is the constant realization of the living facts of the spiritual world. Never to be blind to the vision is the best possible way of assuring ourselves that we shall not neglect the vision; hence, we have to remind ourselves unceasingly of the daily meaning of the mysteries of the Faith. It is just this that the presence of our Lord at the right hand of the Father memory tends to produce. It makes me see that the work of Redemption is still carried on, in that the appeal of the Wounds and outpoured Blood cries without ceasing to the Father. Let me make myself forever conscious of the eternal value of the facts of the Incarnation.

[26] Heb. 7:25.

∾

The Holy Spirit reveals
God's undying love for you

The Third Person of the Blessed Trinity is the most mysterious; about Him we seem to hear least and to understand most vaguely. The work of Father and Son, their place in the economy of the divine plan, is simple and evident, at least in its main lines; but of the Holy Spirit it appears as though His precise purpose had not been sufficiently described to us. He is the equal of the Father and the Son, of the same nature, power, and substance, eternally existent with Them, participating in the same divine life, forming with Them the ever-blessed Three-in-One. He represents to our human point of view that wonderful mystery, the personified love that proceeds from Father and from Son forever, and by this act completes the perfections of God.

We can conceive of no further addition to that being, save power and knowledge and love. Yet we know also that He has His place, not only in the interrelation (if the word may be allowed) of the Godhead, but in the relationship (although this phrase is certainly inaccurate) that exists between God and us. For since God is one and indivisible, His love for us cannot be other than the love that He has for Himself. In Him there can be no distinction at all. Hence, we discover that He loves Himself and us in the love of the Holy Spirit. His love we see to be nothing else than Himself, unchanging, undying, without shadow of alteration. Sin as we may, we cannot make God love us less. Children though we be of wrath, He cannot help but love us, for the gifts of God, especially the supreme gift of Himself, are without repentance.

God cannot cease to love me. That is the most startling fact that our doctrine reveals. Sinner or saint He loves and cannot well help Himself. Magdalen in her sin, Magdalen in her sainthood, was loved by God. The difference between her position made some difference also in the effect of that love on her, but the love was the same, since it was the Holy Spirit who is the love of the Father and the Son.

Whatever I do, I am loved. But then, if I sin, am I unworthy of love? Yes, but I am unworthy always. Nor can God love me for what I am, since, in that case, I would compel His love, force His will by something external to Himself. In fact, really if I came to consider, I would find that I was not loved by God because I was good, but that I was good because God loved me. My improvement does not cause God to love me, but is the effect of God's having loved me. Consequently, even when I am punished by God, He cannot hate me. It is His very love itself that drives Him (out of the very nature of its perfection) to punish, so that Dante spoke truly when he imagined over the portals of Hell the inscription "To rear me was the work of Immortal Power and Love."

Each of us is, therefore, sure that he is loved eternally, that, from God's side, that love can suffer no change. How, then, is it that we grow evil, or lose the familiar communion that we once had with Him? It is because He has given us the terrible power of erecting, as it were, a shield between ourselves and His love. He loves forever the same, but it is we who, by our sins, have the power to shut off that love from effecting anything good in our souls.

Surely there is something overpowering in the concept of this work of God, this unceasing and unchanging love. I talk of fidelity in friendship as being to me the most beautiful thing of earth. The sight of a lover, faithful, despite disillusionment, to his beloved is the most wonderful thing in all the world; this loyalty of soul for soul, despite every toil and stress, good repute and evil; beyond all degradation and above all ambition, when soul has been knit to soul.

> *Love is not love*
> *Which alters, when it alteration finds,*
> *Or bends with the remover to remove.*

Yet this is but a feeble representation of the ineffable union between God and me. Sinner though I be, He is my lover always. Even my sins cannot break His persistence; it can only set a barrier between me and it, can only, by the dangerous gift of my free will, prevent its effect from being seen in my soul. But the love of God is with me always, "in me and within me and around, in million-billowed consentaneousness, the flowing, flowing, flowing" of the Spirit. How can I hold back, howsoever wrongly I have acted? For His love is the same forever. As I was deep in His love when I was a child, so also does He love me now.

∞

The Holy Spirit enlightens your mind

The work of the Spirit has been outlined in the Gospels. Our Lord
at His Last Supper, when His teaching seems to have expounded
in the full splendor and height of its tremendous mysteries, when,
if ever, the Apostles could truly say that He had passed out of the
realm of parable and had come into the deepest ways of truth —
our Lord at His Last Supper said that His going away was necessary
for the coming of the Paraclete. He had to die and rise and ascend,
and then, from the right hand of the Father, His own work would
continue in a ceaseless intercession for all the children of men. On
earth, however, His place would be taken by the Holy Spirit, who
would teach the Apostles all things and bring back to their minds
whatever He had taught them. In this way was guaranteed the infallibility and growth in doctrine that are the work of the Spirit.

Our Lord had certainly to temper His doctrine to the minds of
His hearers. He could not from the first reveal to them the full
meaning of His words. In the beginning, indeed, the need was simply for the main ideas to sink gradually in; then slowly the other
less important although necessary truths could be added. The little that He did teach was not too clearly retained, so that He frequently had to be upbraiding them with not having understood
His meaning. The length of His stay with them had not made

them always grasp of what spirit they were. What would happen when He was gone? He answers that only His going will set them on their own strength.

As the Church grew in the range and depth of her doctrine, so must she forever grow. The problems that distract her must increase; with each generation, they change their expression, for the forms of thought are the most mobile and uncertain of all human construction. A cathedral lasts longer than a philosophy; a haunting song outlives the latest system of metaphysics. Questions are settled only that the restless mind of man may add another difficulty to the solution that allayed its previous doubt. Rapier-like in its power to find the weak joint in the armor, reason, sharpened by scientific criticism, picks here and there at the composition of the Creed. New conditions, new discoveries, new languages, require new attitudes, new difficulties, and new adjustments of old principles.

Obviously it is not sufficient to know the rules of the art; the great trouble and anxiety comes in their application. So, too, is it in the Faith. The articles of belief seem at times to suggest contradictory answers to the problem that happens at the moment to perplex our minds. According to one mystery, one solution; according to a second, another. How to choose and select, to decree without fear or favor, without danger of mistake, is the work of the Church. Not merely in the broad line of the Church, but in the individual soul, the same task must go on — the balance between what has to be discarded as of passing significance and what is of abiding import. I have to discover for myself which is the mere adventitious dressing of some bygone form of thought and which is of enduring truth. Yet not indeed for myself, since in the Church abides forever the indwelling of the Spirit of God.

Thus came the Holy Spirit on the first Whitsunday. He came, we read, in the rush of a great wind and in the form of fire, to typify the illumination of the mind by faith and the impulse given to the will by love. He came to teach all things, to recall to their minds the full doctrine of Christ.

At once after their reception of His grace, the Apostles become changed men. No longer timid and frightened followers who fled at the first sight of danger and denied with an oath that they had ever known the Name of Christ, they now become glad missionaries, declaring themselves willing to suffer in defense of that Name. In council chambers and before kings, they announce the Gospel. So, too, when perplexities come as to whether or not they should force on all Christians the ceremonies of the Old Law as being of binding value on the conscience of the New Dispensation, they assemble, discuss, and decree in a phrase that clearly marks their own appreciation of the place they had to take in giving to the world the message of Christ: "It has seemed good to the Holy Spirit and to us."[27] They and the Holy Spirit are fellow workers in the apostolate of Christ.

The revelation made to them by their Master was but a grain of mustard seed compared with the full development that should come after. It would grow from that until it included all truth, but the knowledge of every detail of that truth would not at once be necessary, so the gradual unfolding was left to the work of the Spirit.

The work, then, of the Holy Spirit is twofold: to inflame the love and to enlighten the mind. Let me wait patiently for this illumination of my spirit by the Holy Spirit, putting no obstacle in the way, praying daily for that illumination which shall light, as by a vision, my view of life.

[27] Acts 15:28.

Through the Holy Spirit's gifts,
your actions can be worthy of merit

The real difficulty experienced by most of us in keeping up our courage in the unceasing battle of life is that we realize how utterly we depend upon ourselves. Of course, it is true that the grace of God will be always with us, that it is never withheld, and that there is always a sufficiency of it for us to meet and triumph over every assault of the evil one.

Yet even so, the disquieting thought comes home to us that it is always we ourselves who determine our own actions; so much so, indeed, that if they are worthy of reward, it is we who obtain the reward, but if of punishment, that it is we who suffer. Says St. Thomas with stimulating paradox: "Not partly by God and partly by man, but altogether by God and altogether by man." That is to say, I have to reconcile these two separate truths: I cannot will anything without God's grace helping me to do it; yet God's help does not take away from me my responsibility in the act, for its moral value will be adjudged to my credit or demerit.

It is, then, to repeat, just in the second part of the paradox that the difficulty lies. Conscious as I am of my past failure, I can hardly look forward without dismay to future troubles. Consequently, I turn to see if there is anything that the Church teaches that can relieve me from the burden of this discouragement. Is there any doctrine that gives me in any way at all an escape from the terror of my own responsibility?

To this the Church makes answer that her doctrine of the indwelling of the Spirit of God by means of the sevenfold gifts does go a long way to remove the load from my own shoulders, does suggest to me a perfectly true sense in which my soul is ruled not by me, but by another. As far, then, as these things can be stated in human language, we may say that the gifts differ from the virtues in this: the gifts are moved into operation not by me, but by God. When I perform an act of virtue, it is obvious that (not excluding God's grace) it is I who perform it, and acquire merit in consequence; but in the movement of the gifts, it is not I but God who is the mover. He is the sole mover. In the actual movement of the soul under the influence of the gifts I cannot claim any lot or part; I cannot claim any merit at all. It is He who has His hand on the tiller, who guides, steers, propels. Hence, it is He, not I, who has control of my soul.

With the four gifts that perfect my intelligence, He illumines my mind; with the one gift that perfects the will, He inflames my desire; and with the two that perfect the passions, He strengthens with His intimate indwelling my emotions of love and fear. By the instrumentality of the gifts, the soul is keyed up to the level of God, tuned to concert pitch. Or, to vary the metaphor, the soul is made so responsive to the divine influence that, like some delicate electrical receiver, it registers every passing breath of God. I must remember always that it is His doing, not mine.

Must it therefore be admitted that by the gifts I merit nothing? Surely if this is so, it would seem as though I had therefore no need for them. If their influence on my life was only to leave me no better off than before I received them, I might just as well not have had them at all. If, in them, God is the mover to the exclusion of myself, then it would be absurd for me to expect any reward for what has been absolutely no work of mine. This is true. I do not merit by the gifts.

Yet to this I must also add that I can profit by them. The Holy Spirit lights up my mind and enables me to see, or refines my perception of and responsiveness to His least suggestion. That is His doing so far. Illumination and refinement are entirely His work. But my part comes in later, when I act up to these suggestions or in accordance with this vision. Then I am profiting by the gifts. Suggestion and vision alike are from God. He opens my mind, and I see Him everywhere, in a flower, in trouble, in the soul of a sinner. If, in consequence of seeing Him in the sinner, I turn to that sinner and speak kindly of the love that never fails, or if I help him even by my sympathy, even if I speak no word of spiritual significance, then the good I achieve, or at least the good I am trying to do, becomes my way of profiting by means of the gifts. This indwelling of the Spirit of God, while it takes from me the control of my soul and hands it over for the moment to God, yet gives me something by which I can again love and be rewarded. I do not merit by the sevenfold gifts, but I do merit through them.

∞

The Holy Spirit's gifts enable you
to see God in all things and events

Out of the Holy Spirit's sevenfold gifts, there are four that perfect
the intellectual side of man. They are wisdom, understanding,
knowledge, and counsel. Of these, it is obvious that the last is
chiefly given to me for the benefit of others, the first three for
myself.

The gift of counsel means quite simply that I receive suggestions from the Holy Spirit as to what advice I am to give to those
who come to consult me. I am made so responsive to the Divine
Wisdom that I at once perceive what is best for others, in a way
that, without the gifts, I would be wholly unable to do. Thus, it
sometimes happens that I am suddenly conscious of words apparently suggested to me from outside that are as much a surprise to
myself as they are of evident comfort to my hearers. The very
phrase for which they have been longing, and which alone seems
to have the power to enable them to see straight into the entan-
glement of their affairs, comes trippingly to my tongue, even
though I am perhaps unacquainted with their circumstances, except for the little that they have been able to tell me.

The gift of knowledge enables me to see God in the natural
world of creation, in reason, in the arts and crafts of man, in

nature. It is an understanding of God, learned from the material things of life. On the other hand, the gift of understanding allows me to see Him in the supernatural world of faith, in truths and mysteries, while wisdom further acquaints me with the interrelation between faith and reason, nature and supernature.

In these ways, God, by means of His gifts, lights up our minds. Under this illumination, I now look out upon creation and find it to be alive with the traces of God's presence. Nature becomes at once the very loveliness of His vesture, and I say to myself that if I can touch but the hem of it, I shall be made whole.[28] Even in the relentless preying of beast on beast I see somehow the wonderful work of God. The machinery of man is no longer a sight of ugliness, but becomes colored by the brightness of His power. It is the child's toy that reproduces on an infinitely smaller scale the creative energy of the Creator. The linked reasoning of philosophy is the imitation of an infinite intelligence.

Then I lift my mind higher to the ampler regions of faith. Here surely is the very splendor of God. In the depths of mysteries that my intelligence is too faulty and finite to fathom, lurks the wonder of His truth and the ways of His wisdom. Justice, mercy, loving kindness, and overpowering majesty are all crowded upon my imagination by the thought of all that He has revealed to me of Himself. Here, if anywhere, I can at least understand that God is altogether above me. Then, again, the highest gift of all floods my soul with even clearer light, and I see the interrelation of all things. I see how the death of a sparrow, the sunset, and the Incarnation are all parts of a perfect whole. It is not an uplifting of the soul from earth to Heaven, but a perception that earth and Heaven are themselves the fragments of a larger scheme.

These, indeed, are visions such as the gifts that perfect the intelligence evoke in the mind. But it is our business to see that they

[28] Cf. Matt. 9:21.

do not remain barren visions. Just as faith is allowed us that it may lead to life, and as we shall be the more straitly condemned if we do not carry into practice what faith reveals, so also will our judgment be the more severe if, with all the light that is vouchsafed to us, we yet prefer to walk unheeding in the midst of this wonderful world. There are very many who find life dull and religion altogether a thing that bores them. Perhaps the reason is that they neglect the vision; it is there before their eyes if they would only look.

But for me, the world must become transfigured. Life, then, will be found more easy, less vexatious, will lose that dreary outlook that is the most depressing of all temptations and that makes me consider it not worth living. I shall at least understand that there is a purpose in existence. Evil and suffering are seen to be parts that need to be handled carefully so that their places in the design may not be overlooked; not ignored but acknowledged, they are found to be the stepping-stones to greatness. Success and failure have no separate meaning, for the need is for them both.

So, in all, patience is discovered to be the most perfect virtue to have achieved — patience with others, with oneself, with life, with God. Nor is this state of soul due to a disregard of the circumstances that attend our time on earth, but to a more thorough appreciation of the terms of existence. I see life fuller, enjoy it more. It is the patience not of the wearied voluptuary, but of the enraptured lover, who is so sure of his love that he can afford to wait through all time for eternity.

∞

God's nearness gives you courage

The gift that perfects the will is that of fortitude, which, as we have stated in general terms, must be carefully distinguished from the *virtue* of fortitude. This gift is entirely under the direction of God and excludes altogether on my part any action at all in the operation of the gift. This exclusion of all human cooperation seems harder, perhaps, to understand when the will is in question, as it is in the gift of fortitude. It seems altogether impossible to imagine that God can direct the will and yet that its act should be voluntary. It is clear, indeed, from the Catholic doctrine of grace, that it is possible for God to move the will so powerfully as to determine, not merely that the will shall act, but to determine also that it shall act freely. God is so intimate to the will that He can, so to say, save it from within. But this is different from His control of it in the gift of fortitude.

In the intellect, a light can be present that is none of our own; but in the will, how can there be a force that is not itself of the will? In other words, we have to reconcile two ideas apparently contradictory — namely, a will that acts yet does not merit. I am apparently and actually perfectly free, for God does not compel the will unwillingly. Yet with all my freedom, under the guidance of the gift I cannot acquire merit. That is what we said was the very characteristic of the sevenfold gifts: that they were, in their proper operation, entirely the work of God.

To grasp the way in which God thus works, we can describe it only as a sense of firmness imparted to the soul by the perceived presence of God. A comparison, however inadequate, suggests to us in what manner this is effected. The mere presence of others gives us a courage that alone we would probably not have experienced. A child having to undergo some slight operation, some test of pain, is usually willing to bear it patiently if only his mother will hold his hand. It is, of course, not that the pain is in this way rendered any the less, but only that a feeling of bravery is imparted by the mere presence of the mother.

So, again, in a still more striking way is it with children in the dark. They are frightened by the loneliness of it; but if another is in the room, even though he may not be seen nor heard, without any sensible appreciation of the presence and sustained only by the knowledge of the nearness, the child becomes at once reinforced by a courage that springs entirely from the other's proximity.

An invalid will grow querulous when he knows that he is alone. The mere presence of an onlooker will nerve him to bravery without a word being spoken or thing done.

In some such sense, our soul, by the perceived presence of the Holy Spirit, is encouraged, despite its natural or acquired timidity, to persevere. Thus it will be seen that the paradox has been reconciled. The perception of the presence has not been our own doing; still less has the nearness of God been through any merit of our own. But the mere indwelling of the Holy Spirit has itself refined the perceptive faculties of the will so that they are strengthened by the Divine Friend.

This, then, is the precise purpose of this particular gift — a perception, apart from all the ordinary methods, of the proximity of God to the soul. Not, indeed, as though it meant nothing more than the appreciation that God is everywhere, but rather just one aspect of the appreciation — namely, such an idea of it as will enable the soul to gain courage. Always the gifts mean, according to the teaching of the Church, such a refinement of spirit as shall enable us to perceive the least passing breath of God. So still has our soul become that the slightest stir ruffles the surface with ripples of a passing presence. So delicate is my soul that instinctively I am conscious of the indwelling of the Spirit of God and nerved in consequence by a corresponding strength that is no result of any determined act of will, but is, as it were, forced on me by the very nature of the case. Neither presence nor strengthening are in any case my doing, nor do I participate in either. But when I take the further step and proceed to act in consequence of them — when, in virtue of a strength that is not my own, I banish fear and face resolutely the difficulties of the good life — then has the gift led to the virtue, and out of something that was divine has blossomed something that is human.

Surely it will be of the utmost consequence to me to realize this nearness of God, and the courage that its perception will give. In all my trials, none are so hard for me to bear as discouragement and depression. How, then, can I now shirk my duty and the disagreeable necessities imposed on me once I have made use of this Divine Friend, whose hand is always locked in mine?

∞

The Holy Spirit's gifts shape
your attitude toward God

Besides the intelligence and the will, there are other faculties that, although they are numerous and diverse, can be shortly grouped under the heading of the emotions. Sometimes they are called passions, in the philosophical meaning of the word; that is to say, the movements of the nonrational portion of our being. Sometimes we speak of them as sentiments, especially when we wish to imply that they are to be considered weak and effeminate. Under both categories there will be meditations on them, for they constitute a very considerable force in human life. Here, however, we have only to consider them as perfected by two gifts of the Holy Spirit.

For this purpose, it will be necessary to say that these emotions, although various, can be themselves divided into two main headings, such as fall under the general name of love and anger.

Under the first would come joy, desire, and so forth — namely, all these sentiments that have upon us the effect of drawing us toward something or some person and giving us expansive feelings toward all humanity. The chief result of these, even physically, is that they widen our sympathies.

Under the heading of anger, we would place fear and the other set of feelings, the effects of which are to chill the soul, to contract the emotions, and to produce upon us the feeling of numbness. Even physically we know from experiments of psychologists that the result is to stifle action. The one set shows that our mind has been attracted, the other that it has been repelled.

Piety, then, is said to perfect the attitude of man toward God and toward the things of God, by giving to his relation to his Maker the appearance of friendship. Fear of the Lord, on the other hand, inclines him rather to look upon God in the character of a judge. The one sanctifies the feeling of love; the other hallows the feeling of fear. And in the life of the soul, there is room and need for both. Indeed, it may be said not unjustly that together they produce in the soul that instinct of reverence that is begotten of both. Love that knows no reverence is not love at all, but passion; and fear that cannot climb to revere the object of our fear is altogether inhuman.

So, too, from the opposite standpoint, it can hardly be questioned that the chief obstacles that get in the way of our perfect service of God are the two characteristics of hardness and independence. We do not respond to His appeals; the Passion and the ever-flowing love leave us cold, because our hearts are so hardened by the interests and the cares of our daily life, and that deep respect that we owe to the Master of life becomes too often irritation at the way in which His commands cut across our pleasures. We object to the manner in which, through His ministers, we are told to do something that altogether revolts us — not because it is something very great, but because of its very pettiness. He treats us, we are often inclined to think, as though we were children. Fear of restraint is a natural instinct in men and animals.

Reverence, then, suggests that there is needed in us somehow a feeling of tenderness toward God, a softening of the hardened edges of the soul, and at the same time a subjection, an avowal of our dependence on Him. The Holy Spirit is, then, to be considered as perfecting by means of these gifts even that borderland of man that lies between the purely reasonable and the purely sensual. The vague stretches of man's consciousness are, by the indwelling of the Spirit of God, made at once responsive to the slightest communication from it.

Psychology in our own time has made its greatest progress by exploring all the really unknown lands that are in each of us. The phenomena that are produced by hypnotism and spiritualism are evidence of many other things that are at present as closed to us as the regions of Tibet. But in this connection they explain to us how whatever lies beyond the influence, or rather, direction of reason and will must still be brought into subjection to the standard of Christ. We have, therefore, nothing to fear from the researches of professors, for they are but giving us opportunity for extending in our own souls the territory that must be handed back to Him who made it. This communication and susceptibility to the movement of God is His work, not ours. The virtue must be added to the gift, must follow it as man's contribution (not, of course, to the exclusion of God) to the work of his salvation. It is not sufficient for me to feel this presence or to be conscious of the reverence due, but I must further add to it the love and fear of my heart embodied in action — namely, in thought, word, and deed.

Part 2

∞

The Blessed Mother

Mary's special calling
makes her a powerful intercessor

Since the Council of Ephesus, in 431, the Church has unhesitatingly proclaimed her faith in the divine maternity of our Lady. There had been much discussion on the point at first, for it was only gradually that the Christian people began to consider how our Lord could be God and man at the same time. Heretics had arisen to assert that He was either one or the other, so that the Church was forced to define precisely what was the true teaching of our Lord.

Then, when He had been declared to be God and man — one single Person subsisting in two natures, human and divine — the further point was immediately raised as to whether it was to be judged correct to speak of His Mother as the Mother of God. Only by degrees did this come up for discussion. It was clear, indeed, that our Lady could not be the mother of the Godhead. God, as God, could not have been born of her, since He was of eternity, and she but a creature of time. As God, He could not be her son, but as man, He was obviously her child.

Now, did this constitute her His mother in such a way that she could rightly be spoken of as the Mother of God? It was a question, in other words, of precise terminology, for in all these matters, it is common knowledge how careful the Church has always been to be perfectly accurate. The position, then, was to discover the tradition of Christian people, and it was in Ephesus that the bishops were gathered together who were to announce what had been the constant teaching of the Church.

It was a coincidence that at Ephesus this decision had to be made, for it was at Ephesus that our Lady had lived after the Apostles had been dispersed. When she had been confided to the care of St. John by our Lord on the Cross, this had been interpreted to mean that the young apostle was to have charge of her while she yet remained separate from her Son. When, then, John came himself to settle at Ephesus in the position of bishop or chief of the Christian community there assembled, it was only natural that she should accompany him and live with him. This, at least, is the ordinary account that is given us of the matter, and still at Ephesus is shown "the Virgin's house."

The decision of the bishops can be easily guessed. They declared her to be rightly acclaimed the Mother of God, and since that date, the title has been unfailingly assigned to her in the official Liturgy of the Church. The basis of this claim is the doctrine of the Incarnation. Our Lord came to redeem us, to atone for the sins of the human race. This He could not do unless He was at once God and man: man that he might suffer, God that His sufferings might have infinite avail. Moreover, before He became man, He was already a person, being indeed the Second Person of the Holy Trinity; consequently, there was no reason He should take to Himself a new personality. The divine personality alone could enable Him to fulfill all justice. Consequently, when He was born, He was born as man, but it was a divine Person who was born as man. Man by nature, He still retained His unique divine personality. Our Lady, therefore, is the mother of Him who is God.

The importance of this decision can hardly be overestimated, since it is absolutely on it alone that rests the whole reason for our especial devotion to our Lady, above the devotion that we show to all the saints. Her whole position in the Catholic world depends upon the acceptance of this truth.

We believe, that is to say, that if she was chosen to be His mother, she must have been fitted for her work. Whoever is singled out by God for a special place on earth is no doubt prepared by every necessary grace for that place. If, then, out of all humanity He fitted our Lady to be His mother, it is obvious that she must have been made ready by every possible grace for her close relationship to Him. To no other was it granted to have such intimate acquaintance with Him. For months He abode within her womb; for years He was tended by her alone, left to her sole care and control. Surely, then, we have a right to assume that she must have been fitted above all others to sustain so absolute a trust. He would not have permitted one so closely related to His own body to see corruption, for of her very flesh was that body formed.

From the moment, then, that she accepted her high destiny from the angel's voice, there shone in her eyes the light of motherhood. Without human intervention or concurrence, by her sole union with the Deity, was born her Son. Surely, then, with truth did the angel hail her as full of grace.

Because she is the Mother of God, we draw to her with confidence, assured that from her own humanity will spring her wish to help us, and from her close union with God her power to do so.

∞

Mary's perfection is a gift from God

The law of Original Sin was relaxed only in one single case, for one soul that needed redemption. Upon the whole human race that was to be born, the curse was pronounced that no descendant of that first pair could escape the need of the Redeemer — however holy or sacred, however allied in kinship or work to the Incarnate God, however destined to precede or follow, to herald or remind the world of its Savior. Each created human soul stood in need of a redeemer, required the Blood of Christ to be applied to itself before redemption could come to it. This none could avoid.

The privileges of our blessed Lady were many and great, but they could not include any such gift as that. God could not really allow her to be saved without the intervention of her Son. As much as I, so much did she, require the saving merits of her Son to be applied to her.

Our Lord Himself alone out of all created nature needed no such justification. By His own power redemption had come; God as well as man, He stood in need of no redeeming. It was He, indeed, who was offended against, not He who had offended; but apart from Him, no other could escape. Even His Mother must fall under the universal law. She, too, had to be ransomed, and any doctrine that implied her freedom from this requirement would be blasphemy against the word of God.

This much must be borne in mind, then, before we can hope to understand the meaning of this privilege; unique as it was, it did not exempt our Lady from the need of redemption.

The difference, then, between her case and mine was not that I had to be redeemed and she had not, but only in the different ways in which that redemption was applied. We were both of us, our Lady and myself, redeemed — both cleansed from Original Sin. But with her, it was, so to say, a preventative cleansing; with me, a cleansing after the stain had already been made on the soul.

Original Sin, we must remember, is transmitted by means of the body. The soul comes to us straight from the hands of God. It is the only thing that is directly created by God. Everything else comes into the world through the mediation of secondary causes. The soul, since it is from God, could not arrive already laden with sin. There remains, therefore, the body, which is produced by means of the joint action of my parents. All flesh and blood (formed from them and thus descending, ultimately from the single pair whence came the human race) brings with it the taint of sin. Not, of course, that the material could be sinful, but that it brings sin in its train.

Nor, again, are we to imagine that at any moment the body exists without the soul; according to the ordinary scientific opinion of our time, the fetus, from the first moment of existence, contains human life. But although soul and body come together in an immediate embrace, it is still correct to say that it is from the body and not from the soul that the stain of sin comes, and for this reason: that the soul is of God, and the body of man.

By the privilege, then, of the Immaculate Conception, we mean no more than that our Lady was redeemed by her Son and that the application of His merits to her soul was made in a way different from the way in which they were applied to others. She had a privilege, a special exception to a general law. Through no merits of her own, long before she was able to merit or demerit, solely through the action of her Son, she was preserved from all contagion of sin. She was already redeemed before she was conceived in the womb. Without in any way interfering with the work of His divine atonement, at the very moment of her conception, the power of God warded from her the least stain of sin. In virtue of His sacred Passion, as yet only foreseen, her baptism was wrought without any ceremony and at the instant that her body and soul were united in an eternal embrace.

Thus it is seen that, so far from her privilege detracting in any way from the power of God, or her sinlessness being in any sense due to herself, God went out of His way to deal with her. She is, as always, the highest example that we know of the supreme mercy of God. Sometimes, perhaps, we are led to think of her as though she were in some way less beholden to Him than we are. Really she has received much more at His hands and owes Him love and gratitude that are far greater than ours. By the very splendor of grace with which He endowed her from the first instant of life, and by the never-failing spring of grace that grew greater from day to day, she has become the greatest miracle of all creation, the one part of creation that more than any other owes to Him debts beyond the possibility of humanity to repay.

Salute her, then, my soul, because of her excellence, but salute God more for the existence of such perfection shown to our eyes, and for the wonderful thing that He has done for that human nature that she bears in common possession with us.

∞

Mary, the Seat of Wisdom, can help you understand divine things

There are two things necessary to wisdom: opportunities for acquiring knowledge and a mental capacity to make use of the opportunities afforded us. The first resolves itself, more or less, into the need of someone to instruct us. This may, it is true, in quite a number of instances be adequately offered through the means of a book. There are special sciences or branches of learning in which a quantity of reading is necessary, without which it may be altogether impossible to grasp the subject. Thus, we might say of the study of history that it is almost entirely built up of materials that demand our closest attention and scrutiny.

In other kinds of knowledge, the need may be only for a capable master to instruct us in the main lines and principles. This is especially true of those who are concerned with abstract knowledge. In philosophy, many of the greatest have dispensed with books, taught by their own minds and the stimulus of conversation and discussion with congenial, although opposingly-minded, friends.

In the sacred knowledge of God, it is, above all, obvious that we require instruction rather than books, a master rather than a library. But there is also, again, the necessity for a certain amount of intelligence on our part. Said Dr. Johnson on a famous occasion, "I can supply you with arguments, but not with the wit to understand them." Hence, it is clear that the best master in the world will be altogether unable to effect anything on those who are incompetent to follow him. In fact, the better the master, often, on that account, the worse the pupil.

Now, in the case of our Lady, we notice that she was gifted in a marvelous way. She had at once the greatest Master of all wisdom, and at the same time the best mental capacities for that wisdom. The Son of God, who is the Eternal Wisdom of the Father, was in her company for thirty uninterrupted years, during which time she is recorded to have pondered over the words that He let fall. We are always talking about the effect on children of being brought up entirely in the company of their elders. They are exceedingly precocious, acquire the very phraseology of their parents, and have a view of life that is original and fresh. Whether we consider this an advantage or not, we are quick to see the influence that grown-up people receive from their acquaintances; we judge a man by the company he keeps. What, then, must have been the opportunities that lay in the path of the Mother of God! Her acquaintance with the economy of the divine plan must have been profound. The questions and answers of the Doctors could not be compared with her manifold communication with the Substance of the Brightness of the Father.

Moreover, not merely had she the unique chance in the world of obtaining knowledge of the things of God, but she had also unique opportunities of making the best use of them. She had, that is to say, out of all the world the mind most fitted to understand the words of God. We consider always that children have glimpses of God that are lost to us; we judge that their communication with God is so intimate and natural, so innocent and pure, that they must have helps to give us in their chance and broken remarks. All that Child ever had was hers. The innocence that came from the Immaculate Conception, an unsullied soul that never knew the least stain of sin — where in all the world was anyone so divinely gifted?

It is, then, no mere poetry to speak of her, as does the Church, as the Seat of Wisdom. Over her were outspread the wings of the Spirit of God. United to the Incarnate Word, prepared with angelic purity to understand the divine messages, responsive to the voice of an angel that our grosser ears would not at all have perceived, unclouded by the weakness that sin causes to the intelligence, passionless, without even the dullness of old age, she stands at the head of the long line of the wise who lead onward the children of men. Surely, then, we know where to go in our perplexities of mind.

All, in some way or other, must be puzzled by the intricate problem of life. There are so many things in this amazing world that we do not understand, so many stories of the dealings of God that we cannot reconcile with what we have been taught of mercy and justice and truth. There is as well the outstanding perplexity of ourselves when in the mood we consider our place and purpose and daily failure. There is, finally, the whole of life and death and afterlife, the Incarnation with all that follows from that stupendous mystery, and the meaning of the Church. Where else shall we carry these things that so disturb us, save to the Mother who knew and asked, and in her heart pondered over all these things? Of surpassing intelligence, she shall be our refuge to her Son. For she is but the Seat of that Divine Wisdom which is in her, but not hers. Her Wisdom is not her own, but His to whom we beg her to lead us.

∞

Mary is the Mother of Mercy

There seems to have been no parable that so much attracted the early Christians as the parable of the Good Shepherd. They have scrawled over the walls of the catacombs the figure of the Divine Master, carrying upon His bowed shoulders the wandering and rescued lamb. Even when they set out to depict the figure of St. Peter, the vicar of Christ, they show him also as continuing the role of his leader, and in their forceful art have carved the apostle in the guise and at the work of a shepherd. The Child Jesus Himself in their best and most charming statue is the boy David, with a sling, yet at the same time with the poor and familiar load of a sheep.

Then, as though they could not conceive of any more beautiful idea in which to sum up the work of God's maiden Mother, they have in one case represented her by the side of the Good Shepherd, feeding with her hands a crowd of fluttering birds; she, too, has the high and sacred office that comes to those who the more nearly approach to Christ, of succoring the distressed. We, too, hail her under various titles that so proclaim her kindly privilege: she is Our Lady of Perpetual Help; above all, the Mother of Mercy.

Now, mercy, about which the poets have said such beautiful things (especially Shakespeare in several of his plays; *The Merchant of Venice* and *Measure for Measure* both have passages of peculiar and affecting loveliness), implies, on the one hand, a power of sympathy, and on the other, a position to show that mercy to others — the fellow feeling of sorrow and the ability to help.

In the case of our Lady, it must be evident that she has an understanding of all distress. We speak of her as the Queen of Martyrs, the Mother of Sorrows, because we regard her as having touched the depths of all human anguish. The whole progress of her life was a progress in suffering from the moment of the birth of her Son, through the early anxieties that the massacre of the Innocents entailed, the words of Simeon, and the losing of the Child and His seemingly upbraiding words about His Father's business. The shadow of the Cross during all the thirty years of intimacy, the leave-taking, the known plottings of the Pharisees, the detailed pains of those last days, and the terrors of His agony and death and burial have marked out her burden as above the burdens that have fallen to the lot of the cursed children of Adam.

Is there exaggeration in the way that the Church applies to her the words that the prophets spoke of her Son, that there was no other sorrow to be seen like unto hers? Indeed, apart from His sufferings, which more than any other human being she was able to realize, there have never been sufferings such as hers. Desolation, distress, disappointment, and bereavement were the constant attendants of her life: no one, then, can approach her without feeling that she will understand their own woe. And if she understands as none other can, will she not also desire to help as none other can, since she is the mother of Him who was all love? If His saints are distinguished by love, caught from the fire of His heart, certainly she, more than all the others, must have in her nature the wide sympathy of Christ — the sympathy, and also the will to aid.

Not, then, alone as the spring-head whence broke the waters of wisdom, but as also the nearest and most faithful follower of the

Divine Fount of mercy, we come to her in our distress. Confident, indeed, we are that she will understand by the sad experience of her own troubled life on earth; confident also that, understanding, she will desire to help, we turn to her. The love of God, which has worked the great deeds of pity since the world began, cannot exist in her without effect; the kindness that she saw for thirty years on earth cannot have left her outlook on life untouched. Mother of Sorrow, she is also the Mother of the pitiful Heart. Not merely does she sympathize with sorrow, but she is filled with longing to ease and allay it — the consoler, we say, of the afflicted. Finally, she not only understands and desires to help, but she has far more than any other the power to show that in the fullest way.

The Chroniclers tell us that when Edward III had made up his mind to destroy the burghers of Calais because of the harm they had wrought upon his subjects, and had refused to spare their lives, even at the request of his best soldier and his favorite knight, the Queen of England hurried from her court across the sea to add her petitions to the same cause. Wrathful at her arrival and at her demand, he could only answer: "I can deny nothing to the mother of my son."

In applying this to our Lady, is there not in this purely human view of God and His dealings with men, something of comfort? He does not, indeed, repent of His commands, but He may well have willed to spare at the request of the Mother of His Son.

Part 3

∞

The unity of God's creatures

∞

Angels play a part in your life

Two truths are quite clear to us: that God has arranged the whole of creation into an ascending scale of being, and that it is one principle of His divine governance of the world to work upon the lower by means of the higher. The first principle that has just been stated is perfectly clear; every day it is made even clearer by science. The various kingdoms of which we hear in our elementary studies in the physical sciences are themselves set in order; then, within the domains of each kingdom, the several kinds and species can themselves be grouped in a scale of perfection. There is no need to set this out at length; all that will be necessary will be to note that the ascending grade of nature is measured by the diminution of its dependence on matter.

Thus, the mineral is entirely immersed in material existence and cannot be said to have any real life (although that word itself seems almost incapable of definition). Above this is the vegetable world, having certain properties that, although material in the sense that they can be materially described, are yet endowed with a freedom and a motion that are denied to minerals. Above this comes the animal kingdom, which obviously again is material in its manifestations, and yet has that about it which raises it altogether above the merely material order: the swift guidance of instinct lifts the life of the beast to a higher plane than the vegetable can be said to have reached, although even with the latter, careful observers have discovered something that looks like the rudimentary beginnings of instinct. Above the beast is man, whose glory it is that he can rise so much superior to all other material creation, yet whose shame it is that, with all this, he can also be brought so low.

We continue this principle by expecting to find that there is above man, and on that account even more removed from matter than he, a race of spirits; for man, with all his powers of mind, made even more wonderful by his elevation to the supernatural order, is still a body composed of flesh and blood. This race, then, of spirits superior to man, because more full of life and less immersed in matter — in fact spiritual in its nature — will, on the second principle enunciated, be the means through which God works on the soul of man; for it is evident that God's way of dealing is as far as may be to carry out the whole design of creation by means of creation itself.

Obviously there are certain things in God that are altogether incommunicable; but for the actual continuance of the universe, He has endowed it with a power of recuperation, material and spiritual, that requires always the instrumentality of God, but conveyed through created channels. Thus, the very law by which He began the life of the world was that, of itself, it should increase and multiply. So, again, the mineral world is brought out to its perfection not directly by God, but mediately by the hammer and the tools of man. So also the beauties of nature's fruits and flowers are enormously affected and are at times even necessarily dependent on the instrumentality of the winds and insects and birds and man; while the wild life of the beasts is itself guaranteed by the interference of man. He may have caused the destruction of the animals that he fears, or the animals that please his palate, but he is also no less the preserver of many others. Finally, in the Sacred Scriptures, we find that it is through the instrumentality of angels that God works upon the souls of men.

Surely, then, there is comfort for me in this. I have been told by God Himself that the very hairs of my head are numbered, and that neither the least of His creatures nor the greatest can fall without the separate decree of the Father of all.[29] Then I find that in other places He tells me that the very prayers of the saints (presumably the blessed ones on earth) are carried to the throne of God by the ministry of angels and that the very care of the children of men and of the nations is committed to the protection of spirits whose business it is to "post o'er land and ocean without rest."[30]

Near to me, yet above me, filled fuller with the radiance of life, lit up with a greater brightness than I can boast, fired by a more splendid love, there is an attendant spirit that has been entrusted with my goings and comings. If my eyes were really open and I could see the heavenly messengers on their way up and down from earth to Heaven, and from Heaven to earth, I would find the whole of the universe alive with these bright workers.

Our Lord warned me from harming children or doing them scandal because their angels saw the face of God in Heaven. And my own angel? Should not the thought of his presence, alert, loving, wise with the very wisdom of God, help me in my struggle against the troubles of my life? Patiently he awaits my movements, whispering in ten thousand ways, by these angel voices, by the cries of nature, by the beauties of man's own making, by the friendships of life, giving me frequent counsel. Am I grateful? Am I even conscious?

[29] Cf. Matt. 10:29-30.

[30] John Milton, Sonnet XIX: "When I Consider How My Light Is Spent."

∞

As part of the Communion
of Saints, you are never alone

It seems like a strange vision in the book of Revelation to conceive that vast intercommunion of living and dead, such as the Catholic doctrine of the Communion of Saints proclaims. To unite in one single body the living who follow the teaching of Christ, and that vast crowd of dead who, in Heaven or in Purgatory, follow forever the Lamb, is an idea that is overwhelming in its very extent. That all these should have one common bond seems beyond the power of man to imagine and of God to invent. The dwellers over all the earth, different and even antagonistic, in language and climate and culture; and those suffering souls, bodyless, expectant of release, glad in the midst of all their woe, longing for the end of their exile; and that throng who praise God unceasingly and look down with brotherly compassion on the repentance of sinners on earth — how or in what are these to be established in unity?

To construct a vast empire is a perilous undertaking, which, for the most part, achieves its success only so long as there are sufficient enemies against it to give it solidarity. But here there is the far greater ideal of uniting into one whole, not only the several members of a single kingdom, but every kingdom of the world; to knit together into a perfect whole the armies of nations drawn up against each other in a far-flung battle line; to supply a common code of communication between the fleets on every sea, and — despite war and its rank fury, despite commercial competition in every form, despite racial differences, despite the conflicting aims of life, despite the very brazen portals of death, despite even the high-reaching battlements of Heaven — to leave no nook or cranny in all creation that could be so great or so small as to escape from the wonderful net enclosing within meshes of gold every soul in all the world.

Where shall we find this common bond? It is not in faith, for, in Heaven, faith has passed into knowledge, and the Church has no jurisdiction beyond the grave. It is not in hope, for there can be no hope where the higher gift of possession has been obtained. It can be only in love expressed by prayer. It is, indeed, by prayer that all these are made one.

This conception under which we view the world is really marvelous; it gives an entirely new outlook upon life, for we see how between Heaven and earth are passing ceaselessly great streams of prayer, petitions from wearied and anxious souls rising upward, borne along by the hands of angels, strong cries and tears from hearts in anguish that beg for courage to bear their cross or for the chalice to pass, the grateful thanks of those whose voices have been heard and their favors granted them, and those whose words are no more than a great paean of praise at the marvels wrought by the mercy and majesty of God, and a conscious acknowledgment that God is wonderful in His saints. So, too, from earth and Heaven steal up to the throne of Omnipotence the prayers of sinners and saints for their dear dead; there are hands uplifted in worship, hearts afire with friendship, sufferings of mortal life gladly borne for the hastening of their loved ones' release.

Nor is the intercommunion of prayer and love a mere cry of asking or thanking; there is also the gladness that comes to the soul when it is in the presence of its friends; there is, that is to say, the wonderful pleasure that springs from a silence that is more intimate than any speech. To feel in the company of the saints, to feel our oneness in Christ with all Christians, to be sure that death does not sever or part is indeed consoling to man, whose greatest fear is the dread of loneliness.

Surely, then, it will bring courage to my heart to be certain that with me and by my side marches the following of Christ. If I stand upon a hill and overlook a city, I know that by faith I can see the angels passing up and down from earth to Heaven and from Heaven to earth, mounting with cries of sorrow and anguish, descending with mercy and consolation. I can see the brightness of their trailing glory and almost hear the beating of their wings. The long rows of dreary houses, the crawling smoke, the sounds of manufacture and transit are made alive with a new significance. They are the sounds of earth, but they awake echoes in Heaven. Over all the world that is split into different languages, there is still one common tongue to every Christian.

Here, then, surely I shall get to feel that there can be no real loneliness; that I am not solitary in any sense, for about me always are there prayers of the saints, whether here on earth or there in Heaven. I am not left alone to fight out my battle, for there are countless hosts who watch me, interested in my welfare and applauding my efforts. There are the well wishes of my fellows in the Christian Church who pray daily, as I pray for the whole Church. Day by day, my steps have been kept from slipping through the intercession of saint and sinner, of souls I have known and loved or released, or to whom I bear a special devotion. Not merely is there help and comfort but dignity also in the idea.

I consider myself now, not as one who is of no value in life, of no consequence for my fellows, for I am, indeed, part of a vast band, and my prayers, too, have a place in this great harmonious chorus. While earth sleeps or wakes, through the busy day and the long watches of the night, this wonderful commerce goes on through the medium of endless prayer.

∞

Your prayers can assist the dead

The Communion of Saints is a most comforting doctrine, for it links together the living and the dead. We believe so intensely in the life beyond that, for us, death does not make the huge difference that others would have us suppose. Those who have crossed over to that other life are themselves alive. We call it life, and a real life we believe it to be. For us Catholics, indeed, there is no such thing as death in the sense that it means the absolute cutting off of all regard for the life that is this side of eternity.

We ask the prayers of those whom we know to be beloved of God, nor does it much matter whether they be alive or dead, since we suppose them always to remain human enough to be interested in human things. Even when they have put off mortality, mortality must have forever a meaning to them. Hence, we ask the good to pray for us when we meet them in our life here; and when we learn that they have gone over into the fuller and ampler life that is above, we do not say that then they cannot be asked to help us, but rather that their prayers are far more likely to have weight with God, and that they will be more interested in our welfare. Hence, the Catholic Church has always advocated prayers to the saints. Just because the saints are dead, why should we cease to beg their intercession?

So, again, is it with those who are in Purgatory. I prayed for them when they were alive; in their troubles, in their day of trial, I remembered them before God. Why, now that they are still in a state of trial, should I put aside their claims on me?

How do I know that my prayers can be of any avail to the dead? How do I know that when they were alive, my prayers were of any use to them? I trusted in the mercy of God and followed the practice of Christian Tradition. So now I trust in God's compassion and adopt the Christian inheritance.

Let me consider, then, that belief in Purgatory and in prayers for the dead allows me the privilege of friendship continued beyond the grave. Surely it is part of the blessedness of friendship that a friend bears as much as may be of his friend's troubles. Indeed, the way that love best expresses itself is not in the external signs of affection, even if these are sweet, but more especially if, in sorrow, I can, by some loss to myself, relieve my friends of their pain. The mother is most pleased when, by denying herself, she can give an extra treat to her child, the friend when he can halve his friend's trouble and, by his sympathy, double his joy. It is, that is to say, one of the great gladnesses of my love when I can, at the cost of my own ease, purchase for my friends some consolation.

Thus, as our blessed Lord proclaimed, no greater love could be expressed than that a man lay down his life for his friend, for this means the very last extremity of sacrifice taken joyously to save the life of those whom he has loved. Love, therefore, can, at its best, express itself in no other way so well, or with such pleasure to him who makes the sacrifice, as by obtaining relief for another by means of our own discomfort. After all, we should consider that when someone has given us his affection, we can never make any repayment; it is a thing so valuable because so sacred, that we have a debt of gratitude that is a debt always; consequently, we are glad of the little opportunities afforded us, not of repaying (for this is impossible), but for acknowledging our indebtedness, for even to acknowledge is to make both of us realize how great the thing is that has happened. The very largeness of the debt is recognized and, by being recognized, is best returned.

Now, it is just this that prayers for the dead imply. They make us see that friendship is, as Scripture made us aware, stronger than death.[31] It has a hold so firm that it lasts beyond the grave. The "mortmain" for the medieval lawyers was the clutch that the dying hand never relaxed, and in the same fashion, we hold that the dead do not let go of us; death does not part, but unites us. By our prayers, we can help our friends who are dead; and more, it is not prayers only, but everything borne patiently for the dead can be offered up for them so that their time of purgation may be shortened. I cannot tell for certain whether God has accepted my pains for theirs, but I am assured that, if He judges fit, what I have suffered may be taken as for them. Just as the whole Christian inheritance supposes that vicarious suffering is part of the divine plan, so that our blessed Lord could take upon Himself the sufferings of the whole world, so, in a lesser way, we know that God does allow the children to suffer for their fathers' sins, the innocent to make expiation for the guilty. Certain indulgences — that is, certain penalties of the older penitential code that I can now satisfy by the saying of certain prayers or by doing certain pious exercises of charity — can also be offered up for the dead.

The advantage of all this is that life, with all its troubles, becomes a thing easily borne with. Gently I become resigned to the will of God, which I cannot change; I offer my own daily annoyances and anxieties in satisfaction for the sins of my dead friends and, by my loving sacrifices, speed them into the Presence. The fascination of life can be thus renounced for love, human in its origin, but divine in its consummation.

---

[31] Cf. Cant. 8:6 (RSV= Song of Sol. 8:6).

∞

You have a unique role
in Christ's Mystical Body

One idea to which St. Paul frequently returns is the comparison between the faithful who are in Christ Jesus and the members of a human body. He makes use of this metaphor several times to prove several things — for example, in one place, that each has a separate work to do and, in another place, that each separate work is dependent on the rest. But while, in this fashion, making use of a comparison that has occurred to many writers before his time and since, St. Paul gives it an elevation and a nobleness that raises it above the dignity of a mere literary device. For him, it is evidently a real truth that is to be of help to a person in his outlook upon life.

We must remember, first of all, the circumstances in which St. Paul found himself. He was a convert from Judaism, where he had been brought up in the very strictest form of the Hebrew faith. He was "a Pharisee of the Pharisees"; that is, he belonged to the narrowest, most fanatical, most exclusively nationalistic of the various parties of his nation. Then had come his sudden and miraculous seizure on the road to Damascus, and all the old fierceness was turned now into a burning and impetuous love of Christ. His education, while certainly designed with care under Gamaliel to lead him to a wholehearted acceptance of the Law, evidently brought him into touch with Greek and Roman culture. He quotes passages from the poets and, in his address to the Athenians, shows considerable sympathy with the nobler side of paganism. Moreover, his missionary tours among the Hebrew communities in the Greek cities of Asia Minor made him realize that not these communities alone, but all the world was longing ("groaning") for a new and more perfect revelation.[32] His missionary venture thus became more and more an appeal, not to the circumcised (for these had their own valiant apostles), but to the Gentiles. St. Paul took, that is to say, for his own portion, the most degraded religion with which he came into contact.

Now, what is his method of dealing with these poor souls? He at once endeavors to make them realize their own value in the sight of God. He tells them that they are all members of Christ. These people who have been accustomed to worshiping idols, and who have looked upon gods as heroes of very doubtful morality, who have never been assisted to rise above their own surroundings or to improve their stunted spiritual life, are now confronted by the ideals of Christianity, which certainly must have appeared to them more dazzling and even more impossible than they do to us, who are familiar with the character of Christ.

And while, in this way, they suddenly found life become very much more difficult, and were contrasting their old natural or unnatural practices with the new purity and continence demanded of them, St. Paul, instead of telling them that they are sinners and upbraiding them with their failures, is at great pains to point out to them how God, by becoming man, has raised man to God. He reveals the whole story of the Incarnation in its culminating mercy of the Crucifixion. They have been bought at a great price; if man has not valued them, God has. But not merely has Christ died for them; He has made them one with Himself. The sacraments knit

[32] Cf. Rom. 8:22.

95

them to Him; the Eucharist is a memorial of that death, transfigured to an abiding presence. Matrimony is but a type of the union between Christ and each single soul; and the ensuing love is so fierce and vehement that it breaks down every barrier, sweeps aside every obstacle, and makes each one with Christ: "I live now, not I, but Christ liveth in me."[33]

Here is comfort, not for them only, but for me as well. I am a member of Christ; I have been purchased by the Blood of God. So I am of value in His sight; He thinks me worth troubling about. But not only has He redeemed me, but He has given me the grace to be a member of His Church, a member of His Mystical Body. I have, then, a certain definite place in this organization and do a work that others, indeed, might have done, yet which He has confided to me alone.

Not only have I thus my own vocation; because I am the member of a body, I have a definite function to perform, but one that needs the cooperation of others. They and I are interdependent. We require each other, and every single Catholic has demands on me, on my good works, prayers, and so forth.

But even more than I am dependent on my fellow members, I am dependent even on Christ and He on me. To me, miserable, poor, foolish, and sinful, it is also given to "fill up what is wanting in the sufferings of Christ," for if "one member suffers, all the members suffer."[34] He is my Head. Yet surely this ought to inspire me to go on with my struggle in life. This should give me courage to persevere. Just as I find that I can hope to reform others — children, sinners, the poor — only by making them realize the good they can do and the goodness that is really in them, so is it also with myself. I shall surely do better when I realize my own dignity as a Christian soul. I, even I, am a member of Christ. So I shall take

---

[33] Gal. 2:20.
[34] Cf. Col. 1:24; 1 Cor. 12:26.

care not to sully my reputation or lower myself. I shall have an *esprit de corps*, a loyalty to my chief, that will keep me conscious that in my hands is the honor, not of myself only, but of all my fellows on earth and in Heaven, and of God Himself. For if one member suffers, all the body suffers also.

∞

Every person possesses dignity

The whole force of events in every civilized country has surely been to make us recognize the dignity of the human soul. In matters of social organization, in the economic labor market, we can see that one chief means of the present terrible oppression of the poor has been the wanton and deliberate neglect of the individual personal worth of the worker. In the ordinary manuals that are issued on the social question, the arguments for both sides are seldom taken from any view of the individual, but from social reasons for the betterment of the community, or from the exchange between work done and wage paid.

"By himself," says a modern economist, "a man has no right to anything whatever. He is part of the social whole; and he has a right only to that which it is for the good of the whole that he should have." This is obviously a very splendid basis for any act of social tyranny. One has only to prove that society requires one part of the workers to be underpaid, to find sufficient argument of defense for sweating. Nor is this a mere surmise, for another economist writes, "There are some men whose maximum efficiency per unit of food is obtained with small consumption and small output. These go into lines requiring neither exceptional strength nor exceptional skill and remain poor because the best commercial economy in such lines is obtained by a combination of low output and low consumption." Thus are the cruelest cases of underpayment approved!

This case of political economy is symptomatic of a great deal that is present in modern life — a desire to exalt the community at the expense of the individual, springing from a disregard of Christian teaching. For the Catholic, there can be no such method of argument. Society may fall in ruins, but the individual must be saved. Of course, as a matter of fact, society will become much more prosperous when the individual dignity of human personality has been recognized. Yet, certainly, regard for the individual must precede regard for the whole community. The doctrine, for example, so popular in the novels of George Eliot and in the philosophies of the nineteenth century, that the individual was to care nothing about himself (since he was mortal and his soul faded with him), but was to work for posterity alone, has become recognized as a foolish, although nobly intentioned, philosophy. For, if the individuals were of no worth, then neither could the sum of them be worthy of a man's labor. If I were to put aside my own pleasure, since I was the creature of a day, for the benefit of other creatures no less transitory than myself, then was I to waste the little time that was mine on others, who were no more worthy of it than I?

To belittle the individual is evidently to belittle the society. But to exalt the individual is to make of a society something "almost divine," says St. Antonino. Christ came to save the whole world, because, under His teaching, the individual soul alone would have been as worth the ransom of His death as was the race.

In all these things, then, in the whole of my outlook on life, in my attitude toward others, and in the care I should have of my own soul, I must continually realize the supreme value of the individual man. Some saint has said that one soul alone would suffice for a bishopric, that the thing that is deathless, that is exalted by grace until it becomes a partaker of the divine nature, that required the death of God for its own ransom, must be indeed worthy of the highest possible attention and reverence. There cannot, indeed, be any conflict between the good of the individual and the good of the society, for the advance of the members must advantage the whole.

But I must begin with the human unit, with myself. I can never value others, nor act charitably toward them, until I am fully conscious of the worth of my own soul. Without that appreciation, I can never be of real service to any of them. Once I have perceived my own dignity, I can perceive the dignity of others, and realizing the importance of saving my own soul, I shall be led also to help others to save theirs. The proverb is indeed justified: "Charity begins at home." The very basis, therefore, of all Christian virtue, of any attempt to be made by man to achieve something greater than himself, must rest upon this stable foundation: the value of my own being, its high call and destiny, the very divinity that inhabits me, the spark of God that remains inextinguishable to kindle again into flame the dying embers of my life.

Part 4

∞

Human life and its reward

∞

Sin creates a state of loneliness

The gravity of sin comes from its being an offense against God, but its effect on the soul is to be measured neither by the guilt nor by the temporal punishment inexorably affixed, but by that deep sense of loneliness it brings with it. Scripture is full of the comparison between the soul and a waterless desert; in one place comes the phrase "the desolation of the wicked." Now, this represents a quite apparent effect that sin has upon the soul. It makes a man realize as nothing else does the terrible loneliness of life. It is possible that, after a while, this perception wears off and the soul becomes in this way, as in others, hardened to the sense of sin, but at first, when the conscience is still delicate and refined, after an offense against God, human nature feels itself to shrivel up and become cut off from the rest of the world.

Notice children when they have done wrong — how difficult it is for them to face their fellows again; they seem to have severed themselves from the companionship of those with whom they are wont to play. A scolding drives them entirely upon themselves, and the punishment of solitude that grown-ups rather thoughtlessly inflict on little people is as nothing compared with the terrible desolation that has already overspread the tiny nature. There was a picture in the best and most pathetic of our humorous papers that — with the skill, not of artist alone, but of a human heart that has understood human nature — makes the child cry out against the mother for scolding and making "all the room so dark."

The sense, then, of sin brings with it a feeling of loneliness, when the first pleasurable excitement has worn off. This loneliness our Lord Himself submitted to in the hour of His dereliction.

Nor is it to be supposed that the desire that so many saints have shown for solitude is in any way a contradiction of this. Really it is a further proof; for it is, on the whole, just the saints who do desire solitude; the sinners are far too lonely to find a desert at all suitable or even tolerable.

Notice who those are that spend most of their time rushing from one distraction to another; they are those who have felt the torment of loneliness so fiercely that they cannot endure to be by themselves. So lonely are they that they spend all their time feverishly pursuing one pleasure after another or one work after another — anything or anybody that will take their minds off the torment of themselves. The oppression that sin effects in them makes them anxious to live to the utmost their lives in the full stream of human existence. Pleasure is heaped up in crowded hours to make them forget the aching void of their hearts. Indeed, it is their greatest punishment that they finally succeed, until they lose at last all perception of their pain, whereas the saints are so full in themselves of love that they must draw off alone to be away from all others; so accompanied are they by the dear presence of their Friend that they cannot stay and waste (as, to them, it seems) the precious hours with any other thought than of Him. Thus sat Mary at the feet of Jesus, while Martha, busied over many things that were unnecessary, hurried to and fro, sometimes in His presence and sometimes out of it.

This does not mean that we can show our love only by retiring out of the world to the cloister; but it does imply that only those can stand the loneliness of life who have their hearts aflame with the love of another; while the effect of sin is to produce a feeling of loneliness that irks humanity.

Sin's loneliness is evident, and the cause of it no less clear, for by sin the presence of God, made perfect by sanctifying grace, is removed. After all, God is the most intimate neighbor of the soul; no other power can creep so close to the heart and tangle itself so cunningly with the roots of our desire. The will is at His mercy alone, so as to be moved by Him without in any sense destroying its freedom. Every movement of goodness is effected by the special impulse of His virtue, and every thought that turns to the things that are more excellent must have been inspired by His illumination. For Him, then, was my soul wholly formed, and without Him it is balked of its purpose and reduced to a hungry longing for what it cannot achieve. Thence is it restless until it finds its peace in Him; thus is it lonely, deprived of all that is most required by its several faculties.

Man, in other words, was made for love, the diviner part of him for divine love. By sin is all this love dried up. The parched and thirsty soul feels, therefore, the need of the dew of God, and rushes madly as the beasts wander in the jungle looking for the water they cannot find. The soul by sin is thus made solitary. I must therefore in my heart see that the grace of God is not removed and the life of my soul destroyed. When I am feeling particularly the loneliness of life, perhaps the cause is that I lean too little upon God; perhaps it is that my sins will not let me feel that inward presence that is the sole real source of peace here below. I was created by Love for love, and when by sin I act contrary to Love, my heart must necessarily feel His absence.

Even in death, God is with you

The great effect produced in the soul by sin is an intense feeling of loneliness brought about by the very offense against God, for, by the fact of sin, the deep consciousness of the intimate union between Him and ourselves can no longer be experienced. After all, no one can be blind to the traditional reverence that we have for the Divine Spirit who governs the race. All men, since historical knowledge and memory begins, have realized this sovereign of the universe to be the most intimate and familiar being to every human child. In our fear, in our success, in the moments when the beauty of things has come home to us, we have turned instinctively, to address not someone without, but the spirit within. However far we go back, that is instinctive to man.

Sin, therefore, which breaks this bond, cannot but impress on the soul its loss; and since death is the penalty that God has attached to sin, it would seem natural that the terror of death should come precisely along the same line of loneliness. This, too, has been the age-long attitude to death taken by the race; just as it has always slunk away to hide after its sin, so it has faced death as the great solitude.

Even in prehistoric days, this view of death impressed the mind of man. As far back as we can trace his life and habits, we find that he buried his dead with their most treasured possessions. Near the right hand of that earliest boy, whose grave has been unearthed at Le Meustrier, a flint knife was found, doubtless his favorite belonging, something laid by the loved one's side to allow some semblance of companionship, of treasured gift, to break in on his loneliness. So, too, were wife and slave buried with their lord, lest he should be lonely in death's great silence.

Indeed, solitary as life can become, death must be yet more solitary. Life comes to us as members of a family, as units in a great social organization; as perhaps blind, and deaf, and dumb to the outward concerns of others, yet as the object of their persistent and tender solicitude. But death must leave us alone to ourselves. From the love that springs between two, the child is born; thus others herald it into the light, but it goes out from the light alone. Death works that change at least; whatever other rest or peace it will one day bring us, that loneliness is always its portion. It is the very pathos of a deathbed that the long shadows of the loneliness of the tomb are already being cast upon the soul. The voice of the dying person has to travel seemingly along endless cloisters before it can reach our ear. We have to stoop to catch the whisper of his failing breath. The constant chafing of the loved one's hands, the soothing pressure, is evidently only very slowly felt, perceived, and realized. It seems as though the soul had already retreated from the outposts of its dominions, and had shrunk back in fear to the keep, the citadel, the last strong place where alone it may hope to baffle the advancing foe. The communications are almost severed; only by the merest and most uncertain rallies does it still hold parley with its friends, who watch, hoping to hear the last request, the final farewell, the ultimate human recognition.

Yet, despite all this loneliness and solitude and aloofness, the souls of the just are never quite lonely in death. We gave, indeed, as our reason for supposing that death would be lonely, that it was the result of sin; and sin, we explained, meant cutting apart the two intimate things: my soul and God. But with the just there is never such severance; God and the just are always one. When other friends have to say to us, "Farewell," He says, "Welcome, come, ye blessed of my Father."[35] Nay, because of my loneliness, He clings closer to my soul and, in the sustaining Viaticum, hastens to guide me through the shadows of the valley of death. The sacrament of Communion is given to me for the purpose of strength that springs from the nearness of His presence, and never is that presence more required than when I go out alone from life into the doors of death.

For me, then, the vision of faith will light up that valley, that I may see upon the hill the crowded forms of those who come to bid me enter into joy. I die, indeed, alone, but only that I may pass into the company of the elect of God. The prayers that are said around the bed of death repeat the thought that there is a welcome beyond, and that I shall not be left lonely in the dread moment when most I need the assistance of others, their comradeship, their supporting affection. Freely, then, I shall face whatever befalls, conscious of that hand held in mine, trusting in His own blessed words that I shall not be left forsaken, but that to the end of the world He shall be with me always.[36]

---

[35] Cf. Matt. 25:34.
[36] Matt. 28:20.

∞

Trust in God when you face
the death of loved ones

I meet death not merely in myself, but many times over in others. At first, the hearing of it comes as a shock to me. I know, indeed, that all must die. My pets in my childhood have died, and I have buried them with some pomp and have thought of them as having gone to some place of pleasure. Even so, however, it may well have happened that I did not altogether realize how irrevocable their departure was. In a vague way, I said that I would not see them again, but there remained always the hope that, in the end, they might reappear after an interval.

Then I heard next, perhaps, that a familiar friend had been called away, and I learned later that he was dead. What that meant I did not fully know. Black seemed somehow an appropriate color; it fitted the temper of my mind, but I was conscious only that I would not see that friend again, and his name was added to a list that came up each morning and evening at my prayers.

That is probably the remembrance of death that comes to me when I look back on my childhood — a vague notion that there was now a gap where once people stood. But after a while, as things went on as though nothing had ever happened, I lost my appre-hension of it. It became hardly more than a blur that gathered around certain faces, and it was a subject that on the whole I found it better to avoid. Prayers, of course, were to be said for the dead, and during November I was no doubt busy over my indulgences for the holy souls; but all that was intensely impersonal.

Perhaps the thing that really most seized my imagination and made the idea a thing of reality has been the sight of the dead. There is nearly always something unpleasant in the presence of the dead, something that makes us shrink back from their sight. Our intense love for them may in given cases overcome the feeling of distaste, but that is so clear an exception that it almost revolts the thoughts of those who watch. The very idea of going into the room, for most people, is in itself repellent, partly perhaps from the knowledge that they have no business to be afraid. The dead can do us no hurt, yet we have instinctively a dread of them, lying so still and silent. The drawn features, their waxlike glaze, the curious odor of death, haunt the imagination. We kneel and say a prayer, then hurry out as soon as we can with decency.

Then suddenly there comes the thought that the fear of death is really a fear of the separation that it causes. Life and love go hand in hand, but death casts a shadow on the plumes on youth and brushes into disarray the elaborate ornaments with which friendship decks out its lovers. Death, indeed, means separation, divorce made absolute.

Why should God, I ask complainingly, take friends from me? What have I done that He should thus crush my one consolation in life? Hostility to Him is often the first result of the death of a friend. The loss is always sudden in the end, and the poignancy of my regret finds its simplest outlet in a declamation against the Ruler of Life.

Whither, then, shall I now turn for comfort against this terrible peril? To my crucifix. That is, indeed, the sole refuge for those who are in distress against the ways of God, for His manner of dealing with the children of men has not been to turn to us and beg us to have blind confidence in His love. He has never made so heavy a demand upon my faith and love. He has never put my trust so severely to the test, for, like the kind Father that He has ever been to me, He first gives definite proofs of love, and only then ventures to ask something of me in return. He waits for signs of my affection only after He has Himself given pledge of it.

Now, it is just in the crucifix that we find best of all the whole summary of this method with which He deals with me. There, indeed, I can look and see how He has first died for me. Then He can speak to me from that seat of love, and bid me see, if I can, whether greater love than that could be shown me. There is no question, be it observed, of blind faith, of closing one's eyes to see what God will send us, as children play among themselves; but it is with our eyes wide open to His wonderful display of love that we can turn again into the path of life and go forward with courage and trust. He has given Himself as a hostage to us for His good behavior.

Yes, of course I am disturbed when those I love are taken from me; if I were not, I would not be human. But at the same time, I must allow that God is wiser and more loving than I am, for His wisdom and love are of eternity. I must, therefore, go on in perfect trust: His death and the remembrance of it stills the fear of my soul. Although those whom I love have gone down into the valley of death, neither for myself nor for them shall I fear evil, for He is with us.[37]

---

[37] Cf. Ps. 22:4 (RSV = Ps. 23:4).

Christ will comfort
you at your judgment

Perhaps, for many, the terrors of death are as nothing compared with the terrors of judgment, for all that affrights us in death is found far more fully in the awful moment that succeeds it. The loneliness of death, which is its chiefest horror, its most over-whelming fear — that utter separation from our life and from that part of us, our bodies, which we have come to regard as so partic-ularly ourselves — is followed by a still more bitter separation, a more cruel divorce: for our judgment must be solitary, isolated, alone. Even the saints can do little for us, for the judgment must be righteous and just, and this means assuredly that God cannot go out of His path of justice because of the pleading even of those whom He holds dear.

What else, indeed, is the judgment, as far as we can grasp it, but the naked setting of our soul as it is now at this moment in the sight of God? He knows absolutely the state of my whole being. He knows what I do not, whether I am worthy of love or hatred. To me, that blinding vision may be a tremendous revelation, a rolling back of all sorts of hidden curtains with which I had shrouded my soul from my own gaze — all the little deceptions that I had prac-ticed on myself, the little ways in which I had hoodwinked my conscience and pretended to myself that I did not really think that, in certain things I had done, there was any great sin. Many times I had salved the conscience pricks of my heart by distinctions and devices. Now, in a flash, these are all laid bare.

Nay, so lonely shall I be that even the very judge may be none other than myself. To the Son, indeed, is given all judgment. He must apportion the praise and blame, the reward or punishment. Yet, in that moment when the veils of ignorance and conceit are torn from my eyes, I must become awfully conscious of the pageant of my life. I can need no external voice to point out to me the evils of my life, for the loud cry of conscience itself will be the sole decisive voice required. The scenes through which we have lived will return to our remembrance, and we shall be face-to-face with our lives.

In the accounts of many of those who have gone so close to the doors of death as almost to have had a sight of what takes place beyond them, we are repeatedly told that they have seen then the whole forgotten vision of their lives. The whole past record has filed before them as though they sat as spectators in some theater and watched the acting out in dumb show of every detail of another's tragedy or comedy. From manhood back through the dim reaches of childhood the vision sped. Nothing was omitted or passed by; the whole appeared as it had been. Would there be any need than this for further judgment? Would not the soul itself sum up by its own loathing and distaste what it thought of this record? Deserted, therefore, even by oneself, one's pride, one's conceit, one's fond hopes that all was well — oh, the biting, piercing loneliness of that utter isolation!

Yet even so is there consolation for us. There will be One who will be to us, then, a comfort, a refuge, and a hope. The very figure of the Judge will be itself the sole sight that will give us any gleam of brightness in so horrid a scene. The five wounds — will not their light illuminate even the dark corners of the stricken soul and give it hope in the weary waste of its bitter isolation? Through Him will all our good actions take on an infinite value.

The comfort that He Himself has given in His own wonderful description of that day is found in the gracious text: "As long as you did it to the least of my brethren, you did it to me."[38] Whatever good we have done will have its reward from Him. The great doctrine of the unity of all Christians into a sacred body of which Christ is the Head will give, even in the horrors of that moment, supreme relief. All the devotion that I have shown to the saints will there have been gathered up and regarded as devotion to Him; for to a Catholic, reverence for the saints is exhibited only because they are His friends, so that in reality (as we hold) those who have shown them reverence have really been showing reverence to Christ. The kindnesses of life, the little we have done for others, will be remembered for our reward. Thus, through the terrors and horrors of the awful judgment, there will always be the light lit by friendship. The unswerving love that we have shown to Him who is ever faithful will not be forgotten. There can be no loneliness so long as He is there.

[38] Matt. 25:40.

∞

God's mercy allows a chance
for purification after death

The Protestant Reformation abolished among its adherents belief in Purgatory. It has found that, by so doing, it is bound also to remove from among its disciples a belief in an everlasting Hell. The Gospel is so welded together in truth that if one part or article is renounced, the rest is at once deprived of meaning. To deny one single tenet of the Church is impossible, for the denier is at once brought to see how some other teaching that, in itself, he is willing to admit, is at once rendered void of all sense.

To deny Purgatory was to set an alternative between Heaven and Hell, so sharp as to be too painful for faith, hope, and love. As a result, under the name of Hell, a sort of caricature of Purgatory is now taught in the Protestant churches. Consider what it must mean to believe that souls must be either perfect and wing their way straight into the presence of God, or imperfect and be condemned to eternal perdition! Surely, the more we think of the blinding purity of God, the more conscious do we become of how few of even the best and holiest on earth are fit for that spotless presence. Is God expected to take into the eternal vision of Himself those whose lives have been full of imperfection? Can I honestly say of myself that I am in hatred of God, or, on the other hand, that I feel myself ready for an immediate approach to Him? Gradually, therefore, the idea grew that Hell was nothing more than a place of preparation for the final reward of the vision of God.

This remark is not introduced from a controversial motive, but merely to bring out into clearer relief the teaching of the Church. For us, then, Purgatory is not a halfway house between the two, but it is set right on the way to Heaven. Its meaning can be best described by a true understanding of the judgment. The soul then, one must suppose, sees exactly its state, contrasting its weakness and long list of sins with God's spotlessness. It feels that it cannot, just as it is, straightway after death venture into that presence, for "nothing defiled shall enter Heaven."[39] Consequently, it turns eagerly to find whither it may go to get cleansed from its stains. It flies to Purgatory.

We must not look upon this as though it were some place of punishment, some prison-house in which the poor soul suffered fearful torture in order that the justice of God should be avenged. This view of God would seem to be childish. He does not want to make us love Him by the sole method of punishment. He does not act by coercion in order to draw us to Himself and keep us immured in Purgatory until we are ready to say we love Him; but He allows us a place where we may be purged of our sins and rendered fit by the fires of love for an entrance to the Beatific Vision of His beauty. It is, indeed, a state of pain, but not of sorrow; it is suffering, but in utter gladness; for the doors of Purgatory lead necessarily to the pathway to God.

I must not think, therefore, that my dear dead are in anguish. No doubt they are restless and eager for their release, but only as a lover might be restless who did not find himself fit to meet his beloved. He would wish, indeed, that his time for approach might be hastened, but he would be far from wishing to enter straight into

---

[39] Cf. Apoc. 21:27 (RSV = Rev. 21:27).

that presence without being fitted for it. For love, too, makes its demands upon us. Love, too, has its ceremonies more rigorously enforced than the ceremonies of court or altar. The suffering soul is certain of its ultimate reward, the sight of God. It has no feeling of fear, no anxiety as to whether it shall in the end be able, as its time approaches, to leave the purifying fire and draw near to the presence of God. Surely, then, must its joy, the reward of the perfect knowledge of its Maker, already have overflowed into the soul.

Hence, there is pathos, but not rebuke, when it turns itself to beg the supplication of my prayers. It is established in the way, but it cannot now help itself. It is certain of its release, but it cannot, in any way that we know of, hasten the time of it. It is left in that regard entirely in our hands, at our mercy. It is, as St. Thomas reminds us, the supreme expression of friendship that the friend bears the sufferings of his friend. If we could take upon our shoulders the pain of all our friends, surely they would always be at peace. Here, then, that course is open to us, and we can truly save them from their penalties. They are waiting — not impatiently, for they cannot cry out against the will of God — but it is in my power to help them. Let me see to it that this is done, and the law of love obeyed.

∞

In Heaven your happiness will be full

Here on earth, we are always lonely, nor can the best of us avoid that feeling, for we were made for friendship, human and divine, such as here can never be wholly realized or perfectly satisfied. To its full realization there are innumerable barriers we cannot remove. We look forward to the meeting of friends, and we find that often there is something that comes between us, not in the sense that we disagree, but that the very limits of our being prevent that utter absorption of the lover in the loved one, for which instinctively we yearn. Despite our eagerness and their sympathy, we are conscious that absolute oneness is impossible. The presence of those we love is enjoyed, but it fails to satisfy the longing of our heart; the very limits of space and time seem often to put us apart.

Hither and thither we run, turning to this friend or that, glad that we are still responsive to the call of affection; yet this very energy of our nature, which never is sated, tells that it was made for things that are better able to fill our hearts. Our hearts, indeed, were made for God, and they can never rest until they rest in Him. From the existence of this desire for friendship alone, one could prove the need of man for intimate union with God; one could show that nature itself proclaims the idea of love as the only thing that can finally satisfy us.

In Heaven your happiness will be full

To rest in God eternally is the supreme joy of Heaven. Indeed, Heaven has no meaning but that. As of Heaven, so of Hell, poets, artists, and saints have told us many things: they have described under various allegories both the delights of the one and the pains of the other. They have let loose the rein to their imagination and have conjured up scenes of surpassing loveliness or grim and awful suffering. The harmonies of music, the appeal of color, the delicious charms of perfume and taste have all been laid under contribution in order to express as energetically as possible the wonderful joy of Heaven.

But we know that these are in reality but the imaginings of those who are endeavoring to depict truth, but know that they are incapable of doing so. They would not pretend that they were doing more than putting into sensible form things that lie outside the range of the senses; for, after all, the joy of Heaven is no other thing than to see and know God. To stand face-to-face before Him and know Him even as we are known; to be able to detect, line by line, the features of His divine beauty; to trace the splendor of that divine life that, from all eternity, has sufficed for God's perfect happiness; to study unendingly that marvelous harmony of justice and mercy, strength and tenderness, love and wisdom — the anticipation of doing this must always fascinate man's reason. Then swiftly the will must follow the lead of the reason, for knowledge will not stop until it has passed to love.

It was spoken truly that it is not good for man to be alone. Here are we always in exile, weary strangers, sojourners who have come as yet to no abiding city. Here we seem as if, like Dante, we wake to find ourselves in a dark wood. Yet, as to travelers there comes cheeringly the gleam of a distant light that streams in the dark from some cottage window and makes glad the path, gives elasticity to the steps and hastens into regular rhythm the swinging pace, so must the thought of that true home encourage our progress here on earth. We should have the feeling of loneliness that comes on all wanderers in exile. The very joys of life that might otherwise distract our thoughts from heavenly things, should appear now in their real significance, as foretastes of that everlasting joy sprung from everlasting life. Human love and the delights of friendship, out of which are built the memories that endure, are also to be treasured as hints of what shall be hereafter.

Heaven, then, is simply the vision of God. True knowledge unveiling for us the sacred beauty must perforce drive the heart to love. Over it, while it gazes on God, must break and sweep the fullest tide of rapture, a divine espousal, a union so intimate that the limits of our personality must be strained to breaking point. Yet it is not that we shall enter into all joy, but that all joy will enter into us.

∞

Hell is the eternal solitude
of those who turn away from God

Hell is the most terrible of the Christian mysteries. The progression of loneliness in sin and death and judgment reaches to the furthest limits of possibility in the awful loneliness of Hell. It has all the horrors of eternal solitary confinement. That is the real torment of Hell, although there are others. Dante and others before and after him have imagined for themselves a place of torture; they have set to work to describe what in the most frenzied of human thoughts such a life must be; they have bidden to their assistance all the known and the unknown horrors that the most morbid imagination can suppose.

The effect has been at times, not terrible at all, but revolting: these writers who can imagine nothing save physical pain have often succeeded merely in giving one the idea that God gloated over the writhing bodies of His children. Very often the harm done by some so-called pious books is incalculable; the harrowing details given even suggest that the authors themselves have taken pleasure in describing these tortures. But all these accounts, whether by canonized writers or not, count for nothing, since they know no more of that afterlife than we; they know only, as do we, that the real punishment of it is the loss of God. Our Lord Himself used the word *fire,* so this must, therefore, represent the best possible description of the torment of the damned. But no one can suppose that he can fully understand what was meant; the precise significance of the phrase is beyond us.

This, then, is all that we know: the essential pain of Hell is the loss of God to the soul, which at length knows what God means. Here, on earth, it is perfectly possible to go through life in more or less comfort while the thought of God is wholly absent from the soul; it is sometimes the easiest way to forget and ignore God. But death brings with it a knowledge of things that our philosophy here ignores. It brings to the soul a knowledge of God and a realization that our nature was created for Him as the purpose of its existence. Hence, the punishment of Hell is the utter and eternal and conscious frustration of the soul's crying need. It is as though in a flash we had at last understood what everything in life was for, discovered the meaning of everything that had befallen us, found the solution to all the perplexities that had worried us — and then realized that our own previous ideas, and the practice that had followed them, had resulted in our complete inability to make use of life: a perfect nightmare in which one knew the use of everything, but could use nothing to its purpose. This torment, then, can come only to those who have died in revolt against God — not those who seemingly die in sin, for, in the last ebb of consciousness, who knows what mercies God has in store? But if any such pass out from here hating God, in revolt against Him, then, flung out as they are into eternity (an unchanging "now"), they must remain forever hating and losing, and conscious of their incalculable loss.

Am I worried over this? Does it come to me as opposed to the idea that the New Testament gives me of the character and ways of God? Then, assuredly, there is this much to be granted: that I can never hope to adjust in abstract method the justice and mercy of God in perfect balance. I can never hope to understand, still less explain to others, how Hell is compatible with the Crucifixion. I may, indeed, see how the one necessitates the other, how love alone could build up Hell; but that is only a fleeting vision that never wholly satisfies. I must be prepared, at any rate, to go through life unable to answer the questioning of my own soul, clinging only to His divine revelation, and gladly confident in His mercy toward all the children of men. If I have so much compassion on the most guilty wretch on earth that I cannot in my heart wish him so terrible an end, then God, whose love is infinite, must be still less willing to see men in such straits. Indeed, is not Calvary a sign of the extremes to which He would go in order to safeguard man from it? In the case of my own soul, of which alone I have real knowledge, I see that He has continuously restrained me by grace from the edges of the pit.

For others, then, I am full of hope. But for myself? The thought of Hell should not be often in my mind, for, please God! I have no need of fear to lead me to His side. In times of overwhelming temptation, perhaps once or twice in a lifetime, I shall need to think of Hell; but in my daily trials, let me rather, although reverent and believing in His word, try the path of Love.

∽

Your body will be resurrected

It is obvious that the resurrection cannot apply to the soul, for the simple reason that to resurrect means to rise again, and the soul cannot rise again, for it cannot fall; it is immortal and must live forever. When, then, we profess in the Apostles' Creed that we believe in the resurrection of the body, we can only suppose that the body will at some future time be rejoined to the soul, and that both together will be lifted up to the enjoyment or punishment ordained.

This doctrine, therefore, implies two distinct things: first, that my body will decay, and second, that it will one day rise again; one, that it will cease to be, another, that it will again take on existence. For the first there is no need to produce any evidence. It is indeed the lament of the poets that the fair and beautiful body, fearfully and wonderfully made, with all its intricate machinery and its marvelous faculties, is destined, despite every care and every cure, to pass back one day into the same earth from which it sprang. That body which gives the zest to life and makes life itself worth living; that tired frame that, with its long, drawn-out agony, makes life a tiresome existence; the body, whether young, hardened into perfect manhood, or worn out with the ravages of time and work — back to the earth it must go. The poets lament, and those in suffering, perhaps, hasten themselves unauthorizedly to that consummation, but toward it we all are tending. "What shall we call this sojourn of ours here: a living death or a dying life?" asks one of the Fathers of the Church. Does it very much matter? The result is the same.

Yet to this also we must add as Christians that death does not end all. The body goes, but it will as surely return; it dies, but it will live again.

How, then, can this be done? How can that mortal frame that mingles with the earth until it becomes part of some other organism than itself, once more put on the vesture of human life, be quickened into a new human existence? Change seems to be so essentially its nature that it is difficult to conceive any relation between it and the wonderful everlasting life that is described to us as unceasing, yet always present.

But the difficulties in the way of this resurrection are more than a mere incongruity of imagination; for the body itself is changing all through life. Is it not within seven years wholly renewed? If, then, in life this change takes place continuously, so that we end with a material body that is altogether different from the body with which we started, how can it be possible for us to suppose that after death the body that we had can be brought back to us? For when put into the grave, the material flesh and bone passes into all sorts of other forms of life, mingling with the grass and the flowers that wave over the place where all that was mortal was interred.

Struck, therefore, with the note of change that runs through all material creation, its growth and its decay, we wonder how it is possible for the body to be clothed with immortality. How, we ask, can the same body after centuries come back into life?

St. Thomas makes reply that we speak of the same body, despite its endless changes, just as we speak of the Thames or of London, although, as we speak, the water of the river has all changed, and the inhabitants of the city are passing out from it. The change is not in either case sudden, but gradual, and this justifies our use of the same name for that which is always in a state of flux.

But the real point, that the second objection more nearly touches, is that it is the soul that makes the body ours. According to the teaching of St. Thomas, it is the soul that gives the body its right to be considered human at all, since of itself it is a dead and inert thing, like the corpse is when the soul has gone out from it. Life and all that life includes is due to the indwelling of the spirit; hence, my body is mine simply because my soul inhabits it. Consequently, when we talk about the resurrection of the body, St. Thomas says expressly that we are not to mean that the identical particles of matter constitute the newly risen body, but that whatever material substance becomes informed by my soul becomes itself at once my body.

From this I learn that, just as I may not deny the existence of spiritual beings, even though I cannot see them, so neither may I deny the holiness of the body, even though I do see it. Both make me man, and neither of itself can wholly constitute me. Nor should I be led away by the seeming mysticism of those who would make out the body to be a mere symbol of other things; it is to be reverenced for what it is in itself. It is the creature of God as surely as is the soul, so ennobled, indeed, by the Incarnation that the fair flesh of the Son of God, marked with the prints of nails and spear and scourge, redeemed me, pleads for me, and can be worshiped. The coming dignity of my body should incline me to the utmost care for it, realizing that one day I shall put on immortality, and that with my own bodily eyes I shall see my Savior.

∽

Eternal life is an everlasting "now"

Eternal life is the common inheritance of every soul. To each, in virtue of its spiritual nature, is annexed immortality as a participation in the prerogatives of God. The conditions of that life may differ vitally, in that for some it is to be a reward and for others a punishment. But although in this way it is evident that those who are possessed of it may be very variously placed (even such as are rewarded by the vision of God's face being capable of unequal measures of knowledge and love), yet it is eternity as some sort of duration that is to be the same for both. To grasp it may be beyond the power of man's imagination, but the intellect can formulate truths about it without necessarily pretending to comprehend them. But of this much the reason can take cognizance: that the eternity promised to man is the free gift of God.

The idea of annihilation, repugnant as it seems to be to human nature, is a course that is in the abstract possible to God; for the whole basis of the spiritual life supposes that the divine power was not only exercised to call us into being, but is continually being exercised to keep us in existence. Nor is this need of being upheld caused in any way by the fall of the race. It is no punishment for sin that we have to be supported by the hands of God; it is, rather, a consequence simply of our position as creatures. Just because He alone is the uncaused existence, He alone exists of Himself; and annihilation, therefore, is averted, and immortality secured, by the free promise and fulfillment of God.

Definitions of this eternity are various, and from the nature of the case must be inadequate, but eternity may be best described as a persistent "now." Just as for those whose attention is very steadily fixed on some absorbing matter, time has no meaning and the seconds and minutes slip by unnoticed, so, in the absorbing interest of eternal happiness or pain, there can be no idea of the passage of time. This is taught by those old legends that have so caught the fancy of many poets, of monks hearing the song of a bird of such entrancing loveliness that, when they returned to the cloister, they found that a hundred years had elapsed since they had begun to listen to the music. There are tales even more descriptive in the pages of mere psychologists, where the same idea of the riveting effect of attention is steadily insisted on. The whole idea, therefore, of duration has been transferred from the mere notion of the distance between passing moments into the perhaps vaguer notion of fluidity, movement, and change.

Now, in eternity we assert that all "the dull monotonies of change" will have ceased altogether, and life will be definable not in terms of growth, but only as sublime consciousness. Perhaps the very idea of eternity having no end gives the unpleasant sense of boredom with which certain people seem to regard the notion of life everlasting, and has subjected it to light raillery. No past is possible, no future to be expected, because of the very absorption in the present. That is all we mean.

Perhaps this will help me to understand what is the difficulty in the idea of Heaven and Hell. Fling into eternity a man who dies in revolt against God, fling him therefore into an absorbing idea of hatred, and what possibility is there for his repentance or ultimate forgiveness? It would be as absurd as for one who was engaged in the vision of God to fall from the love of God. Quite sincerely we can say, in the full meaning of the expression, that there is not the time either in Heaven or in Hell to do so. There is no time at all, no change, but a ceaseless "now." There can be no future. Even the soul in Purgatory does not suffer change in its ultimate destination. As it crosses the threshold of the next life, it knows its final reward and can no longer be turned from the love of its Maker. Thenceforward there is no merit and no demerit; no increase can be made in the volume of divine love, only the fettering chains broken, the stains washed clean, the debts fully paid.

For me shall be one day this changeless existence, this everlasting "now." Shall its persistence be joy or pain? In this life of time, I must make up my mind and fix my duty, for there I can neither repent nor fall. But the point that needs most insistence is the consideration of what precisely is meant by the ceaseless "now." Just as, when my attention is taken up with anything that absorbs my interest, all notion of passing time is lost to me, so the meaning of the eternity of Heaven is made intelligible to me on earth.

In Heaven you will see God face-to-face

In his teaching as to how the Beatific Vision is achieved, St. Thomas proves the richness of his intelligence. The glory of Heaven, the essence of its joy for me, will be to know God even as I am known. The intimate acquaintance God has of my whole nature, His deep comprehension of my passing thoughts, His perfect and subtle understanding of my strength will be somehow paralleled by my own true knowledge of Him.

But how is this to be done? How am I, a creature, to get into my limited reason a perfect idea of the infinite? Whatever I do know comes to me by means of an idea; that is, I obtain my knowledge of things, not by directly taking them into my mind, but by seizing in them the essential constituent of their being and formulating it in a sort of mental word of definition. The result is a kind of mental picture that contains the barest elements of what I am understanding.

Hence, the perfection of my knowledge of anything depends entirely upon the adequacy of my idea of it. If that mental picture corresponds to the thing itself really, then my knowledge is all right; but if there is no such correspondence, then obviously I have not grasped the meaning of what has been presented to my mind.

In Heaven you will see God face-to-face

Now, it is evident that by no manner of means can any idea represent God adequately. He cannot be cramped into any human idea. Hence, it would seem that I could never see God as He is.

Then at once St. Thomas points out the way in which the difficulty is overcome. It is really simple, but overpowering. No idea can perfectly represent God. So God must Himself take the place of the idea. No longer shall my ideas in Heaven be, as here on earth, the mere fabrication of my own intelligence, but, in the case of the vision of God, it is He Himself who enters familiarly into my intelligence and so impresses Himself upon its surface that He becomes part of its very mechanism. So intimate is He with its texture that it is He who is its light and its informant.

In other words, and to repeat, my idea of God in Heaven is not as my idea of God on earth. Here I have seized it for myself, and have fashioned from what I have been told, and what I have read, an idea of what He is in Himself. I have gathered together notions of a self-existing Being, who is just, wise, truthful, powerful, loving, merciful, and so forth. I have gotten more or less vaguely impressions (even though I cannot properly express them) as to what wisdom, justice, mercy, and so forth mean. These I lump together and form for myself, under the light of faith and reason, an idea of God.

But in Heaven, there will be no such process. God is at once in Himself our idea. Hence, the souls in bliss see Him adequately, fully, wholly, for they see Him by means of Himself without symbol, sign, or representation, but with His single and immediate presence. Not as in grace are we made partakers of the divine nature, but He is almost a partaker of ours.

I shall in Heaven see my Maker, yet not lose my own individual being. I shall be absorbed in Him, see Him steadily face-to-face. All the veils that at present hide Him from me shall be rent asunder, every separating influence, every reflecting mirror or darkened glass (lest His glory dazzle my weak sight), shall be ruthlessly cast aside, and in the absolute contemplation of Him shall my happiness find its complete satisfaction. He shall be one with me, yet without His strong, overwhelming being making me cease to be myself. He shall live in me, yet shall I myself live. It is all a very great wonder — this perfect knowledge, complete, adequate, obtained by no act of mine, but by the infusion of Him into my soul. As St. Augustine noted it: "Not we shall enter into all joy, but all joy shall enter into us."

Nor can this end in mere wonder, for there is to follow, consequent upon such a vision, the utmost rapture of love. The heart will itself break out into perfect songs of love. But it is the vision itself by which the soul attains perfection. The apprehension is an act of intelligence, a seeing, a beholding of God.

Oh, how careful must I be of that frail, faltering reason that must one day be possessed by God! How clean must be that temple which God shall one day enter! How guarded must it be from the profane defiling of evil thoughts, how ceaselessly defended from evil assaults! Here I must prepare for that ultimate embrace.

Part 5

∞

The Christian life

∞

Christ calls you to follow Him freely

The very phrase "following Christ" shows how voluntary our service of Him must be. He recognizes the freedom of choice He has Himself given us. There must be no compulsion, no being dragged after the chariot wheels of His triumphal car, no long line of captives grimly led behind Him. His own ministry among men — although it might be at the behest of His Father ("I am come to do the will of Him that sent me"[40]); although even His death, according to His own phrase, might be "necessary" — was yet the free and willing service of His subjection. "I lay down my life," said He; no one took it from Him.[41]

The imagery of our English poets such as Milton and Dryden, who have attempted to depict in language the offering of Himself made by the Son as a propitiation to the Father in atonement for the sins of the world, shows Him as stepping forward in the divine presence and offering to take the proffered burden from which the angels shrank in fear. This is, of course, purely metaphorical, for to none other than Him could the office of redemption have been suggested. But it is true insofar as it expresses the doctrine that the

[40] Cf. John 5:30; 6:38.
[41] John 10:17-18.

whole tragedy of the Incarnation was freely undertaken by the Second Person of the Trinity. He became man of His own choice, without any necessity from His own nature, acting in this way, not from any inherent compulsion (such as that from which the Trinity proceeded), but by the simple decision of His will.

As, therefore, His own ministry was freely undertaken and pursued to its own sublime end, so of the same nature was His own appeal to be made to those who wished to come after Him. The purity and strength of His life, the fathomless tenderness of His love, the keen agony of His sufferings, the winsome appeal of childhood and boyhood, the charm and fascination of His manly grace and bearing, the wonder of His language, the sympathy of His heart, the boldness of His denunciations of hypocrisy and cant, His love of freedom, His passion for justice, His devotion to truth — all these, we say, compel our love and our affectionate discipleship, but it is the compulsion of free service.

This marvelous appeal to human nature is the sole secret of His power. What alone He asks of us, or would be willing to accept, is the devotion of a son, not the forced labor of a slave. His parables and sermons and prayers are full of this idea of sonship; and through His Apostles, whom He had instructed in His own principles and teachings, He is forever insistent upon "the glorious liberty of the sons of God."[42] We are free, therefore, in our choice; we can take or reject His yoke. At the most and best, our highest title must be that of follower — that is, of one who comes behind, perhaps a very long way behind, but who deliberately and of set choice, without any penalty of force, walks in the footsteps of love.

Yet if there is any penalty, it is the penalty not of force but of love, since although the choice is free, the cost must always be paid. And the cost here is the yoke of Christ. The yoke is sweet indeed, and the burden is light; but for all that, there is a yoke and a

[42] Cf. Rom. 8:21.

burden. There is something to be borne by us, some difficulties to be overcome, some disappointments, some agonies in the garden, some cross-carrying in the busy streets, some loneliness, some betrayals, some jeers.

We are free, yet have called ourselves followers, and He will take care that we do follow Him. Perfectly conscious of what will meet our eyes on each day's awakening and of what will form the retrospect of our working hours when we turn to our sleep in the evening, we yet freely follow in the footsteps of love. Not spasmodically, like Peter — at one time zealous and promising to die for Christ, at another denying all acquaintanceship with Him — but, deliberately and with full knowledge of what the consequences are likely to be, calmly striving to keep up to His stride and pace, we hurry after Him.

Certainly we shall never catch up to Him. He will go forever swinging down the great highway, His figure heading the great Crusade. Right away, His form showing against the gray and dusty pathway, can He be seen leading His followers. But at least I am going in the same direction. Stumbling, failing, footsore, hot, tired, weary, it is a blessed thing for me to be still following with a glad heart.

∽

Christ is the model of manhood

Man's great gift and greater responsibility is his manhood. As a child, he sets his face toward it; and when he reaches the season of its arrival, he stands or falls by his acceptance or repudiation of it. It is a thing that does not come of itself. Each must achieve it for himself, for there are many we meet in life who do not seem ever to have won their manhood. They have drifted through their days; they have existed rather than lived. "It is easy to be honest enough not to be hanged. To be *really* honest means to subdue one's party spirit, one's vanity, one's prepossessions, ideals — stating things fairly, not humoring your argument — doing justice to your enemies, whether you are stronger than they or not; making confession whether you can afford it or not; refusing unmerited praise; looking painful truths in the face, and not merely seeing 'the inmost part of them'; knowing what one means, and knowing when one has no meaning, and shaking off one's plausibilities, and fifty-five things which men see with pleasure and which the angels see through."[43]

All this clear-sightedness is what is surely expected from a man as part of his manhood; yet it is something also that does not come

[43] Aubry de Vere, *Memoir*, 103.

by the mere passage of years, but by the very definite overcoming of nature by supernature, or, perhaps more accurately, it is the true evolution of nature when developed by supernature. It is not a thing that one becomes, but a thing one ultimately and definitely acquires — indeed, it is precisely that which man is put here to acquire. He is human just in proportion to the degree in which he attains to this ideal. He has, that is to say, the dominion over himself, the lordship that reason and will can alone secure.

The possibility, of course, is rooted in man to start with. But long ago his nature received a severe check from the Fall; all the stately ordering of its several parts was disturbed by that dread catastrophe; the nice harmony and balance were disturbed. The springs of man's beautiful nature were diverted to other ends than that of his real destiny, and the noble generosity of his nature was warped by the terrible disease of selfishness. Meanness, pettiness, the desire of his own personal satisfaction to the utter disregard of the convenience of others took possession of him and dominated his life. He no longer appeared as the lord, but as the pirate, of creation. The fine upright nature was gone, and in its place came a low-aiming instinct for pleasure and preservation.

Yet all the while, the older ideals remained beneath the new and distressing selfishness. From time to time, he felt that he was made for better things, felt the movement to a better life, felt uplifted by emotions that rather puzzled him by their greatness. He saw self-sacrifice and proclaimed it divine, watched the mother in travail for her child's delivery and declared it to be itself something worthy almost of worship. He found that truth was a god, and lying an evil spirit. Gradually, through that "light that enlighteneth every man that cometh into this world,"[44] he began his upward struggle to something more worthy of him than the Fall had reduced him to. In the revelation of the Old Testament, in the fragmentary

[44] John 1:9.

gospel of the Greeks, he felt himself being led to a greater and nobler vision; for the whole of creation groaned, feeling itself working toward a new birth. Then came the fullness of time, and the Perfect Man was born, lived, died, and became the model for all generations.

This is the very purpose of Christ. Of all the instructive yearnings that paganism and even Judaism could not satisfy, Christ gave a definite approval and a finer example. He was the desired of nations, the figure of the substance of God, the exact reproduction of the ideal that, through all the centuries, had been ill-expressed and largely unconscious at the back of the human heart. Man had waited and tarried for the morning, and now the day was breaking. He found set before him the perfect figure of a man — gentleness, self-sacrifice, hatred of hypocrisy and cant, sympathy with the frailties of human nature, and the fierce love of justice, truth, and innocence. Suddenly he discovered that the wonderful word, which his mind had vaguely formed for itself as the ideal of human nature, was made flesh and dwelt among us.

Here, then, is for me the perfect manhood or manliness at which I have to aim. Obviously it will not be without a great struggle that I shall get anywhere near the goal. But just as men nowadays take as their model some statue or picture that represents for them the perfection of the human form and, by careful exercise, endeavor to reproduce the same perfect development in their own bodies, so is it also with the soul. I have to guard against the supposition that I have come close up to Him, or that when I give way to beastliness, it is different in me from what it is in others ("I am really not that sort"). And I must guard against the opposite fallacy of thinking that I am utterly unable to follow Him. I must take my life as an artist takes his clay, and out of it form as great a masterpiece as my own powers and my material allow.

∞

Your body is a temple of the Holy Spirit

From our childhood we are taught that we must take more care of our souls than of our bodies, that where their interests clash or come into opposition, preference must be given always to the soul. Our Lord Himself has repeated this for us on many occasions, with His "What doth it profit a man to have gained the world and lost his own soul?"[45] and His exhortation to fear rather those who can hurt the soul than those whose power is limited merely to the body.[46]

But all this proves more than the simple supremacy of the soul, for it implies as surely that to the body as well certain duties are of divine command. If I am ordered to pay more attention to my soul than to my body, then at the same time it is clear that I am expected to pay at least a certain amount of attention to my body. Indeed, this is also evident from other reasons, for my body, too, was given to me by God. It is the most intimate gift from His hands, and the influence that it bears upon my whole life and upon the conduct and even temptations of the soul is so enormous that no one can neglect it without peril of great loss. The account that I

[45] Cf. Matt. 16:26.
[46] Matt. 10:28.

shall one day have to render to God for all the gifts of which He holds me the steward must include as of very great importance the care and culture that I have bestowed upon my body.

Wonderful it is, too, in all its ways. Compacted together, intricate and marvelously made, there is nothing that man has invented that comes near to his own frame in the delicacy and refinement of its texture, its mechanism, its perfect form, its coloring. When some genius has constructed an automaton, the world wonders; yet how few stop to think of the still more marvelous thing that they possess from the hands of God.

Now, it is a strange thing that with all the asceticism that Christianity has taught, it has probably done more for the reverencing of the body than any other forms of religion. The old pagan creed was, it might seem, an absolute worship of the flesh. It exalted the present time, it made the pleasures of life to be the purpose of life, and it repeated that joy was the end of all things and that the gods themselves had delight in their godhead because it freed them from the responsibility of any other claim than that of their own desire. The crimes of the gods were more terrible than had ever been the crimes of men, just because the gods could give free rein to the cravings of the flesh. With all the poetry of their mythology, there was a degradation about it that shocked the better type of minds and made them find mystical interpretations for what was obviously merely bestial.

Yet in spite of this wonderful worship of the human form divine, we turn the pages of pagan history written by pagans, and we find it one long lament. The historians of the Greek cities and of the Roman Empire are all full of the terrors and the horrors of life. They might have deified the joys of the body as the sacred instincts of man, but they found in actual life that these joys could not be found, precisely because they were sought. They had meant to exalt the body; they succeeded only in defiling it. They began by worship; they ended by profanation. They considered the physical side of life as the most perfect, but they degraded it by a filthiness that has hardly been equaled and never been surpassed. Even men like Socrates and Plato have left records that make us almost despair of the noble character of man.

Then came our blessed Lord with His gospel of mortification of self-denial, and of the renunciation of "the lust of the eyes, the lust of the flesh, and the pride of life";[47] and suddenly we find as a paradoxical result that never since the world began has more been done for the body than has been done in Christian times. The very existence of hospitals is a thing that the followers of the Crucified have originated. The whole modern worship of charity and philanthropy, which, with all its absurdities, has been on the whole nobly meant, is a legacy of Christ. The care of the sick, of those in sorrow, of the fallen — the care taken to improve the physical well-being of people — date precisely from those times when first the Cross was hoisted as the ideal of human life.

After all, the Master Himself, who upheld suffering in His own life as the most perfect expression of love, was also the most eager to remove it from the lives of others. He went about always doing good. He forgave their sins, but He healed their bodies — nay, in His wonderful description of the Last Judgment, He seemed to make the whole future of the soul to depend more on the corporal than on the spiritual works of mercy.[48] He began the splendid tradition that has done more than anything else to defend the Christian name.

And the reason for this apparent worship of the body? It is because the most splendid thing that has ever been said about it is the Christian belief in it as a temple of the Holy Spirit. This body of ours, with all its fleshly feelings and instinctive desires, is yet the very dwelling place of God. It is the shrine of divinity, a shrine He

[47] Cf. 1 John 2:16.
[48] Matt. 25:31-46.

Himself did not disdain to inhabit. Duties, then, of cleanliness, exercise, and health are of obligation. To pamper it is to profane it, but to mortify is to make it alive, to make the very glory of God shine through its transfigured radiance.

∞

You are responsible for the souls of others

Our Lord said, "A new commandment I give unto you. . . . By this shall all men know that you are my disciples: if you have love one for another."[49] And everyone has noted that in the description that He gives of the Last Judgment, He seems to make the whole future life depend entirely upon the corporal works of mercy. He does not upbraid the wicked for their blasphemy, nor for their pride, nor for their direct refusal to serve God, for they were quite surprised to learn that they had neglected their duty to God; it would seem as though they would at once have done all they could for Him, had they seen Him in any want or distress. No rebuke falls from His lips that they have ignored the sovereign worship of the Father, but only, "I was hungry and you gave me not to eat, naked and you clothed me not, homeless and you did not take me in. . . . Depart from me, ye cursed, for inasmuch as you did not these things to the least of my brethren, you did them not to me."[50]

St. Catherine of Siena[51] tells us that we have a distinct obligation to help our neighbor, so that if this help is withheld, we are

[49] John 13:34, 35.
[50] Cf. Matt. 25:41-43.
[51] St. Catherine of Siena (1347-1380), Dominican tertiary.

guilty of sin. She notes, for example, that in Psalm 18, when we pray to be spared from the sins of others, we are really supposing that the sins of others may be our own very fault, and that it is quite possible that God will judge us not only for what we have done, but also for what others have committed through us.

Thus, upon us rests the responsibility of countless others, of all those upon whose lives, either directly or indirectly, our influence is brought to bear. Surely the prospect is frightening, for who shall say where that influence of ours is to stop? An act is performed in life, and the ripple of the waters it has disturbed widen until they touch the shore.

Parents as well as priests come under this grave responsibility; nor is the wonderful effect of influence for good or ill confined to those who are in an official position of authority over others. All layfolk must be included, for upon each lies the obligation of doing what each can for his neighbor's soul; none are exempt. Indeed, everyone can do a great deal.

The laity, insofar as their lives are fuller of activity, and as they are far more numerous than are the priests, have a much wider field of action. It is difficult to see where the possible scope of their effective power can cease. When we read the lives of such wonderful men as Ozanam[52] and others of his type, we see that there really is no limit to the amount of good that can be effected by layfolk. So closely and intimately are they associated with their neighbors that, at every turn in the road, they can be saying, doing, and living that which must bring ideas to those about them. If each, then, did his best, what a huge change would come about!

Take my own little circle in life. Supposing that I had brought to bear upon all the whole power of which I am capable, what a difference would by now have been seen in the little world that

---

[52] Bl. Frederic Ozanam (1813-1853), founder of the St. Vincent de Paul Society.

forms the boundary of my activity! Then each of these, too, would have become the center of another circle around which revolves another. How many lax Catholics might have been led back to the practice of the Faith! How many young men, when just a word might have saved them, would have been prevented from an evil step from which there was no recovery! How many boys might have been kept close to the reverence of the noble and pure ideals of Christ!

Of course, human respect makes us afraid of acting, for the power of the world springs, as always, from its boldness. By it, bad men create an atmosphere around them. If the good were as bold as are the bad, there would be no bad left, or very few. Every unit tells. If every Catholic were a credit to his religion and openly professed the whole round of Faith, how the evil of the world would be cowed! It is, perhaps, the little things that tell most — grace properly and respectfully said before and after meals, a real Sign of the Cross, lifting the hat deliberately when passing a church, bowing the head at the mention of the Holy Name: these are the things that oddly enough most strike those outside with the true Christian fearlessness.

Laymen should also be keen on their religion and be able to give a reasonable account of the faith that is in them. But the strongest argument of all is a religious and edifying life as a courageous Catholic.

We are responsible, then, if there is a soul we can help toward God who, through our laziness, is thrown off from that direction to a lower plane of life. Of us will God ask, as He asked of Cain, "Where is thy brother?"[53] and it is only a murderer who can dare make answer that we are not the keepers of our brothers.

But what a joy to have been of use to others, to have given them a helping hand over the difficult places of life, and eventually to

[53] Gen. 4:9.

find a ready welcome from the courts of God, where we shall find gathered together those who under God owed to us their presence before Him! Perhaps I have been too afraid of professing my Faith; no one will on that account respect me the more. Perhaps, on the other hand, I have tried to ram my religion down other people's throats. There is surely a middle course of gentle and kindly life, full of the wisdom of charity, based upon the perfect figure of Christ.

∾

Keeping God's Commandments
shows your love for Him

The coming of Christ was not to destroy, but to fulfill. Hence, our Lord never in any way abrogated the moral teaching of the Old Law. Whatever Moses had declared to the people as the moral code of Israel was never to be slackened, but rather, under the New Dispensation of love (for which men had been laboriously trained and educated under centuries of fear), to be filled out in fuller detail. The Commandments were not, therefore, to be lessened, but to be increased. Whatever had been ordained was still ordained; what had been at one time permitted, might not, however, be permitted now.

All this is the inevitable result of a higher grade of holiness. As the soul draws nearer and nearer to the holiness of God, it absorbs more and more of the meaning of sanctity. Things that at one time seemed hardly to suggest a scruple now become considered in a new light, from a higher plane. The soul has become more sensitive, and can detect flaws and defects where before it would have noticed nothing amiss. As we get holier, we think ourselves always worse, for always more pronounced is the great gulf fixed between what we are and what we should be. And what I can see taking place in my own soul has taken place in a larger way in the upward movement of the race toward God. Before, Moses forbade adultery; but now, "I say that whosoever lusteth after a woman in his heart hath already committed adultery."[54] The New Law thus fills in the details of the Old.

It is interesting to see, as a result of this, that without Christianity man would have no real proof of the idea of racial progress. Destroy or deny the truth of Christian teaching, and nothing can be found to show any advance on our part toward the perfect day. The whole doctrine of progress rests upon a supposition that man has grown toward a larger and freer hope. Christianity alone, especially Catholic Christianity, can ratify and confirm this. Abolish our idea of a Redemption accomplished and our notion that Christ introduced new laws and a new sacrifice and new channels of grace through the sacraments, and the whole fabric supporting progress falls to the ground. Apart from the advance made by Christianity upon both Judaism and paganism, there is very little evidence of an upward movement; for neither in art, nor even in crafts, have we — considering the length of time the human race has occupied the earth — made progress. It is difficult for us to improve on the masterpieces of ancient art or literature; and even in technical skill, some of the builders of antiquity were ahead of us. We are simply unable nowadays, with all our resources, to do what some of them have done. Doubtless we have discovered things they did not know, but also how many things have we not forgotten? The note, therefore, of optimism that pervades modern scientific circles rests upon the moral teaching of Christianity.

This, too, is enforced by the Commandments. The new interpretation that Christ has given to the Old Law, the spiritualizing influence He has shed on what was to a certain extent a material view of moral life, are all advances that will be made noticeable to anyone who will take the trouble to study them severally. He

[54] Cf. Matt. 5:27-28.

cannot help but be struck by the huge advance in ethical values that has been made in this New Dispensation. Under the previous code, the whole relationship of God to man in the matters of moral life was a relationship of rewards and punishments. If man was obedient, he would be rewarded; if he was suffering, he had done evil and was but fittingly punished.

But the new code meant, in some ways, a reversing of the old. Suffering and success were now proofs neither of rewards nor of punishments, but of love only. Whatever happens, I am now to find love as the sole solution of life and its problems. I am not to be searching my heart to see wherein I have failed, but rejoicing that, in all, God is showing me His love. The Commandments come, indeed, as restraints to human nature, but as restraints that impose the burden of love. "Decline from evil" is the least and lowest act of religion, the highest and best is "Do good." Man was created, not to avoid sin, but to love God; and we show that love — so He has taught us — not by calling upon His Name, but by keeping His Commandments.

Fortune-telling endangers souls

There is a whole category of odd and fantastic doings and customs that we can group under the name of superstitions. Some of them are merely the foolish traditions that spring up, no one quite knows how or when, although antiquaries may find their traces many centuries ago and can even at times establish relationships in traditions of this nature between the races on many continents. Some probably had once a religious significance, but they have now severed all their connection with religion and merely enshrine evidences of what they had been formerly.

But there are other practices that are far more dangerous. In themselves, indeed, there may be much that a patient and scientific study will one day succeed in establishing as of much use to humanity; but in the meanwhile they are, many of them, full of peril. For the most part, they play just upon the borderline between soul and body, which we commonly call the nervous system. Hence, the physical prostration they produce is often a prelude to a moral prostration, which is, of course, even more terrible.

Nor should anyone wonder at such an effect, since the evil spirits, which our Faith tells us are bent on the ruin of the human race, are clever and crafty enough to make use of every possible means of deceiving our credulity. They have ruined man time and again by the inventions of his own genius, wasting his strength and reason by means of discoveries that ease his pain or drown his sorrow.

Hence, it is not surprising that they have influenced souls by the fatuous superstition of foretelling the future. Fatuous, indeed, this must ever be, since my future acts are free acts and lie at the disposition of my own soul. Even I cannot predict with certainty what I shall do. God only, because He dwells in eternity (and comprehends in His single glance the past, present, and future), can see and reveal them. Fortune-tellers do not ordinarily suggest to us the kind of people whom we can imagine God taking into His confidence.

These fortune-tellers may, by sheer practice, come to discern character very quickly, just as a detective may be able, by the science of his trade, to determine very swiftly, by all sorts of signs that would be unnoticed by others, the temperament of those of whom he has had the opportunity of a good scrutiny. Most people are probably able, by mere practice, to make a pretty shrewd guess as to the characters of those whom they meet; and once the temperament and characteristics of a man are known, it is not difficult to reconstruct both his past and his future. The quick-witted have their own dangers and temptations; the slow-moving and obstinate fellow can be judged to have firm friends, but few of them. And so it is possible — although obviously the game is not learned without some difficulty — to invent details in life that come very near the truth; near enough, at any rate, to impress the most skeptical.

Indeed, so obvious does all this seem that one could hardly imagine how lucrative the trade of foretelling the future has become, nor would anyone suppose how dangerous it may be for certain souls. For some of them, it has become the chief means of discovering the will of God. It is all so simple that it is difficult to see wherein the peril lies. Yet Shakespeare has shown in the marvelous structure of *Macbeth* how an easily moved mind can justify to itself a crime that has been foretold it, just because it has been foretold. It is evident that, had no such meeting taken place on the heath between Macbeth and the "weird sisters," the murder of Duncan would probably never have suggested itself to his mind. Until then, he had been an honest, if ambitious, soldier. But the witches prophesied that he would succeed to two titles, and that eventually he would obtain the crown. He does immediately hear that he has become thane of Glamis and thane of Cawdor, and consequently, his eyes now turn to the royal dignity itself. The opportunity is granted him, for Duncan comes to sleep under his very roof. Here at once he sees the gradual accomplishment of his glorious destiny. It is fate, destiny. How can he oppose himself to such heavenly evidences? His conscience at first halts and boggles at the murder of a guest, but he repeats to himself that he cannot escape, and the evil deed is done.

This is, indeed, the temper of mind that itself works out the foretold future. This is the peril, that a crime, foretold and once become a possibility, may speedily (as a result of the prophecy) be an accomplished fact. It is not foretold because it will take place, but it takes place because it has been foretold.

∞

True fear of God draws you closer to Him

Fear is a weakness and a strength, a sin and a virtue. For most, it is probably an evil, since human nature shrinks from present pain and is the more vividly afraid of what more immediately threatens. For that reason, it would appear that man is more likely to be too much, than too little, afraid in life. No doubt there are many who need to be more circumspect, more cautious; but these adventurous spirits are fewer in comparison than those who find in the life of the soul too much matter for depression and discouragement.

Naturally the real determinant as to whether fear is legitimate is to be sought in ascertaining the object of fear. Obviously the whole question is: "What exactly is it of which I am afraid?" Should the thing feared be, indeed, an evil that it is reasonable to dread, then we are justified in our alarm; otherwise, of course, we are not. Yet whenever there are two opposing menaces, we must be careful in our choice. This must be made under the high light of God's good grace, since, in the deliberate words of Scripture, men "fear where there is no fear";[55] by which it is evident that the sacred writer means only that there is often a fear out of all proportion to the thing feared. The body naturally shrinks from pain and

[55] Ps. 13:5 (RSV = Ps. 14:5).

loss, and consequently, we have always cause for some fear, but not for the excessive fear we entertain about material things. For the body must one day perish, but the soul can never die.

Fear, then, of God must necessarily be ours; nor, when we are conscious of His terrible judgments, can we well help it. The justice of God, and the words that the compassionate Son of Man has used of that "day of wrath,"[56] certainly justify us in being alarmed at all that it entails. Yet love, too, must sweeten and soften it. We have to prevent ourselves from becoming obsessed by the mere shadow of fear, for love and fear must no man put asunder.

We start, then, with the assumption that both are essential to the proper worship of God; but we add as a note of practical wisdom that, of the two, most people need to insist in their hearts more on love and less on fear, since, by nature, one's feelings by themselves incline more to fear than to love. St. Thomas asserts this in more than one passage: "Between the two extremes of timidity and boldness, it is more necessary to overcome the first than the second. For it is more difficult to repress timidity than to moderate boldness, because the dangers that result from the latter are sufficient to make us quick to temper its excess, whereas the thought of the serious evils that result from timidity ends in making us more timid still."[57] Of the two, therefore, fear is usually the extreme that needs least encouragement, for it is already in most people quite sufficiently active — in fact, predominant.

In consequence of this, I may be led to wonder whether, in my own case, my fear is too little or too much, whether it be properly motived, whether it is really the servile fear that God dislikes, or whether it partakes of that filial fear out of which comes love.

What signs can I look for to discriminate between the right and wrong fear? This surely is the infallible test: the fear that is really

[56] Rom. 2:5.
[57] *Summa Theologica*, II-II, Q. 123.

and truly from God should take me nearer and nearer to His feet; a fear that keeps me from His presence and holds me at arm's length from Him can never be His gift.

I think of the Magdalen, whose sins brought her near to her Master, made her come boldly into His presence, and kiss His feet; nay, made her so little timid of Him that in the garden of the Resurrection He had to rebuke her: "Touch me not. I am not yet ascended to My Father."[58] So, again, the fear of Peter that drove him out of the courtyard of the High Priest after his triple denial and made him weep bitterly, could yet extort no other words from his heart than "Thou knowest all things. Thou knowest that I love Thee."[59]

So, then, the true fear of God should hold me to His love and to His reverence. It must prevent me from turning away from the pathway of His commandments, nor should it further disturb the peace and serenity of my soul, nor torture my conscience nor bruise the tenderness of love or lead the enemies of God to speak of Him reproachfully. I may know what is a false fear of God, for it will lead me from Him.

[58] Cf. John 20:17.
[59] John 21:17.

∞

Children should obey
their parents out of love

The first duty of a child is to obey God through his father and mother. For that, we have divine warrant, and in the Old Testament we find that this is insisted on under the extreme penalty of death. The only limits put to this obedience on the part of children are the limits of wrongdoing: "To love, reverence, and obey our parents in all that is not sin."

This strait subjection of the child to the parent, since it is the result of the natural bond between them, should be a subjection that is softened and made easy by love. That is to say, the mere physical strength of the parent is neither the origin nor the measure of that obedience, but both are based upon a definite relationship that is absolutely different in kind to the mere relationship of guardian and ward. Consequently, the sense of ungrudging allegiance must enter in as an essential element. The feeling is to be deeper than mere juxtaposition or dependence, and to be derived from an almost instinctive appreciation of each other's affection.

Whether or not this affection exists emotionally should not make an appreciable difference to the duty. It is, unfortunately, possible to find parents and children sometimes at open war, due, apparently, as much to incompatibility of temper as to anything else — an incompatibility arising often from sheer family likeness. But even so, the child has duties of obedience to his parents, precisely because they are parents.

It is needful to notice that the child has these duties, for the law of obedience affects the child only while he is a child. No one has said that men or women are bound to obey their parents. Obedience, in the direct meaning of the word, ceases when the age of childhood ceases; for as children, their lives seem, by a law of nature, to be not altogether severable from the family life. The dependence is so great (greater far and longer than the dependence that exists in the animal kingdom between cub and mother) that physically the whole group can be considered as one.

So, too, in the moral view of the family, the effect of elder upon younger is so intimate and so intense that, again, for practical purposes, the child is sanctified in the faith of the father. But later, when the child has become old enough to determine himself fully as a separate existence, he must settle for himself the details and main movements of his own life. Obedience has ceased to be a necessity and would become a hindrance. Reverence and respect remain always; influence may survive, but authority has departed. In matters of religion they can no longer dictate to me; they have no longer on them the charge of my soul. For myself and by myself, I sink or swim. It is I who choose my partner in life, not they for me. They can, and should, no doubt, offer me advice. It is advice and nothing more, to be listened to with attention, the more because they are my parents, but not for that implicitly obeyed.

So long, then, as obedience claims me in childhood, let me look to it that this obedience is given ungrudgingly, that it is not spoilt by incessant grumbling. The weariness of life, springing at times from the very closeness between my parents and me (for this mere physical approximation, while it usually stimulates the emotions of love, may at times cause an increase of irritation), must never force me to renounce that duty of obedience which the

Commandments of God ordained and the life of my Master preached. But when I have outgrown the dependence of childhood and am of sufficient age to think and act for myself, in the interests of my own soul, then obedience may have a cramping effect upon my character.

The very purpose for which I was created was to serve God with all the individual faculties — such as they are — with which He endowed me. Now, if I allow myself to be overridden by any other, I may do more work in the world, but not such as I alone can contribute. My personality has been lost, and the account I render is not for my talent, but for another's. The intelligence, experience, richer nature, and greater moderation of my parents must be to the end of my life a law, "not a force, but a perfect guidance with perfect love"; but my life is always my own and God's.

Hence, to their warnings and promptings, I must ever show patience, respect, consideration, and gratitude, but I cannot hope to plead their commands as an excuse for my actions to the judge, any more than I could the orders of the state or the counsel of the priest. The ultimate responsibility of a man must lie always with himself.

∞

Parents are responsible for their children's physical and spiritual well-being

It is a platitude in moral science that rights are founded upon duties. Consequently, whenever we claim that others have certain obligations to perform toward us, we can feel perfectly certain that we have corresponding obligations to them. My children must obey me, so it is my duty to look after them.

Nay, we can go further than that and insist to ourselves that God surely expects from us a deeper consciousness of our responsibility and a more exact fulfillment of it than He can possibly hope to find in those whose judgment and power of realizing the difference between right and wrong is in so many ways infinitely less developed. We may suppose — indeed, it is the frequent claim of parents — that their experience is fuller and their opportunities of better judgment more assured. We must suppose also, in consequence of this, that a more strait account will be exacted from them as to how they have carried out the trust confided to them. Hence, I must first (before I venture to discover for myself wherein those duties lie) impress my mind with the seriousness of my position and the extreme responsibilities that these duties of parenthood impose on me. Besides, in my failure or neglect, not only is my own soul at stake and brought to ruin, but precisely because of my parenthood, I may drag others with me in my fall. Fathers and mothers have in their hands the plastic matter of young life. They may, by clumsy handling or by mere negligence, allow this to become hardened in a fashion inimical to itself.

How, briefly, may we note wherein chiefly these duties lie? Perhaps the simplest way is to recall to mind what exactly the parent gives to the child. First, *being*: the formation of the offspring depends, at least to a considerable extent, upon the parents.

Second, *nourishment*: the physical well-being of the child is also at the mercy of father and mother. Even in the womb, the unborn baby may be affected; and through his early years, the evil done may be incalculable. Sufficiency and the right kind of food must be studied by both parents, although here probably the instinct of the mother will be most generally right. Anyway, the whole material care of the child must be rigorously and vigorously attended to.

Third, *education*: this implies the whole development of that which is rational in the child. His intelligence, his memory, his imagination, the power of will as exercised in the formation of character, and his knowledge of God, of His revelation through the Church, and of the story of the Incarnation are all included as requiring training by the parents either directly or indirectly. Then, as age advances, they must prepare the child for a profession or life ahead.

All this obviously is a distinct obligation that falls on parents in regard to their children for just so long as they are children. For the measure of duty is right, and the measure of right is duty. Hence, if, when I have obtained a certain age, I have no longer to obey but to act for myself, it follows also that my parents are equally no longer obliged to attend to my wants or engage further in preparing me for life. If I consider myself able to judge for myself, then I have thereby released them from any need to worry themselves further about me. When my children can refuse to acknowledge my authority, I can simultaneously refuse to support their indigence.

Obviously no such thing will take place. The child will continue to listen and follow advice long after the time has come for him to claim independence; while the parents will continue to maintain the child long after the time when their obligations have ceased toward him. But always the measure of right is duty, and the measure of duty is right.

Moreover, what I have always to bear in mind is that the purpose of my responsibility is to train my children to be independent of me. The mother must forbear to lavish her affection when she sees that it is weakening the child's character; the father must restrain all overpowering of his children's judgment. Train, yes; but crush, no. "In great states," says Ruskin, "children are always trying to remain children, and parents wanting to make men and women of them. In vile states, the children are always wanting to be men and women, and the parents to keep them children." Advice and guidance is mine to give, but dictation (when they have ceased to be children), never.

∞

Christ models loyalty to one's country

The devotion of a citizen to his country is a natural virtue, felt instinctively by the heart. A critic might trace its origin to a mere lust for possession and make it arise out of some clannish feeling that made primitive peoples hold what they held against the world. Various material suggestions of this kind have been made to account for it; but their truth or falsehood is immaterial and is, indeed, utterly beyond all proof or disproof, being a pure hypothesis incapable of verification. Moreover, it is, indeed, of very slight importance to discover the root from which a thing has sprung, since what was born of earth may well be fitted for a place in Heaven; it is not what things were, but what they are that most concerns us.

The fact, therefore, of the existence of this feeling of loyalty to our particular central group, whether local or national or international, cannot be contested. Even those people whose constant critical attitude seems to belie any such spirit, would justify their own strictures on the very ground that they love, and wish to correct because they love.

It is, then, this mere fact of patriotism that is of momentary interest, rather than the cause that produced it; for it is an axiom or principle of Catholic theologians that nature never acts in vain nor is wholly wrong. Whenever we find a very strong belief in the race as a race, there must be some real meaning to its belief. Custom may have distorted or caricatured the original, but there must have been some original.

But it is not merely a natural expression of primitive feeling, for nothing has been left that is that only; no department of human life has been abandoned, but all have been made sacred by Christ, our Lord. So, too, He has dignified patriotism. For while He denounced the narrowness of national religion, He, who was Himself man, felt the bonds of national love and pride. Over the far sight of His own fair city He wept, when, in His knowledge of the future, He beheld it straitened and battered on every side. He wept over Jerusalem not merely because He foresaw the ruin of a great city, but because it was the chief city of His nation. He was human as well as divine.

So, again, throughout His life He was splendidly loyal to every organization that could have conceivably any claim upon Him. He spoke unhesitatingly of the hypocrisy of the lives and of the narrow outlook upon religion of the priesthood of His own nation, but of their power and jurisdiction He spoke only to acknowledge them. Their example He could not praise, but their precepts He did. Even of the huge Roman Empire His guarded utterances could not be construed into any antinational declamation, so that, while the Pharisees never dared to rouse the people by saying that He was subservient to Rome, their attempts to curry favor with Rome by insisting on His antagonism to Caesarism could be backed up only by an impudent falsehood.

Loyalty, therefore, to my country and to my people is a virtue that I learn from my Master. I have no right, if I take my teaching from Him, to denounce it as a weakness, for even when (if ever) Socialism establishes internationalism in government, police, and trade, it will find that the national feelings and desires will be always there. They may be diverted to useful ends, but they can never be destroyed.

Yet loyalty, as our Lord also teaches, does not mean a blind sub-servience to every act of my own nation. The genuine patriot, just because his patriotism is genuine, may be obliged to denounce the evil and unjust courses of his own people; and the greater his love for his country, the more passionate, in all likelihood, will be his appeal to it to follow after justice and truth. For patriotism, like every other good quality, must be subject always to conscience, and cannot dictate to conscience. Its promptings must be carefully censored by prudence, justice, fortitude, and temperance.

But allowing all this, I must recognize that my country has certain definite claims upon me. It affords me protection; it provides for my convenience and allows me peace. In turn, I must render to it a willing service, a respect, a love even that will drive me to do my best by her for her spiritual and temporal prosperity. Nay, I shall see that the nation is really nothing more than an enlarged and greater myself; for a people is the sum of its individuals, the continued development of the personality of each one of us.

∞

Anger is sometimes justified

In itself, anger is neither good nor bad. It is a passion, and although this word *passion*, like the word *anger*, ordinarily is interpreted in an evil sense, it does not bear that meaning in its original significance. Primarily, it implies the movement of our nonrational nature; that is to say, it means simply that the faculties lying partly in the body and partly in the soul (if the inaccurate expression may be allowed) are in operation. Hence, if they operate under the direction of reason and will, they are reasonable and therefore to be justified. If they obscure reason and will, they are unreasonable and to be condemned. Still, the fact that the expressions are so often interpreted in an evil sense suggests to us how very easily they can be turned to abuse.

Now, therefore, we must begin by realizing that we can sin by being angry when we should not be; that is, anger sometimes rules us — does not give the reason time to deliberate, but blinds it in the rush and fury of its movement. Instead of being instant in obedience to the will and to the reason as directing the will, it takes up an attitude of command and dictates to both. Thus, in an English Chronicle we read that King John was "subject to ungovernable fits of temper." That simple sentence reveals the whole moral significance of anger. It is an evil when it is "ungovernable," when it "subjects" us to its dominion. The king was himself a slave, obedient and tied to the flare and flash of his own temper; and to dethrone reason is to destroy in our souls the Vicegerent of God.

But this very view of reason suggests to us another, perhaps more important, idea. Not only may I sin by being angry when I should not, but I may sin by *not* being angry when I should be. If my reason tells me that it is right to be angry, then I disobey God when I refuse to give place to wrath; for, as the New Testament teaches, it is possible to "be angry and sin not."[60] Our Lord Himself, when need arose, roped together a bundle of cords and drove from the Temple those who trafficked in the House of Prayer, and down the front steps He flung the tables of the money-changers.

Perhaps for most of us, the fault is not that we are too angry, but that we are not angry enough. Think of the evils that are in the world, that are known to all, admitted to exist by public press and on public platform. Would they have survived thus far, had folk all shown the indignant anger of Christ? Hypocrisy, cant, and the whole blatant injustice that stalks naked and unashamed in national life — may not our own weakness and silence have helped to render impotent all efforts to reduce these terrible things? We are convinced that a living wage is necessary; our mind is made up that the traffic in souls should cease; openly we repeat to each other that it is uncomfortable to hear people making their laughter out of the ideals of Christ. But what is the use of conviction or determination unless they are driven by the fire of anger? Dirty stories, uncharitable gossip, perpetual criticism — it is my meekness that keeps them alive.

I have got to make myself realize that anger is itself neither evil nor good, and that it can be either. Hence I must pledge myself to see how far I allow anger to rule me when it should not, and how far I overrule it when I should give it a free hand. Revenge is,

[60] Eph. 4:26.

of course, unchristian; the quick thought that leaps to the brain, the natural instinct that wishes to get even with an opponent, the desire to retaliate by harsh language, or clever retort, or deeply wounding attitude of disdain, or ironic politeness have all to be swept aside by the gentleness of Christ. The prayer of Christ for His executioners, the general spirit taught in the Sermon on the Mount, the rebuke that He addressed to St. James and St. John who wished to call down fire from Heaven on the villages that had refused to welcome Him — all point the way of gentleness and peace. He Himself summed up the essential expression of His own teaching in words that will probably make all Christians bow their heads in shame: "By this shall all men know that you are my disciples: if you have love one for another."[61]

Even the spirit of the Old Testament, with its rigid justice of eye for eye and tooth for tooth, could yet feel that vengeance must be left to God, who would Himself repay. The law imposed justice, but the individual practiced mercy. But all that is to be noted here is that all this gentleness is not contradicted by teaching the need of anger. Gentleness is not a sense of weakness (for cowardice is unchristian), but of strength; and anger against injustice and hypocrisy is a sense also of strength. How often must not Christ have been angry, yet how always must He have been gentle!

[61] John 13:34, 35.

∞

War is necessary in this
world, but should be justified

For every follower of Christ, the slaying of a fellowman is a terrible thing. That one nation should have to march out against another and compel it by sheer force to refrain from evil and do good seems quite contrary to the spirit of our Master. His Sermon on the Mount, so full of its high idealism of "turning the other cheek," of submitting to, rather than repelling, violence and giving the coat to him who takes the cloak,[62] strikes the whole note of the Gospel, yet can hardly be made to fit in with the traditional practice of Christian nations. The figure of Christ in its austere gentleness rebukes the swaggering truculence of actual Christians.

It is true that there are phrases, too, in the New Testament that imply the opposite, startling and broken expressions about swords, not peace, as the gift He gave;[63] injunctions to sell clothing and to purchase weapons;[64] metaphors about war within the family, and parents and children set in fierce opposition.[65] Even as a child, it

[62] Matt. 5:39-40.
[63] Matt. 10:34.
[64] Luke 22:36.
[65] Luke 12:53.

was predicted of Him that He would cause sorrow to His Mother, and that many should fall as well as rise in Israel on His account.[66] But these do not seem at all to disturb the even tenor of His other teaching. Through all their violence and fierceness still echoes the gentle voice that bade men learn of Him, for He was meek and humble of heart; and the octave of Beatitudes are surely the true notes of His perfect harmonies, for the law of fear has at last given way to the law of love — not the fierce slaying of the enemies of Israel, but the conversion of their hearts to the Lord their God.

But just as we have had to realize that it is possible to be angry and yet not to sin, so it is also possible to make war and yet not sin. To grasp how this can be, for the word *war* substitute the expression "employment of physical force." Now, here it is obvious that the very observance of law requires physical force as a necessary adjunct. Legislation is worse than useless unless it can be enforced; and to enforce legislation is quite simply to employ force in the carrying out of its enactments. We may not personally obey the Acts of Parliament or Congress because of the policeman, but the policeman is essential to the Parliament in case we do try to disobey. For the same reason, it is futile to oppose arbitration to "the employment of physical force," since the weakness of arbitration consists precisely in this: that it has no soldiers at its back to carry its decisions into effect. The Hague Tribunal, while merely a tribunal, will be a standing travesty of peace: consequently, even if international wars were abolished, international law would still have to be enforced by international police. Armies and navies will be forever necessary, at least to carry out the awards of an international judiciary.

It follows, then, that the employment of some sort of physical force may not be denounced as unchristian in itself. Force and law are necessary for righteousness. Hence, when the Church blessed

[66] Luke 2:34-35.

the Crusades, she simply turned war from its evil course; she did not destroy it, but tried to sanctify it.

Therefore, while war, whether as a protection or a punishment, must always be necessary in this sinful world, very much may be done to mitigate it. The Church herself insists upon three conditions to be fulfilled before any war can be called just: the matter of the quarrel must be grave, for the price of it is the most costly of all prices; all other means of adjusting the difficulty must have been tried, because physical force is the final and ultimate method of affording either protection or punishment; there must be some considerable hope of success. This last condition sounds at first cynical, in that it appears to justify all rebellion and only rebellion that is successful. But the real meaning of the proviso is that it is foolish to spill human life and undertake terrible risks of enterprise, unless there is some chance that goodwill eventually be effected. If it is impossible to right the wrong, then it is foolish of me and unjust to others if I rouse a whole people and end by leaving their condition worse than it had been. I am forcing on them an evil that can have no reasonable justification.

Then, too, it is incumbent upon all who are in any sense responsible, to take care that the fever for war is not fanned for political purposes, still less out of party politics. In matters where the consequences are so appalling, special care and deliberation are required, even when the cause itself is righteous. Wars of aggrandizement, wars of partition, and wars that are based only upon religious differences cannot bring ultimate peace. My influence for justice must necessarily be limited, but the united influence of each is supreme.

∞

Avoid giving bad example

In ordinary English, the word *scandal* has taken on a meaning that is altogether different from that attached to it in the Church's sense. Conversationally, and even in exact literature, *scandal* signifies nothing more or less than gossip, true or false, that reflects evilly upon character. "Talking scandal" is our phrase for indulging in the tittle-tattle about our neighbors or the prominent men of our world, which forms the staple produce of many of our conversational efforts. To refer to the corrupt practices of a politician or the maladministration of some public fund is commonly done by alluding to such and such a "scandal." Matrimonial difficulties and immoral practices are also spoken of as scandals when they have been described in some detail by the public press.

But for the most part, the significance attached to the word may be summed up in the idea that it supposes the revelation of something hitherto hidden or hushed up, which, when known, seriously injures the good repute of an individual or of individuals. In other words, *scandal* means that some culprit has been discovered and is being discussed.

Now, in the Latin signification *scandal* means nothing of this at all. It implies rather that something has taken place that will in all probability be suggestive of evil to others. It does not simply mean the discussion of someone's misdeeds or the publication of them, but it means that these misdeeds have caused others to follow their example. In the ordinary phrase, *scandal* implies sin on the part of the speaker; in the ecclesiastical phrase, it implies sin on the part of the doer. It means those actions of ours whereby we lead others into sin; hence, it is usually bracketed with "bad example."

It is undoubtedly true that our Lord uses the word thus when He denounces so strenuously in the Gospel those who would scandalize little children.[67] He pointedly and fiercely anathematizes all who lead astray those younger, more innocent, than themselves and bids them prefer maimed lives to such a train of captives to their evil example.

Scandal, therefore, means that there is such a further addition to evil acts, as that they not merely concern the perpetrator, but also, through him, have an influence upon those who may come to the knowledge of them. When I have done wrong, I may imagine that I alone suffer the penalties, whereas, in reality, by my very act I may have started others also along a like career of wrong. Or it may even be that my wrong actions do not so much lead others to copy me, but raise in their minds thoughts against the value of the sacraments or against the divinity of the Faith. People looking on may well say to themselves that if I, who go daily or weekly to my duties, am no better than I am, they had better not attempt to improve their own negligence; or if Catholics do no more than I, then there could be no reason for converting men to it.

Further, it is necessary to remember that this sin of scandal can be perpetrated unintentionally. It is quite possible that without considering the effect of what I am doing or saying, I am really and effectively "corrupting youth." Carelessness and ignorance do not make a sin less, simply because we do not choose to remember who

[67] Matt. 18:6.

is watching or listening, or to whose ears our sin will come. We have therefore to consider how far what we do is not merely sinful, but likely to lead others into sin.

Of course, we are not responsible if people unreasonably are scandalized at us, for there would seem to be certain souls who consider it to be the test of their own goodness that they can find so easily evil in others. It is almost worthwhile thinking just for a minute or so whether I may not myself possibly be counted among that number. Things that are in themselves innocent, even charitable, may yet be interpreted by narrow and suspicious minds into misdoings. Now this, obviously, I cannot help and have a right to ignore; nay, it is more than certain that it would be wrong of me to allow myself to give any encouragement to such baseless ideas. It is sometimes said that this readiness to be scandalized is a particular vice of pious people; but the answer is that people who do indulge in it are certainly not pious, whatever the outward semblance of their lives appears.

Still, in spite of all this false and hypocritical "scandal," I must never forget the responsibility that attaches to life. To a very large extent, from the very nature of human existence, I must live in the full view of my fellows, who are quick to repeat as well as watch, and who will find in my age, or better education, or higher position, or Catholic belief, a justification or excuse for imitating my shortcomings. I must certainly never set out to edify people, for so I would probably never succeed in doing any such thing, but would merely become a hypocrite myself; but I must, all the same, be continuously careful of the influence I cannot help exerting on the minds of those with whom I come in contact. I must beware, lest I prove a scandal or stumbling-block by my sins.

∞

Purity calls for knowledge

Here, as elsewhere, our Lord set up a new and more astonishing ideal, harder, more sublime than had yet been taught in the Old Law. In word, work, and thought, the gospel of purity was to be insisted on. The commandments had, indeed, shown that sins of the flesh could be committed in thought before the flesh itself had been corrupted, but the Christian view of marriage and the attitude to be adopted toward the "sex problem" were new importations into the scheme of revelation. Nor was it by the mere promulgation of a law, but still more brilliantly by the flame of example that this teaching was made plain. The Virgin Motherhood of Mary, the chastity of Joseph, the innocence of the Beloved Disciple, the very treatment of the Magdalen were new ideals.

The lesson, indeed, in the last case was not lost, for everywhere that the gospel was preached, the love of the Magdalen was to be made known; that is, our Lord was desirous that all His children should realize the splendor of this new gospel, which, while setting out something higher than nature could have imagined, taught nothing that was impossible to nature steeped in the grace of God. The Old Law in some ways aimed as high, but the motive it suggested was fear — the penalties attached being the chief deterrents. But a new system was to supplant the old. Love was to take the place of fear. Whereas love had been kept sacred by fear, it was now to be sanctified by itself. Love was to be realized as something so divine that sins of passion were crimes against it.

It is this healthy attitude that I have most need to cultivate in my soul — not to be forever trying to curb and control the wild emotions of my heart or the foul imaginings of my mind by appeals to the judgment to come, but simply to set before myself the high value of love. The love of kindred souls is indeed a great mystery, but it is a mystery profaned when passion is made its purpose. Passion cannot be excluded, but it must not be intended; it will be a concomitant, but not the aim. The very blessings that love was designed to bring will be found to have disappeared if innocence is lost. Chastity thus contains more love than does corruption. And if purity is represented as white, this is not because it is snow-cold, but because it is white-hot.

I am, indeed, as God made me; and in myself, as I came fresh from His hands, there is in me nothing of evil, apart from my own desires. Nor can there be anything wrong in my knowing my powers and the purposes for which my functions were intended. In knowledge there can be no evil; in lack of knowledge, which is the mother of curiosity and the fellow of sin, there may well be much. Purity therefore, to repeat, cannot consist in shutting my eyes to facts about myself that God intended me to use for His greater glory; indeed, it is possible for me to miss the purpose of my existence. I may lose the whole responsibility of my life by ignoring these purposes of God.

When, therefore, I have attained an age sufficient to be dimly conscious of disturbing elements within me, it is my duty to ask and get instruction on those points. My parents are the proper guardians to whom I should turn, for to them I am especially entrusted. I have also my elder brothers and sisters, and the priest to whom I am accustomed to confess. All these I may, and one or other of them I must, as of duty bound, consult so that I may acquire these truths from lips that shall instruct me unto honor and not unto dishonor. Know them one day I must, and it is perfectly possible that I may have formed in ignorance habits that are hostile alike to body and to soul. Innocence is to be found in the knowledge and fulfillment of the law. St. Thomas Aquinas, the most learned of the saints, has been made, by Pontifical decree, patron both of youth and of chastity. If, then, I find that questions I inadvertently ask are shelved or suppressed and answered with embarrassment, I should seek out someone whom I can trust and of them demand full knowledge lest I err: for ignorance may be the cloak through which innocence reaches its end.

Or if I am a parent or a guardian, then realizing the sacredness of love, let me see how I fulfill my responsibilities to my children. Do I look to it that I explain, as gradually as their gradually opening minds allow, the mysteries of life, or do I leave them to discover by means, fair or foul, the purpose of their existence? Perhaps through fear of exciting curiosity, I may have allowed them to fall into evil ways; for although passion is not the aim, it is nearly always the concomitant, of love.

∞

Discipline of body and
soul helps you avoid sin

It is commonly said that there is one set of temptations with which
we should never attempt to argue, and these are temptations
against purity. So long as they are upon us, we must avoid everything calculated to excite us in any way and turn swiftly to anything else that is likely to call off our attention from the thought
that has come into the mind; for the very fact of struggling with
ourselves, insisting upon the degrading nature of impure thoughts
and all that kind of thing, means really that instead of succeed-
ing in expelling it, we are driving it deeper in. At all costs, we must
move the mind abruptly away. As soon as we are conscious that
some foul imagination is present to us, we should breathe a brief
prayer to our Lord, or our Lady, or our angel guardian, and then
betake ourselves at once to some hobby or distraction.

It is often said that it is when we have nothing to do that these
thoughts most disturb us, but their frequency does not depend on
that so much as on other conditions of life. But this is certainly
true: it is in moments of idleness that we experience greater difficulty in escaping from them, simply because the very state of idleness prevents us from turning at once to an absorbing topic. Hence
the enormous importance of never allowing ourselves moments of

idleness or of becoming listless, for then it will be hard to think of anything sufficiently stimulating to take our thoughts off the evil thing. People who have not enough to do, or who enter into nothing with any zeal or energy, are just the people who are most likely to be especially bothered. The mind grows tired from want of exercise.

Obviously, then, true asceticism begins with thoughts. Asceticism itself does not signify the mere renouncing of desire, for desire is as much a human need as love; nor has it essentially any connection with a minimum of food or a maximum of contemplation; but it does mean the mastery of self, achieved by the gradual control of the will. It means an eager, watchful spirit, perpetually alert; it means a sensitiveness to sin, a delicacy that turns instinctively from every suggestion of coarseness. Thus is the gateway of the soul forever through the mind. If this can be kept pure, there can be little fear for actions or words; these follow exactly the lines of dalliance.

So I must, even at times when no temptation is about me, be at pains to impress on my heart a great love for chastity, try to look upon it as so supreme and delicate a virtue as to become transparent in the expression of a face, and to hush into silence the evil conversation of others, and by its freshness bring a sense of steadiness and ease to those who are tormented.

All this implies meditating on the lives of Christ and of His maiden Mother and exalting the high atmosphere of the Holy Family. The way of human nature is to repose not on fear, but on love; hence, it is foolish to suppose that dread of punishment can normally, or for long, influence the will when opposed by any impulsive passion. The pleasure that is present will seem more attractive than the future pain is repellent. To be pure, I must really love purity and learn to appreciate it.

Then it further implies that I must avoid all those occasions which my sad experience tells me have brought these trooping imaginations upon me. People, books, places, pictures, and dances that I have personally found dangerous I must personally avoid. General rules, anyway, are practically impossible; the whole affair becomes individual for each conscience.

When I find myself beset by thronging thoughts of evil, I must put them away from me. The healthier I am in mind, sometimes also in body, the less likely am I to have impure suggestions. A life that is reasonably hard, that allows no mere indulgence to the system, that is eager and alert and disciplined, that exercises its will-power by sheer effort of will and makes every endeavor not simply to drift through life, has in it the seeds of true asceticism. The hardier the body, the safer the soul. It was the bracing discipline of the hair shirt, the vigor of the fast and early rising, and the fierce austerity of solitude that were aimed at by the monks; and sin grew rampant in the cloister when ease and convenience became the tests of monastic prosperity.

What is true of the monk is true of us all. Hence, even athletics have their place in the science of the soul. To many a man, the confessor in his whispered advice suggests bodily exercise and out-of-door occupations as means of working off the overcoming humors that otherwise torment and make weary the soul. The influence of matter on spirit is an experienced fact that the race had recognized in Eden, but all this is of no avail unless the thoughts of evil are expelled. When these unclean things appear, let me, without scruple or argument or disturbance, put them from me.

Part 6

∞

The ages of man

Youth must develop self-control

In a certain sense, youth is less perilous than age, for it is more open, more generous, and more easily touched by love. The idealism and romance that fire and awake boyhood are kept alive throughout youth — the golden time when as gods we walk the earth. Yet it has in spite of all this, nay, perhaps because of its very perfections and its wonderful powers, even greater dangers. It is more full of blessedness and more full of perils. The corruption of the best is worst, "and festering lilies smell far worse than weeds."

The very fearlessness of youth, its love of independence, its fine belief in the nobility of the race, and its utter disregard of every criticism directed against those whom its soul loves, land it not infrequently in difficulties that are largely of its own manufacture. Nor are these difficulties of one sort only. They appeal to the many variously. For some, they come in the form of doubts against faith, for the mind in its dawn of strength realizes far more of its powers and far less of its limitations; for others, against purity, which the very splendor of their manhood itself creates; for others, in a consuming passion for ease and the good things of this world. Life, they feel, is to be lived, not dawdled. They take the day while the sun is up, make use of every moment that comes, and leave willingly to a later day the evil consequences that must follow. Even death they desperately disregard, because what they love is life, and not mere existence. They do not care for length of days; it is not with them (as it is with the old) a mere clinging to life, but a desire to live life to the very full.

Yet different as these temptations are in their appeal and in their manifestations, their cause is nearly always the same: selfishness, want of self-discipline, love of personal pleasure. Oh, that youth, which can be so generous, can be also so mean! Oh, that this golden age of divine perfection, when mind and heart and frame alike seem nearer to our vision of the gods, when the very intensity of pulsating life sweeps with tremulous hand the full strings of human harmonies — that this golden age should turn to tinsel and tawdry show!

The youth that denies nothing to itself denies everything to others. The body is so splendid, the mind so eager, the affections so spontaneous, that they can hold themselves in against nothing. It seems a sin against youth to plot and counterplot against its demands, to refuse it the least of its wishes, to renounce the fulfillment of any of its powers.

So it happens that just that period of life which is most open to generous impulses, which is most unselfish in itself and most ready to espouse the cause of everything oppressed and to right every wrong, becomes turned from the high chivalry of its nature to a terrible selfishness. Parents are sacrificed, their rulings scorned, their advice ridiculed and despised. Even the sense of comradeship between father and son, daughter and mother, is swept aside for some friendship that is none too high. All the parents' long labor of accumulating a sufficient competence for their children is accepted by these, not with gratitude, but merely as a personal tribute due to their powers and importance

Indeed, the young must be heroes. Youth cannot rest in a humdrum life, either in things material or spiritual. It cannot continue to make monotonous and feeble efforts at anything for long. With a rush and an impetuosity it must carry its positions, or it will leave them half-captured and then turn to some other occupation. Its only success is success.

Now, to be heroic means to have self-control, to deny oneself. The body trained is more splendid than one allowed to grow without care: the lean flanks, the straight back, the corded muscles are due to frequent and continued exercise. The perfection of form is not achieved without much violence to the native love of ease. The tired feeling in the evening is often due to too little exertion during the day and is best dispelled not by giving in to it, but by vigorous, although brief, exercise. The mind cultivated by good education is more charming than the boorish brutality of an undisciplined wit. The well-cared-for appearance is more full of attraction than the slipshod and ungainly disorder of an unkempt man.

So must the soul be subject to the rules of love, to daily Mass if possible, to the regular attendance at the sacraments, to the unselfish regard for others' convenience, to the restraint of thought and word and deed that tend to foulness. There alone shall I find that true asceticism which must stamp a true follower of Christ, that knightly denial of all that is evil, and that determined love of all that is fair and beautiful. I must be "the master of my heart, the captain of my soul."

∞

Youth is man's greatest gift to God

God's greatest gift to man in the natural order is his youth. Nothing else brings him so much persistent pleasure, nor makes life appear so full of incident, nor earth so full of gladness. There are other delights, such as friendship, and the fair face of nature, and the very joy of life that comes from work well done and from pleasurable exercise; but these even are themselves dependent upon youth or at least the memories and ideals of youth.

It is youth, indeed, itself that is a necessary condition for appreciating things for the first time; for the delights that we learn only late in our time cannot make the same appeal to us as do the pleasures that come to us "trailing clouds of glory," bringing with them the scenes of our childhood and youth; for life always is as a man holds it to be. Clouds, for the youth, are seen only in their silver lining, and the very forces drawn up against him appear merely as the necessary matter out of which victory must be fashioned. The suppleness of limb, the swing and poise, are typical of a motion of soul that is swift, eager, adventurous, fresh. It is this, then, that makes the whole world appear so beautiful and so worthy of all human efforts. The "eyes of youth" give its proper setting to all life. After all, we find only what we are looking for, and only set out to search for what the heart has already had with itself. Hence, we realize the value of that great gift of youth, for it has a more won-derful power than that of which the ancient classics fabled, since it turns all things else into itself. So, to the young, all the world itself is young again.

As youth is God's greatest gift to man, so is it no less man's greatest gift to God. I can make Him no offering more acceptable or more worthy. The cloisters of a monastery may be tenanted by those who have come wearily out of a disillusioned world, who have seen their ambitions crushed and have lost all sympathy with the faded grandeurs of reality. Yet surely God loves best to find there innocent hearts and loving souls who have come to Him first, not waited until all else had palled.

And what makes a good religious in the sight of God must ap-ply also to all those whose distinct and divine vocation it is to serve Him in the family and at work among the professions of the world. Some of these, too, turn to Him only when they have tasted the bitterness of all things else, and come, already wearied and worn out, to offer Him what is left of their lives; but those surely are the dearer to Him who have clung to Him always by their strength, whose freshness is reserved for Him and none other, and who can consecrate to Him the very fullness of their powers.

Youth, then, as His best gift to us, must be also our best gift to Him. He asks from us our best, and our best alone is worthy of Him.

Not when the sense is dim:
Now in the time of joy
I would remember Him —
Take the thanks of a boy.

The sweetness of childhood must charm God even more than it fascinates man, for He must see in its depths generosity, modesty, and trustful purity that we cannot fathom, but only dimly perceive.

I have, then, not to wait until I have wearied of other things before I turn to Him, but I must give Him of my best. He is so very patient, so eager, so foolish even for my love, that He is willing to take whatever I am willing to give. The New Testament rings with the story of His love for man, and the memory of it made St. Paul, an Athenian in feeling although not in birth, cry out about the foolishness of the Cross. The wisdom of God might indeed be wiser than the wisdom of man, but it was certainly a stumbling-block to Jew and Gentile. So low did He stoop, so exaggerated was He and so extravagant in His way of showing His affections, that in all reverence we feel tempted to tell Him that it is not so that man is to be won.

But He is indeed so ready to take whatever affection I like to show, that He is apparently full of thanks when I toss to Him the worn-out end of my life. Like a boy in the street, He seems content when I leave Him merely the stump of my existence.

Yet if He is content with a deathbed repentance, surely I cannot be. I am not so mean as to presume upon His goodness, to act according to His fondness for me. He has given me this flood of life, this gaiety and elasticity of soul. He has made my life beat high with hope, and scent the fresh perfume of the soul, and see the sun high in the heavens with its golden glory transmuting all things. Let me see how far I can return it to Him. He loves my youth as I love it; let me give it back again. Let me love and serve Him now, when my love and service are of some use to Him, not wait until I am old and useless before I make my offering. Now, while the heart is young and the senses are alive, while youth is generous and attractive, while my soul has the charm and freshness of early morning, let me draw nearer to God, who giveth joy to my youth.

∞

The middle-aged must resist
the tendency to become selfish

Who cares to acknowledge that he has reached middle age? We do not mind in jest describing ourselves as old men, talking about ourselves as becoming feeble, and joking about senile decay. It is so palpably untrue that we feel no reluctance in so doing.

Or again, there are those who are pleased to look upon themselves always as young men. They grew up in a society that was older than they were, or precociously entered among others whose years were more than their own. They heard themselves spoken of as young men and have persisted in imagining themselves always young.

Occasionally there comes a reminder that things cannot now be done that used to be done easily; occasionally we realize that certain pleasures are pleasures now no longer. But we cling desperately to our youth — a proof positive that it is escaping from us; for, to say that we are middle-aged seems a terrible sentence to pass upon our humanity. The charms of childhood, even of babyhood, have been sung; the freshness and attraction of youth is the theme of half the literature of each generation ("If youth but knew"); old age has its artists who depict in soft tones and genial half-lights its venerable appearance and sunny smile; but of the generation that comes midway, the father who stands between sire and son, who has ventured to speak, save as in a scoff leveled at those who would appear younger than they are? Yet through it, too, we must pass, are perhaps now passing. Should we not, therefore, face it consciously, this terrible middle age?

Let us, therefore, realize that we have outgrown our youth. So many things come to us, of which we catch ourselves repeating, "I shall never do that again." Many an exercise or game has to be relinquished; it no longer interests us in the way it did, for we are no longer as energetic or as capable at it as we were. All this does but mean that our youth has gone from us.

I have reached, therefore, that period of middle age when physically my body has attained a certain development. It has become firmer, more set; but it has no longer the swing, the buoyancy, the suppleness that it once possessed. At the mercy of sudden drafts, it has become more vulnerable to its surroundings; but it has also coarsened in fiber.

Now, does all this mirror inaptly the corresponding effect made by middle age upon my soul? It, too, is more set, fixed, hardened, grows less and less adaptable, less ready to welcome new fashions and new methods and new ideals. It remembers the past, but finds itself less and less in sympathy with the movements and ideas that are springing up around it.

I find myself looking upon past and present as the complete work of humanity. I have, indeed, outgrown the ways of my fathers, but am as yet hardly conscious that the generation I myself represent has also begun to be behind the times. Nothing that now appears can I get myself to recognize as a legitimate development of the things I have fought for, but only as an abuse. My tolerance of others seems to have disappeared. I find myself getting mercenary, denouncing enthusiasm, scoffing at ideals.

I am middle-aged. When Dante woke in midlife, he found himself in a dark wood. For us, too, this sudden realization of where we have gotten to finds us very often in darkness, for middle age is the most dangerous age of all. A boy and a youth have so much that is good in them from their very boyhood and youth that we can be hopeful of their triumph. But of middle age, what shall we say, with all its skepticism, its dislike of enthusiasm, its eighteenth-century hatred of anything unusual or unrestrained?

Now, it is not at all difficult for the skepticism that I hold of others' hopes to seize more surely upon my own. I cannot expect to spend my time dampening the ardor of others and yet be able to awaken my own. Not without much difficulty, without very much self-denial, shall I see myself pushed into the background by fresher aspirants to success. My passions may have grown calmer, but is not my selfishness on the increase? Sometimes does it even not seem as though the loss of passion has meant also the loss of generosity? Both passion and generosity are so often the determined results of impulse.

I must look to my faith, my hope, my love. These will be all the more needed by me in my middle age — a faith, clear, unwavering, built on the supernatural, the unseen; a hope that clings to God, despite my failures and follies; a love that takes sacrifice, self-sacrifice, as the keynote of life's harmonies. My prayers must be carefully considered, for my need now is for generosity. Let me make it the subject of daily solicitude, find opportunities for its daily exercise, study it in the life of Christ. The danger of middle age is terrible, not the splendid danger of passionate blood nor the danger of failing health, but the blighting force of selfishness and the loss of all ideals.

∞

Old age should show the fruit of
a lifelong struggle to be faithful to God

A fine old man! How pleasant is the image that so common a phrase conjures up: the vigorous and healthy mind, its gentleness, its serene wisdom, its broad and easy tolerance, its discerning encouragement of others' work, its power of delicate and appreciative sympathy, its sure experience that leaves it with knowledge yet without any tendency to dictate, its understanding of the difficulties of life, and its readiness to condone the faults of impetuous inexperience! How attractive to youth are all these features of the old! How inspiriting as the reward of years well and nobly spent! What fascination surrounds this figure of old age when it is dowered with all these prerogatives that imagination at once attaches to it!

A fine old man! Beside this, even the worship of childhood seems a sentimental dream. After all, children are attractive in spite of themselves. They do not try to worm themselves into our hearts; we call them affected when we find them making any such attempts. They are innocent from sheer impossibility of doing evil; they are trustful from inexperience; they are loving because their little hearts open as naturally and as unreasoningly as do the flowers. They have no wish in the matter. They are children; as such they charm, as such they appeal.

Old age should show the fruit of a lifelong struggle

But the old man who charms us has himself slowly gathered the treasures of his age. He has seen all things, and heard all things, and done all things, yet, through the whole course of his life, he has kept his faith from doubting man or God, his hope from losing courage, his love from all stain and all hardening.

A fine old man has passed by the ambush of young days. It was so easy to meet life with high hopes and high ambitions and wonderful trustfulness of human nature, so natural to bear all things and believe all things and hope all things;[68] and then, when experience has made a man taste of the bitterness of life, when he has found disillusionments in others, disappointments in himself, it is as easy to become cynical in thought and speech. It was so hard when all our kindnesses were turned to evil account by others who did not realize the sacrifices we had made, and grumbled only that we had done so little, to remain through it all so glad to help, so eager to expose ourselves to be misunderstood, still ready to risk our own peace of soul to save another's. It is the hard discipline of the Christian life that entails love of the brotherhood, even when, or rather because, the brotherhood has shown itself to be unworthy of love.

Of course, it never can so show itself, for if I realize that God loves each of us, then each of us must always be worth loving. The difficulty is to keep this steadfastly in mind all the while that one is actually experiencing continual disappointments. Yet, indeed, in all these strivings of faith, hope, and love is a blessed reward even on this side of the grave. After we have avoided for so long the hardening, chilling, coarsening effect of sheer existence, we begin to enter into that last lap of life, serene and gentle and full of hope. It is the golden age of Christ, of those who have passed from death to life because they have loved the brotherhood.[69]

[68] Cf. 1 Cor. 13:7.
[69] Cf. 1 John 3:14.

But old age is not to be considered merely a climax or a crown, nor does it seem, to those who have reached it, a time of peace. The temptations and follies that youth experienced haunt the steps even when old age has been reached. On earth is no peace, no triumph, only an unending struggle; so that in old age we know that care is required, lest we fall. After all, the age that is pictured by the classic writers as the fine end of life can easily be replaced by a crabbed and selfish spleen, full of crotchets, full of fancies, requiring to be waited on hand and foot, living and battening on the lives of children, making grown-up sons and daughters who should earlier have made homes for themselves waste their full days of life on us.

The Christian type of age which is full of faith and hope and love is not acquired without a long struggle; it means a determined effort to secure this genial frame of mind by forbidding the cynical view from influencing us. Yet even when old age has been reached, the same difficulties are to be experienced. Even then, the trouble is not over, nor are the dangers passed. Indeed, are not the passions of youth less full of peril than the lukewarmness of age, the indifference that comes from physical decrepitude? Old age is a thing apart, so much finer than childhood in that it has fought hard and weathered storms and can offer God work well done. Even should it follow upon a wasted and empty life, there is something still to be offered; it may not be worth much, but it is all we have with which to front eternity. After all, the most praised offering was the widow's mite,[70] which can at least be the last tribute of our days.

[70] Mark 12:41-44.

Part 7

∞

Dealing with others

∞

God's gift of friendship
should be treasured

Our lives are made and marred by our friendships. In the worlds of nature and grace, love is more powerful than reason, heart than head, friendship than law. We can easily notice that people have always influenced us more than books. The literature of our time molds us, it is true, but generally only just so far as we find it embodied in those around us or in one particular person who sums up for us the principles of a philosophy. It is the man who matters.

The action of Christ in becoming flesh was motived undoubtedly by the deep knowledge that He had of the human heart. The whole story of the Incarnation is the splendid attempt of God to appeal to us no longer in the formless definition given to Moses — I AM WHO AM — but as a definite personality whose actual features and whose life should really stir humanly the human soul. "He knew what was in man."[71] He proclaimed not so much a code as a personality, not so much stone tablets as a friend. And what He has done in the supernatural sphere shows us also what is going on in the natural — that our lives are made and marred by our friendships.

[71] John 2:25.

These are not, therefore, to be considered evils, nor as things merely allowed us. For the pagans, friendship was the very end and purpose of life. For our Lord Himself, it is a thing right and good. He has His chosen twelve, and out of the twelve a special three, and out of the three one above others, the Beloved Disciple. Then there were the Magdalen and Lazarus; and what He began, the saints have freely copied; in the biographies of so many we read of special friends.

Friendship, then, is allowed and was practiced by the Master whose lessons we try to learn.

Now, the reason friendship is thus powerful in human life can be readily understood when once we have tried to think what friendship means. It is obvious that friendship implies an openness between friends, confidence, the absence of all reserve; between friends there can hardly be any secrets. Friends, therefore, must, in their talk and in their silence, reveal to each other their secret thoughts; consciously, even more unconsciously, they are letting each other in behind the veil that, to outward appearances, shuts off their lives from others. The deepest feelings and desires become apparent; the little touches that are lost upon others are, to each other, revealing.

The effect of each upon the other is incalculably great. By this friendship, the two are made equal; even if one is but a shepherd boy and the other a king's son, yet if their souls are knit as one soul, all such artificial checks and barriers of class, age, ability, temporal goods, and spiritual endowments are brushed aside quite lightly.

Mutual attraction, therefore, means ultimately mutual influence. I cannot go on living with others or feeling drawn to them, and so opening out to them my heart and listening to or watching the language that tells me of their soul, and come away the same as I was before I knew them. I have affected them, and they me; and all the world can tell how much we have in common.

God's gift of friendship should be treasured

The influence, then, of friendship is all-powerful, just because it means the absence of reserve and brings friends to the same level of greatness or littleness in character.

Friendship, therefore, is not wrong; indeed, it is to be found in the Scriptures, in the life of our perfect Model, in the stories of the saints, whose deeds here rather than their words are to be attended to — or rather, perhaps, whose words are to be interpreted in the sense of their deeds. It is even, as the pagans declared, the most perfect gift of God to men. There is nothing else that gives greater joy in life, nor the loss of which makes the leaving of life more easily accepted.

But because of the very fascination of it, for its due exercise certain qualities have to be observed. The most sacred things are the more easily profaned; indeed, you cannot profane that which is not holy. The higher and nobler are our helps, the more dangerous does their abuse become.

Friendship, therefore, must be:

• *Loyal:* there must be no fair-weather friendship, nor any friendship that allows an attack to be made unparried. A man may sit and never say a word, yet leave the room with the shame of disloyalty on him. Rats leave a sinking ship, but that is to be expected from rats.

• *Constant,* for constancy is of the essence of friendship. Those who are always changing their friends, full of affection for one friend today, revealing all their reserves, and tomorrow seizing on another and making him also a recipient of their tales, do not know what true friendship is. To change friends constantly is bad for them and even worse for me. I should have many acquaintances, yes, but many friends, no!

• *Frank:* friendship must be based on sincere confidence and trust, but this does not justify constant correction, which is an overly hasty attempt to reach the results of friendship.

• *Ideal:* I must see my friend as he is and as he might be.

• *Respectful,* for passion destroys friendship by destroying respect, and cheapens the precious signs of love.

∞

Be prudent in the
presence of acquaintances

Beyond the narrow borders of friendship is the vast territory of acquaintanceship. Friends must be few, but acquaintances will probably be very many — innumerable. We elect our friends, but our acquaintances come to us in a thousand ways. Our friends are chosen with care, but our companions by mere chance. And that precisely is our danger.

A friend to whom we open our whole soul, who knows us through and through, and from whom we conscientiously keep back no reserves, is obviously a person whose influence over us must be considerable. We know each other so well and are so frank with each other that the evil of one must almost necessarily tarnish the other's soul, as the good of one must refine the other. The need, therefore, to be careful in our choice is so plain, so natural, that choice will be made very deliberately. We take infinite pains about it and require a good deal of assurance before we really give ourselves into another's hands.

But we are apt to forget that really something very similar is happening even with our mere acquaintances — namely, an appreciable influence on our lives — yet how careless we are about those with whom we mix! Of course, certain comrades are forced upon us by our neighborhood, by our work, and by our relationships; certain people in life we can hardly with decency avoid. But there are numbers of others who have no call or claim upon us and into whose company we let ourselves slide.

There may be no harm in them, but the point is that we make no effort to see whether there is harm or no. And yet how often our sins come from our company! Our friends we cannot always be with; from our company we can never escape. Our friend is tethered to his place of business, to his home, to his several duties; but our acquaintances are with us all the day. At our business while we work they are beside us; we listen to their language, to their views of life expounded without reticence or modification. We stroll out to lunch between whiles and are once again, as on every weekday, with the same set, in the midst of the same ideas, bathed in the same flood of jest and anecdote and latest social happenings.

Does it not seem as though friendship itself (unless it is loyally and unswervingly guarded) would be outvoted in our lives by the circle of our acquaintances? What chance has it or has anything against the persistent, unescapable influence of our company? The endless tales (not quite the kind of thing that becomes a Christian), the gross conversation (coarse and vulgar, perhaps, rather than evil), the uncharitable gossip, the latest ugly rumor, the jealousy, the rivalry in dress and outward living, the small untruths to make ourselves appear just more important than we are, the firsthand information that is really not quite firsthand, all the mean and petty devices and subterfuges into which we find ourselves forced by our comrades: is not companionship the cause of very much that is evil?

I come, therefore, to this point — namely, that the influence of my company is very considerable, and, second, that most of my company is chosen purely haphazardly. Now, it is obvious that some of my acquaintances I cannot avoid. What can I do about these? Be prepared. I know more or less when I am likely to meet them. I know also in what way I am likely to be influenced by their conduct or conversation. I know from experience just where temptation to agree or accept or propose comes to me, and in what particular matter the temptation lies. Very well, then, even if I cannot escape them, I can be on my guard. I can pray for help, courage, and light to see what is right and to say or do it, fearlessly, uncowed, unashamed. There may be a materialistic view to be refused, if not refuted; a disloyalty to faith to be denounced, at least in silence. To be forewarned is to be forearmed.

And when social conventions and the stress of work are satisfied, do I still cling to them, even when I have found their company to influence me and not for good? Do I still seek their presence by sheer haphazard? Am I careful enough in selecting my company? For I must admit the subtle molding influence they must have on me, modifying my views, refining or coarsening my ideals, accustoming my ears and finally my tongue to language and jest and anecdote. Let me look at those with whom I choose, day after day, to have my meals, my work, and my amusements. How far in their company do I defend justice and truth and my friends?

∞

Respect what belongs to others

The sin of stealing is of many kinds. Its most obvious and, therefore, least dangerous form is the direct taking of what belongs to
another. But this filching of gold or of precious things, the ordinary method of burglary, is recognized as sinful and reprobated
by the common conscience of society. Therefore, in all probability, men are not on the whole likely to commit it. Sometimes, it is
true, I may have a terrible temptation to take some trifle that is lying about, especially if there is little chance of any subsequent de-
tection. But at any rate, I am perfectly conscious that this is wrong,
and although mere knowledge of evil is not sufficient to deter us
from it, it is an immense help.

But there are very many ways in which this blatant burglary is
hidden away under all sorts of names and does not seem to receive,
although it more justly merits, the severe judgment of public opinion. The chief way in which it occurs can be grouped under the
name of business, commercial relations, trade, custom, and so
forth — and not merely in the sense of keeping back from people
what is due to them, but as damaging what belongs to another. I do
not steal only when I retain their goods, but also when I harm
their goods. Thus, in business transactions, I can commit theft by
the substitution of false measures and weights, by the adulteration

of the commodities I pretend to supply, by wasting the time that is paid for by another, by scamping work for which I have received a competent wage.

In these ways, although I do not keep what is due to another, I am doing damage to something that does not belong to me. And the same thing comes also into prominence in the various ways in which a man is defrauded of something owed him.

Perhaps in no way is this principle more steadily violated and more highly censured than in the payment of debts. Somehow one's compassion is always extended to the debtor and never to the creditor, whom one imagines to have somehow or other craftily got the better of the other. A man who lends money is always presumed to be a rascal, and the same idea holds the field where no money has been lent, but a bill left long unpaid. It has become sometimes a boast of certain folk that they do not attempt to pay their bills.

Similarly, too, in pious persons the same defect is shown, but in another way; for with them, it is with the best wishes in the world that they give large sums in charity and yet do nothing to ease their creditors; or, rather, they consider that the poor come before their tradesmen. Really, of course, people who are actually starving and who have no other means of obtaining relief have the first claim upon us; but apart from this, to give in charity is always secondary to giving in justice. I may give alms, but I must first pay my debts. I may build churches to the honor of God, but not to the despite of my brother's just claims on me.

The idea, therefore, that it is the creditor who always has gained in the transaction is widespread, but untrue. Indeed, it is far more common in the modern system of capitalistic enterprise to find the creditors poor and the debtor rich. The wholesale way in which companies are fraudulently or at least recklessly floated is a crying scandal of stealing. The extraordinary fashion that will make men gamble with what is not their own is very prevalent.

I have therefore to take more heed in all my commercial transactions to see, not simply that I am not legally at fault, but also that morally, too, what I do is approved. This should be well worth serious meditation — the attitude of my soul in the face of the rights of others, whether my conscience is sufficiently alive, sufficiently delicate. Ruin may have come to another through my reckless expenditure, extravagance, or neglect. For all these, in God's eyes, I am responsible. The very fact of society, whereby we are all parts of one great whole, makes personal relationships a necessary but a serious thing. The interplay of rights and duties gives loophole for so much harm, so much damage done to those about me, for I cannot echo the cry of Cain — "Am I my brother's keeper?" — without meriting also his condemnation.

Nor is it sufficient for me to bewail my mistakes and promise amendment. There remains always the duty of restitution. What I hold that belongs to another must be restored; what damage I have done to another's person or property or repute, I must, to the best of my power, make good. Even if, for the moment, I cannot repay, I must have the intention of so doing at the earliest opportunity.

It is this strait view of theft that our blessed Lord came to insist upon. His whole life and death were spent on the rigorous justice of God. His Blood which ransomed us made us one and therefore forbade even more sternly all attempts on my part to injure my brother. I must look upon what belongs to him as a sacred thing, a thing that is his by the high sanction of Heaven; and I must be watchful always, lest I lose the Christian attitude of soul — "rendering to every man what is his due."[72]

---

[72] Cf. Rom. 13:7.

∞

Private property is allowed
you for your development

When, in the *Summa Theologica*, St. Thomas Aquinas treats of the
sin of theft, he begins by explaining what he means by private
property. This is not quite so cynical as it sounds, for all that he is
at pains to point out is that I can hardly consider whether I have
taken what belongs to another until I am quite settled in my own
mind as to what others and I have a right to possess. Nor is this an
academic question idly disputed, of no practical consequence, but
rather it is one of the engrossing subjects of the day, and in modern
civilization the whole matter is being worked out quite swiftly to a
definite conclusion in no very great length of time. Let me, therefore, under the light of God's illumination, examine the whole
problem and see where the decisions of the Faith step in and
where I am left to settle the details by means of my own political
and social theories.

First, then, it is manifestly obvious that man has dominion
over the things of earth — not, indeed, in the sense of having the
absolute dominion such as is implied in creation and annihilation,
for these are the sole and proper prerogatives of God; man's power
lies simply in the faculty of adapting nature to serve his own particular ends. He has, therefore, the use of nature and can alter its

forms by his skill and thereby increase their utility to him. He has, therefore, the right to possess nature as his property. He can bridle the horse, and domesticate the cow, and reap the produce of the earth, and harness the forces of water, and do all the other thousand things that proclaim him the lord of creation. The right to hold property is, in this sense, nothing more than the development of personality, for when a man has put his own labor into a thing, he has made it almost his own.

It is lawful, therefore, for a man to own property; but that is not where the real problem lies. The social grievance, if grievance there be, concerns the actual division of property as here and now obtaining — that is to say, the whole trouble is not whether a man may possess things, for he must possess some things, but whether there is any limit or any condition to his possessions.

Now, it may be generally stated that by various historical developments, it has become the practice among civilized nations to allow the individual to hold his own private property to the exclusion of his neighbor. From the oldest records and from the survival of certain customs, it would seem that primitively and until comparatively late, the land and capital (if the word can be allowed of a state of things prior to the existence of much commerce) were in possession of the tribe or commonalty, but gradually there came a division of property whereby each individual had something that was so entirely his that it could be inherited, exchanged, or given away. And the reason for this division, arising out of an original holding by the whole community, has been supposed to be the actual experience of the race that in this way things worked best.

Human nature has repeatedly discovered that what belongs to everybody becomes nobody's business to attend to, and that quarrels soon arise over what has no limits and no divisions, for perhaps two or more wish for the same or desire the whole to be employed in another way. To escape confusion, quarreling, and neglect, private property has been devised. This justification, then, for the division of private property given by St. Thomas and most Catholic writers, is therefore based on no moral law or sacred and inherent right, but only on the practical experience of humanity.

But it will also be noted that, in the abstract, it is perfectly legitimate to suppose such a condition of society where these troubles would not arise or would be overshadowed by greater evils on the other side. The justification for this division is based on the experience of the race; if, therefore, such a state of things should arise in which the experience of the race suddenly or slowly discovered that to avoid neglect, quarrels, and confusion, it would be better once again to resort to what is acknowledged on all hands to have been the earlier type of possession, who can denounce such a return as unchristian or immoral?

From the Catholic point of view, therefore, I must look to the moral side of the dispute. The mere community of possession is not wrong in any sense; it has been customary among nations and has been, besides, voluntarily praised by the Church of God. Which suits best the civilization in which I find myself is a matter that I must settle in my own mind, not attempting to define dogmatically what others should do. Least of all should I defend in the name of private property a system in which a certain large class lives always in the immediate vicinity of starvation. It is sheer cant for me to speak of the sacredness of private property when it consists for the moment in depriving many of private property altogether.

The present arrangement of property was adopted because it was found to work. It may, therefore, be again discarded if it be found to have outlived its serviceableness. But my personal concern is to realize that what I have is allowed me for my own development, and I must look to it that it does not hinder my due approach to God.

∞

Give alms responsibly

The necessity of almsdeeds has continuously been insisted on by the Church. She has always regarded it as correlative to her teaching on the need for private property; for without it as an essential condition of possession, greed, pleasure, and selfishness would dominate the world. Hence, the necessity for giving alms corrects the natural exclusive right to hold what is one's own.

In the older state of civilization, when possessions were the common holding of the tribe, this instinctive demand for almsgiving was expressed in the action of hospitality. The tribe held the territory on which it settled; but it recognized that if anyone came to it in want, it was bound by the natural obligations of its holding to allow him what was needful to him. Even in the feudal organization of society, this right to hospitality was definitely and formally recognized, but when the common-ownership theory broke down and the modern absolute ownership of the individual took its place, the need for almsgiving was correspondingly taken off the shoulders of the community and placed upon the individual. He has become very much more obliged to provide for those who are in need. The basis is very clear, for we are commanded to love one another, and this love of the brotherhood would be vain were it not to include the succoring of those who are in want. But to succor those who are in want means to give alms to them; thus, from the very essential tenet of our Faith comes the stern obligation of almsgiving. This obligation may be either of charity or of justice.

Yet just because this is a virtuous act, commanded by the moral law, it is obvious that it must be done according to the dictates of prudence and reason. Hence, we are not ordered to give all we have to everyone who comes to us and asks our help. We have to exercise our judgment, and not give to those whose need is little what is required more terribly by those whose need is very great.

In point of fact, there are two conditions laid down, one on the part of the receiver and one on the part of the giver. He to whom we give must be in want; that is to say, no one has a right to appeal to his fellow Christians for aid unless it is really a necessity to him, and then only just so long as his necessity lasts. Even a charitable institution has no business to go on soliciting help when really it has no real need of help. It is taking from others whose need is the greater. It follows also that the degree of the need itself, extreme, grave, or slight, must to a certain extent justify the actual demands put forward.

Then, on the part of the giver, it is required that he should give out of his superfluities. He cannot morally give away what is requisite for the support of his own family, for he has contracted obligations to them, and their claim upon his individual fortune is the chief claim of all. His money, time, and energy are due first and foremost to him and his. So, again, there is the matter of his creditors. These, too, have quite definite rights over his goods, and he cannot alienate what is their due. It is clear, therefore, that I must exercise prudence in my almsgiving.

Let me, then, turn my thoughts to that great doctrine of Christ, that love of the brotherhood which is the final test by which men can tell whether they are His disciples. How far do the needs of my brethren appeal to me? How far do I realize my obligations to men as part of the great and sacred family of Christ? We are all members of one body, all parts of the sacred and Mystical Body of which He is the Head. My own superfluities — whatever is over and above my own needs and the proper decency of my life — I can really no longer consider my own at all; they are the common property of all my fellows. I listen to the Gospel of Christ: His denunciation of those rich fools who are "not rich toward God,"[73] His straight sayings about the extreme difficulty that the wealthy have of entering Heaven in that lively comparison of the camel and the needle's eye,[74] most of all to the fine eloquence of His own perfect life, which, although not one of actual destitution, was certainly one of poverty.

So, in contrast with all that, I cannot help noticing my own comforts and the ease in which I, like so many other Christians, live. Can I suppose that mine is at all the life He would have wished His followers to lead? Let me put aside all sentiment and all explanations that do nothing else than merely explain away. Our Lord evidently taught that His fellowship meant self-denial; but He nowhere says that it meant also necessarily destitution. But that problem must be largely individual, for if I find myself in the midst of a population that is poor and foodless, cold, pinched, and badly housed, it is my absolute obligation to help them to the best of my power. To see myself as God sees me, I must contrast my pleasures with my neighbor's needs.

[73] Luke 12:21.
[74] Matt. 19:24.

∞

Rights are for the
fulfillment of your duties

What constitutes a right? For the word has a significance sacred in civilization. It is a word invoked by all who are oppressed, and it finds a response in every heart. It is a phrase that crosses my lips very often, but what exactly does it signify? For, although it has been the battle cry of freedom, it has also been used to justify the most terrible tyranny. Every rebel against authority takes to himself the name of right, and every act of authority bases itself on the same sacred claim.

How am I to know in my own case and in the cases of others, what is meant by the word? How can I tell whether I really have a right to this or that? What do I mean by my right to live, to serve God according to my conscience, to hold property, to demand from the state that my children be educated according to my religious beliefs? Of course, I am using these expressions every day of my life, but let me calmly, in the presence of God, try to make out what they really signify.

I am led to this thought first of all: that the word *right* is not primary, but secondary; that is to say, it is based upon something else that is even more sacred. Every right is dependent on some duty that must precede it. I can have no rights except insofar as I have

215

duties; and apart from what I owe to God, myself, and my neighbor, I have no real justification for any of my rights. That is the first and most important idea that I have to impress upon my mind — the intimate relation between the two things — so that I should never in my mind think of one without thinking also of the other.

Rights must, therefore, be described as the means to achieve duties. Once I find that I have a duty to perform, I shall find all sorts of conclusions following at once, and these conclusions establish definite rights. Thus, my conscience informs me that I have certain duties toward God, and therefore I can fitly argue that I have a right to all those things that enable me to fulfill those duties. I claim a right to attend Mass, to approach the sacraments, and so forth.

I find, again, that I have duties toward myself, to the cultivation and development of my own soul, to the application of the various talents that God has confided to me. So, obviously, I have a right to all those things that enable me to carry out these duties.

Parents have rights over, because they have duties toward, their young children; and the children, just because they have duties toward their parents, must have rights also from their parents. Similarly, if I have certain duties toward the state, I must also have claims of my own that are valid against the state.

To repeat, the two ideas are interrelated, interdependent. I may, therefore, quite shortly define a right as the necessary means to achieve an essential end. Once I am convinced that I have something to do, incumbent upon me in my position as a creature or a member of a state or family or church, then I must claim and endeavor to make good my claim to those things which are necessary for my so doing.

This enlarges at once my idea of my rights and imposes a responsibility on me on every occasion that I use that sacred word. I cannot claim anything as a moral right until I can prove that it is necessary for the fulfillment of some essential duty. Hence it is if I can keep this idea well before my mind, I am in little danger of getting selfish in my life. If, whenever I find myself speaking of my rights (even in ordinary conversation), I set to work at once to see whether they are rights at all and what corresponding duties they oblige me to perform, I shall find that I shall not be so quick or so insistent in asserting them.

It is a pity that the word *right* has become so popular a word, and the word *duty* so dull and respectable, for many people cannot stop talking of the one, yet imagine it to be old-fashioned even to mention the other. Duties themselves do indeed demand in their performance some tax upon my pleasure or my will. I must deny myself something; to do what I ought to do, there must always be some self-sacrifice. My rights, therefore, become nothing more than the requisite opportunities for denying my own will. Let me clamor, therefore, through life, never for rights, but for the better understanding of my own destiny, and only assert that I must be allowed to fulfill my duty. Let me never use the word *right* without the swift consciousness of the duty involved, for rights from the very nature of the thing have nothing at all to do with private privileges (which are exceptions on the whole to be reprobated, and seldom if ever to be demanded), but with sacred obligations.

∞

Promote justice in business

Among the other sins that we are told cry to Heaven for vengeance is the defrauding of laborers of their wages. How is this defrauding done? By not paying them adequate wages. Adequate to what? Not to their work, but to their dignity as human beings. Here turns the whole controversy of a living wage; but for Catholics, it is no controversy at all, having been settled by the Papal Letters of Leo XIII.

In these letters it is laid down repeatedly that an employer of labor is obliged, if he accepts a man to work, to pay him sufficiently to support himself and his family; in other words, the dignity of human nature is altogether different from the beasts of the field. A horse is cared for and fed so that it may be enabled to do the work for which its services are required; and when it can no longer work or its work is no longer needed, it is gotten rid of or given a sufficiency of food. But man, to those whose eyes are lit up by Faith, is sacred by reason of his immortality and by reason of the shedding of Christ's Blood. Once I realize in my own person the worth of my soul and the dread price paid for its redemption, I must begin to take a high view of my responsibility to other human beings.

If, therefore, I employ a man, woman, or child in any industry over which I have control, I must see that the conditions of life I offer them are not inhuman, that they are humanly cared for, and that the wage given to them is sufficient to provide them with the decencies of life. I must never attempt to look upon the wage as an exact equivalent for work; but I must consider that the man is dependent on me. Either, therefore, I must tell him to leave my service or take upon myself his upkeep.

The reason for all this is clear. Men's right must be founded on some duty. It is their duty to live. God has put them into the world to know, love, and serve Him. Now, they cannot do these things unless they are physically as fit as they can be. Hence, they have a distinct obligation to live and keep themselves in such a condition as will enable them to obey God's commands. This means further that they must develop to the full the reasonable possibilities with which God has endowed them. They are obliged to put to His service every faculty they can; hence, they have a right to whatever is reasonably necessary for this purpose. In other words, they have a right to existence, not in the sense of bare subsistence, but as including a decent livelihood.

Now, in a wage-earning society, such as exists in every modern state or nation, the only means of achieving or guaranteeing this decency of existence is by a living wage. Hence, if I have men working for me and giving me of their best work (whether they are able to work well or ill does not really enter into the question; it is sufficient that they are human souls and that they give me the benefit of their day), I am bound to provide for them a living wage as a first charge upon profits. Before I recompense myself or begin to talk of what is due to me as owner, I must first determine to pay living wages. It is a solemn obligation lying on me as a Catholic, however small may be the number I employ.

But how does this affect me if I employ no workers? It affects me in this way: that I may not encourage those whom I know to underpay their employees. I may not invest money in firms that I know scandalously sweat their workers. I may not even buy at shops where it is notorious that living wages are not given, unless, of course, it is something that I greatly need and cannot otherwise obtain.

Is it, therefore, my business to inquire of every place I go whether they are recognized as honest and honorable employers? No, there is no such necessity in the ordinary shops that I patronize, to make such inquiries. But if it does come to my ears that certain well-known firms have iniquitous ways of dealing with their staff or their workers, then I must in conscience show, in the chief way open to me, my disapproval of their methods. When it is a question of investing in companies and so forth, I should certainly take ordinary means of finding out what conditions prevail in the work, for I am answerable when I deliberately prolong such conditions by encouraging and helping the promoters of it. Once employers were convinced that their clients were really determined on this course, there would be no further trouble.

Face-to-face with God, I must work out all these problems for myself; and I cannot go astray when I cling to the rules of justice. Hard rules of business may prevail, but besides these I must consider the value of human souls. God made them, redeemed them, sanctified them. It is for me to value in others the dignity that God Himself respects.

꩜

Observe the duties of citizenship

Among the Greeks, it was considered a noble ambition to serve the state. The writings of Aristotle and his fellows and the dialogues of Plato are full of the same idea. To vote and speak, to take part in the assembly, and to become an influence in directing the national policy were looked upon as the highest possible service that man could render to God. For them, our ideal of Church and state, separate and free, would have made no appeal, not because they made the Church into the state, but because they made the state into the Church. For them, there was really no distinction between the two; not because God had become man, and the Divine was to take charge of the human, but because man had become God, and the human was the Divine.

In consequence, every action done for the benefit of the state was itself an act of piety to the gods. Much the same action produced that curious and impossible custom by which, even in their lifetime, the Roman Emperors were hailed as gods: Augustus Caesar prefixed *Divus* to his name and thus added a hereditary title to the Caesarship. This did not mean that he was supposed immortal or incapable of wrong, but only that, as the highest symbol of the state, he became thereby worthy of worship. Foolish as it may seem in its expression, the idea was a noble one, and compares very favorably with the modern cynic who, parrot-like, declares politics to be a dirty business, and politicians to be only "on the make." What has happened to Christianity that it should seem to fall so considerably below the pagan ideal?

Certainly, then, there is this to be remembered: that the state was itself the object of religious worship. It was equivalent to the Church, and in consequence there could be no other moral code to come in conflict with it. The curious position achieved by Aristotle in his book on politics is that he asks the question: "Must a good citizen be a good man?" Here, by the very form of the question, he does acknowledge really what he would not have done in theory: that there was a fixed law of ethics independent of the state. But as a Greek, he was bound to uphold the absolute fusion of the two.

Now, here Christianity has held an entirely different point of view, for while the state remained national, the Church became international, for it was based, not on ceremonies, but on doctrine; not on customs that are local, but on truth, which is ubiquitous. Yet this did not produce any lowering influence on the view taken of national political life. St. Paul and St. Peter both taught subjection to Caesar, when Caesar meant Nero; and St. Paul himself proudly boasted his Roman citizenship as his birthright.

Again, the Church herself consecrated the forms of government, hallowed kings, sat in the seats of judgment, lent her bishops to the national council chambers, and championed freedom of election. Representative government is her gift to the West; so it cannot be said that she has in her teaching neglected politics. Indeed, the accusation is made often against her that she dabbled too much in politics.

How, then, if the attitude of the Church has been to make sacred the forms of political life, has the result of her contact with the world been to create the cynical distrust of all public men? Perhaps the reason for my suspicious view of such men is the very contrary of this: not that the Church has lowered politics, but because politics have excluded the Church, because they and I have been too anxious to keep religion out of politics.

There is always a natural idea that religion loses enormously from being entangled in party strife; but although that may be perfectly true in many ways, it is equally false when it is made to apply not only to the mere party squabbles, but to the whole domain of government and the national life; for religion stands to lose if it remains simply in the sacristy. The Church must play her part in the defense of justice, whether in politics or economics or abstract truth.

Now, by the Church and religion are not meant simply the clergy; the Church is the whole assembly of the faithful. Catholics who denounce modern politicians are often to blame for the low ebb (if it is a low ebb) of political life. Faith alone and the supernatural value of life can give reverence and dignity to government; and to say that a thing is evil and therefore to refuse any further commerce with it does not tend to make the evil become good.

Let me, therefore, go back to my life, conscious that my duties of citizenship are duties that a Catholic should be eager to discharge. Men crowd in time of war to the defense of the state. Why not also in time of peace? Let me not dread the loss of time that may be occasioned by local patriotism, convinced that in rendering to Caesar the things that are Caesar's, I am rendering also to God the things that are God's.

∞

Your Faith must
shape your political action

If the duties incumbent on me as a citizen are to be accepted as a Christian obligation that I owe my fellows and by the fulfillment of which I pay a debt to God, what am I to think of any arrangement of parties in the state? I may object in theory or in practice to the whole party system and may quite carefully have matured schemes of my own that would make things more efficient and more free.

Or, on the other hand, I may consider that, on the whole, taking everything into consideration, the disadvantages of the party system in actual fact are much less than those that other systems would introduce. In either case, I may do what I can to promote my own particular political aspirations, denounce or uphold the constitution of my country, and take my side and persistently work for it. All these courses are perfectly open to me.

As a Catholic, I have to start from certain definite ethical principles about justice, truth, the values of the supernatural world, the sacredness of conscience, and so forth. But once I have acknowledged these as having controlling influence over all departments of human life, I am perfectly free to choose that particular band of politicians in the state whom I consider to be, on the whole, likely to benefit my country best, politically and spiritually.

It is obvious that to neither side shall I be able to give unqualified support. It may even be necessary for me to declare publicly wherein I part company from those to whose support I have devoted myself.

But for all that, it is probable that one or other of the chief political parties will appear to me to be deserving of my allegiance. Indeed, should the need arise, perhaps the joint protests of Catholics of all political creeds, or their solidarity on any one point, is far more effective than the protest of a Catholic party.

So far, then, my Faith leaves me free. Does it, however, in any way conflict with political practice? It need not indeed, but there are certain ways in which quite considerably it may. For even in my political life, I must still remember that I am a Christian, and that charitable judgments are still required of me. I cannot cut up my life into separate compartments and look upon religion as having no concern with my soul outside the hours dedicated to the direct worship of God. All the teaching of my Faith and the whole detailed doctrine of the Commandments have to be applied as rigorously to my political discussions as to anything else. What I have learned about rash judgments (the duty of restoring the good name of an opponent I have wantonly defamed), about the truth alone being expected of me as a child of God — all holds good even in these affairs, since they concern so very much of my time and my interests.

Much of the invective that is to be read in the political press is obviously untrue and not intended to be taken seriously; the rodomontade in which one leading statesman declares his rival to be devoid of all truth, to be willing to hand over his country to the enemy, to be the most dangerous foe that the nation has to fear, cannot be really meant; and if it is not meant, it is utterly unchristian. No doubt I may be so interested in politics that my temper is much harder to keep under control, my feelings are so keen; but boisterous personal attacks are either true or untrue. If the former, why is my action so very inadequate to the gravity of the situation; if the latter, am I a follower of Christ?

It will be seen, therefore, that a Christian must still remember the preaching of his Faith even when he is engaged in political controversy. And it is this disregard for religion, which so generally takes place in political warfare, that has degraded the whole trade of politics. Just because of its heated accusations and irresponsible criticisms, no one can help suspecting leading politicians of insincerity: if they only believed one-half of what they said in their speeches, party politics would become at once civil war.

May I, then, never denounce a measure as unfair, unjust, or wicked? By all means. Let me be as forcible as I like in criticizing measures; only let me remember not to treat motives in the same way. I may say that a certain bill before the House, or a detail in some politician's platform, violates the principles of justice, but I have no means of knowing that he intends to be unjust. I have no right to drag up a man's past, or expatiate on his meanness or his ambitions, or to accuse him of being bought by a foreign power.

But surely it will sometimes be necessary for the public good that these facts should be mentioned, and even motives exposed.

That is true, but only on the supposition that I can offer real proofs. It is criminal of me to denounce on pure suspicion, to bandy charges that I cannot substantiate, to add to the circle of some flying rumor, to mention transactions, unless I can bring forward reasonable evidence for what I say. I must do all to make public life clean and wholesome. But in so doing, I must not transgress the laws of charity, justice, and truth. By becoming a political partisan, I have all the greater need to remember that I do not cease to be a Christian.

∞

Some false accusations
are to be borne with silence

To be falsely accused is to be conformed to the image of Christ. Perhaps the hardest thing of all to bear without complaint is just that final degradation under which our Master died. Other pains and penalties can be borne with lips closed. The sufferings that ill-health brings us and the financial anxieties of life do not touch us so nearly; they are so common and so passing that we can afford to take them easily as part of human destiny. When we have contrasted what we have to bear with what so many others are suffering, we feel the littleness of our character and its timidity, and we are ashamed. Even when we contrast what we have to bear with what we deserve, we find the immense forgiveness extended to us; it is really so small a pain that mere human courage, apart from all supernatural motives, would bid us be silent and bear our pain like men. Even the disappointment in friends, in ourselves, can be looked upon as something to be carried as our Master carried His Cross. Human nature is erring; and love itself gives us the courage to persevere in loving those who have renounced our love.

But a false accusation brings our pain too near; it is too humbling! Its hardness can be tempered and made less repugnant only by the thought of the nearness that it brings us to the life of our

Divine Model. For false accusations patiently borne are the very essence of the sacred Passion; and by our following of our Master, we are taught by love to rejoice. They are the necessary trials of all those who make atonement for the sins of others.

But the reverse seems also to be true — namely, that those who suffer false accusations in patience are themselves also redeemers and make atonement for the sins of others. I, by accepting in silence the false accusation made against me by another, can bear that other's sin. It is all part of that deep mystery of the Mystical Body of Christ. Somehow or other, this wonderful doctrine that we profess in the Creed under the title of the Communion of Saints not merely teaches us the high dignity of our humanity, but enables us to achieve that self-sacrifice which is the chief mark of the character of Christ.

Now, in this instance we have to realize that we are all members of that Mystical Body, and our entrance into it by Baptism means that the ransom of the Precious Blood has been applied to our souls. Yet, says St. Paul, it is possible for us to fill up what is wanting to the sufferings of Christ. This cannot allude to the initial Redemption, which cannot be completed, for the twofold reason that none other is needed and none other could avail. It must seem that, after some fashion, we can help one another and apply to each other the merits that we have individually acquired. After all, there is one desire that follows upon love: the desire to lessen the sufferings of another by our own suffering. Because, then, we are all Christians, bound together unto love, we must offer for each other the torments we undergo. So we can make it into a principle of spiritual experience that not merely must all redeemers be falsely accused, but all falsely accused can be redeemers.

The spirit, then, of Christ must dominate my own, and the attitude I must hold toward life is this: that all those who persecute me are those precisely for whom I must offer the patience of my forbearance. It would have a very evil and unchristian effect upon me if I got it into my head that everyone was persecuting me. I would grow even more priggish than I am. But when I do find others who make my life difficult, I must dedicate to their service the difficulties I undergo, even as my Master died for those who accused Him of evil that they knew could not be laid to His charge.

How far, then, does this silence under false accusations come into my life? It is obvious that some imputed faults I have a right and an obligation to deny. It is freely declared by many saints that the accusation of disbelief, heresy, and so forth must never be submitted to in silence. And we must refuse to acknowledge all such accusations when God's honor or our own, or our neighbor's good, requires it.

But there are many occasions when I can easily be silent, yet I am not. I make haste to protest, for fear of losing my reputation. I am quick to resent any such thing. Yet really I ought to prefer that people should accuse me falsely than truly, for it is written, "Blessed are ye when men revile you and speak evil of you, untruly, for my Name's sake. Be glad and rejoice, for your reward is very great in Heaven."[75] St. Peter Martyr, complaining to his Master of such false accusations, demanded: "Lord, what have I done?" and the answer that came from the Crucifix taught the lesson of Christ: "And I, Peter, what have I done?"

[75] Cf. Matt. 5:11-12.

∞

Reflecting on God's
gifts overcomes jealousy

The meanest of sins is the most secret — jealousy. Yet secret though it be, hidden so that none may suspect its presence, it works terrible poison in life. The very secrecy itself helps this along, for we are ashamed of so ungenerous a feeling and have no desire to take others into our confidence about it. Occasionally, indeed, our feelings may be too much for us, and a broken expression, snapped out in a moment of provocation, may easily tell what has long lain silent in our minds. The sudden outbreak of war reveals the unguessed secret thoughts of many hearts.

Still, the attempt to prevent others suspecting us of so mean a sin drives the poison deeper into the blood; it works a veritable fever. Perhaps if we would only talk, air our grievances, say precisely what we feel, the pent-up and restrained antagonism would be swept away and the animosity at least temporarily relieved. But no, in silence we nurse our hatred of another's success. We have worked earlier, longer, more successfully, but the other is chosen. We have squandered our affection, done everything in our power to ease and help those whom we love intensely, yet the other is chosen and we are left. He has had advantages denied to us, yet in spite of it, no allowance is made for our more determined efforts.

He succeeds, and we are failures, and such a judgment suffices for the world. Or even at times the very fact of his great deserts does not mitigate, but rather increases, our jealousy. And the knowledge that we have failed, because of our own fault, very often makes our hatred the more unforgiving.

But it is also necessary to remember that the sin of jealousy is not the mere desire for equal success with another. We are jealous when we wish to be or do what others are or do, and wish at the same time that they themselves were deprived of their accomplishment. I cannot help contrasting my own poverty or want of decent livelihood with the luxury and possessions of better folk; nor, again, can I help wishing that this gift of nature or grace were mine — their charm or gracefulness or physical strength or good looks. Again, the man who is discontented with his lot and, fired by ambition, aims at achieving a higher position for himself and his children, can hardly be called a sinner.

And when I myself am so stirred by others' success as to venture into rivalry with them and attempt to oust them by fair competition from their place of supremacy and to develop my own artistic or scientific skill, which I know to be superior to theirs, am I in all these ways following after sin? Certainly not. In the case of one who attempts by fair competition to drive out a rival, he is simply putting to use the powers God gave him.

But in this, the whole trouble is the motive of my action. If it is simply that I wish to have what he has, this is not sinful, nor is it jealousy in the ordinary meaning of the word; but if I wish deliberately to deprive him of what he has already got and am pleased at the thought of contrasting my possession with his loss, then that is indeed jealousy. The sin, therefore, consists in the secret dislike of other people's enjoying what I would wish to be exclusively my own.

Jealousy, however, is not merely a sin; it is also a blunder. Just as pride is foolish since it puffs up a man with self-glorification over deeds that are none of his own, so jealousy, in much the same spirit, makes us greedy of the works, not of man, but of God.

When I am tempted to think much of myself because of some wonderful thing I have done, I answer myself by saying that, after all, I was but an instrument in the hands of God; to Him alone is due the glory of the thing. In the same fashion, when I am jealous of another's achievement, let me remember that they, no less than I, owe their success to God. The foolishness, therefore, of jealousy should very easily move me. Once I am convinced that others are no more to be praised for what they have done well than am I for my great deeds, then jealousy can no longer affect me. Truth would drive me to admit the excellence of their accomplishment, but to trace back that excellence to no human origin, but divine. And when I find that others are preferred to me for posts of importance and, above all, are higher in the friendship of those whose love is, to me, the most precious thing on earth, I must remember that the same indignity was set upon my Master.

Whatever advantage, then, others have over me has to be traced to God's greater condescension to them. They possess more than I do, but that is simply because they have borrowed more plumage than I have.

And when, in spite of all this, I feel the pangs of being set aside, let me remember how another was preferred to Christ, and "Barabbas was a robber."[76] In memory, then, of His patience, let my jealousy be healed.

---

[76] John 18:40.

Part 8

∞

Faith

≈

Love of God increases
with knowledge of Him

In our Lord's solemn prayer to His Father for His disciples at the Last Supper, He said, "Sanctify them in truth: Thy word is truth."[77] Now, because to sanctify (or sanctification) is the whole purpose of our lives, our Lord is evidently at pains to impress on us the fact that without truth — that is, without the word of God — we cannot hope to fulfill the object for which we were created. The revelation of God is absolutely necessary for the love of God, since sanctification, or holiness, means nothing more than that love.

It is clear from the witness of the New Testament that the reason which lies at the back of all the Church's ordinances, sacraments, confraternities, and so forth, all the good works done to our neighbor, all the charity and self-denial in the world, is simply the love of God; for without this, our sacrifices are vain and our prayers a hypocritical deceit. "Not he that saith to me, 'Lord, Lord,' but he that doth the will of my Father."[78] "If I give my body to the torturers, and have not charity, it profiteth me nothing."[79]

[77] John 17:17.
[78] Matt. 7:21.
[79] Cf. 1 Cor. 13:3.

And St. Paul goes very carefully through a whole list of good deeds, and points out the faultiness of each, unless they be done from the motive of the love of God. Hence, since sanctification means the love of God, and since truth can come to us only through the illumination of faith, the prayer of our Lord must be interpreted in the sense of these words of the Council of Trent: "Perfect love is based on perfect faith."

Why should this be? The reason is quite simple. It is impossible to love properly unless we know properly. If we have not a true idea about God, we can never really love Him. The pagans and others have such distorted ideas of what God is like that it is impossible for them to know Him as He is in Himself. So again, those, for example, who would give up their belief in Hell would have no doubt an idea of God as all-merciful, but not of Him as all-holy and all-just. Thus, the God whom they would love would only be in reality a caricature of Him, not God as He is in Himself. It is just for this reason that the Church has been so particular, so fierce even, as it seems, against sins of heresy; for false doctrine prevents people from really knowing God and therefore from really loving Him.

Of course, in a certain sense, it may be said that love helps us to know, so that unless we love people and have sympathy with them, we can never understand them. And this is undoubtedly true, for love and knowledge act and react upon each other. But even so, it is always knowledge that precedes, and the knowledge that comes to us from their own revelation of themselves must itself tend to a better love of them. So of God, the more I listen to His voice, the more I learn of Him, and the better I know Him, so much the more and the better will my love of Him be also. For faith must precede love.

Apart, therefore, from merely making acts of gratitude to God for giving me the Faith, I have also to study, according to my ability, the truths of the Catholic religion, for the deeper my knowledge of

Him, the more I must be drawn to love Him. The more clearly I can grasp His revelation of Himself, the more surely shall I be attracted by Him. He is so perfect, so infinite in His perfections, that truer knowledge of Him must end in truer love.

It is as though I was in some darkened room and could see hardly anything at all. Then gradually, as my eyes get accustomed to the darkness, the outlines of things begin to loom out in vague, gigantic shadows; even details, at first obscure, after a while take on definite shape and stand out in clearer relief.

So is it with the deep mysteries of God: they strike us as incomprehensible, as indeed they are; as contradictory, as indeed they are not. But by the sheer light of faith and fixity of gaze, the Divine Beauty becomes apparent, transparent, and eventually transfigures the world with splendor. I have no excuse for my ignorance, in this age of good, inexpensive Catholic books and pamphlets. I must, therefore, endeavor, year by year, to increase my knowledge of my religion, so that my love of God may grow to the perfect stature of Christ.[80]

[80] Cf. Eph. 4:13.

∞

You must make the Faith your own

Since our Faith is intended to be our life and to enter into every thought and action, it is clear that it cannot be a fixed and stable thing, although it must be conveyed to us by means of definitions and formulas that are fixed and final, in the sense that they represent the best terms in human language that express, as far as it is at all possible to express, the mysteries of the revelation of God.

Of course, the Catholic Church has never hesitated to declare that these definitions are always really inadequate, for it is absolutely derogatory to Almighty God to suppose that the facts of His being and life could be fitted into the limitation of human language and human thought. Hence, while the Church claims that she can define as accurately as possible those mysteries of God, she does not pretend that what she has to say exhausts the subject or even represents the actual truth she is trying to teach. It is the nearest to truth that the human mind is at the moment capable of expressing.

Hence, there is such a thing as the development of doctrine, whereby things revealed from the beginning are found to be in the tradition of the Christian people, even though they might require the rise of a heresy to make the people conscious of what had always been accepted. In this sense, therefore, it must be admitted that faith itself is a fixed and final thing, for otherwise it is clear there would be no possibility of acquiring any knowledge of the ways of God. What would be the use of dogma if it were to be constantly changed, disregarded, outgrown? Dogmatic definitions, therefore, are the vehicles by means of which the divine truths are conveyed to our minds.

Yet the real purpose of faith is something more than this. The kingdom of God that our Lord came to establish upon earth was not merely the elaborate or simple knowledge of the ways of God; rather, it was the individual acceptance of truth simply as a means of life. God teaches me about Himself so that, in the end I may be led to a closer union with Him; it is He for whom I am created, not for faith, but for possession.

The kingdom of God, therefore, is something that the individual, from the age of reason to the end of life, must continually realize for himself. He must continually hammer away at the truths of Faith, endeavoring to get more meaning out of them, to find in them the help and guidance that daily life continually demands. The whole series of mysteries will certainly be of no use to me in my endless advance toward God unless I try to make them my own by ceaselessly pondering over them. Of themselves, they are just the bare outlines of truths, yet it is not truths, but the facts that are contained in the truths, that are ultimately to influence my life.

Hence, my first act must be to get interested in my Faith. For most people, it is a dull thing, connected remotely with dull Sunday afternoons, when they learned and recited the catechism as a lesson. All that has been forgotten, and faith has now to be regarded as the revelation to us of the meaning of life, the understanding of life, the effects of life. I shall never become interested in religion until I have come to see that I must make it personal to myself — chew it, digest it, form out of it the sinews of my spiritual being.

Classic Catholic Meditations

Perhaps the reason we think this a hard thing to do is just because we get into the habit of supposing that faith, and the attitude toward life that faith ultimately produces, is something foreign to our nature. I find myself looking at this gift of God as something that is, as it were, dropped on me from outside, something external. External indeed those truths are, in the quite definite sense that nature left to itself would find no record of them here on earth, or at least a record so misty and incomplete as to distract rather than convince; but it is obvious that they can never influence my actions unless they have become transformed from external into internal possessions. I must so unite them to myself that they affect the whole color of life to me.

Religion may be fixed, and stable, but *my* religion cannot be stable or fixed. The truth may be one, final, determined, but my apprehension of it can never be anything of the kind; it is changing continuously. I am always learning more and more, or forgetting the little that I once knew; the meaning grows more definite or more indistinct, but it grows always. I cannot suppose that this alone of all my forms of knowledge remains stationary all through life; and even if such a supposition ever came to me, the facts of life would very quickly disillusion me. My faith must advance or retreat; it cannot remain the same.

The real trouble probably is that I look upon faith as something purely official, and only obscurely realize that there is a personal side of it as well. Now, it is just here that I shall find the advantage of it to me. To be called a Catholic because we accept only certain isolated truths is hardly worthwhile; once I see that it is as it is called in the Scripture, a "way," then I shall find that it opens up large visions to me and reveals me to myself. Notice that the Creed mentions not merely the truth believed, but the person believing: "I believe in one God."

The Faith is full of mysteries

If, as I am taught from my childhood, faith is concerned with mysteries — that is, truths above reason — how is it possible for me to make them my own? It is obviously impossible for me to acquire such intimate knowledge of a thing that I cannot understand as will enable me to obtain any benefit from it. I may remember the phrase used and be careful not to confuse the way in which it is worded, I may be strictly accurate in my definitions, but what else can I do with it? It is above reason; therefore, it is above life. The very element of mysteriousness seems to preclude every effort at making these truths really my own or enabling them, in any real sense, to have any influence over my actions. I can accept them with my intelligence, but they will remain merely truths and have no personal significance for me.

Now, first of all, it is indeed clear that I shall never be able to understand at all adequately the truths of faith. Whenever I come in contact with God, I come in contact with something that is utterly above me. God is infinite and I am finite, so truths about Him can never be packed into my limited intelligence. If I could understand God, I would be at least His equal. We say in English that when we know anything, we have mastered it. That is a perfectly accurate expression; we can know a thing only when we are greater than it is, so that, if I really knew God, I would be His equal or His master. Hence, it is clear that it is impossible for me to understand God's being or His acts. There must be in everything He does a great deal that I can never comprehend nor ever hope to comprehend. Let me begin by realizing that I must expect, when I come in contact with God, to find very much that is above my understanding.

Therefore, it follows that there will always be difficulties in the matter of faith. There will always be very much that I shall be able to understand; whenever God reveals anything to me, He will add to my stock of knowledge, but He will add also to the difficulties that surround my understanding of Him. He cannot help blinding me even while He enlightens me, not because of His limitations, but because of mine.

When, for example, He told me that He was one and alone as God, I could accept that as shedding light on the world; but when He told me that in that Godhead there were Three Persons, He told me a great deal more about His own life, but at the same time He at once added to my perplexities. He taught me, yet He perplexed me — nay, the very fact of His revelation was itself the cause of my mystification. When I knew Him as the Governor of the world and its just Judge, I found in that no contradiction; but when He told me that He had become man, and had died for me, I was grateful for His revelation, but it added also to my difficulties.

In other words, just because God is infinite and I am finite, it is to be expected that everything that He tells me of Himself, while increasing light, will increase darkness at the same time. In those countries where the sun is brightest, there are the deepest shadows; the very brilliance of the sun adds to the blackness of the shadow that it casts.

I must, therefore, repeat to myself that if all the ways of God were capable of explanation, then I would know for certain that He did not exist, but was the creation of man's mind. It is just because He is so difficult to comprehend that I know He is, indeed, a revealer of truth.

I arrive, then, at this: that these mysteries are apparent contradictions. He is all-holy, yet allows sin; all-loving, yet allows suffering; full of mercy, yet the builder of Hell; all-powerful, yet leaving me perfect freedom; God, yet man; innocent, yet the Redeemer of His people; united to the Father by inseparability of nature, yet feeling on the Cross the loneliness of His abandonment.

What have I to do in the midst of all this contradiction? I am to take the mysteries to pieces. I shall find that it is because the two apparently opposed truths are taken together that their difficulty occurs. I must simply cling to both ends of the chain, and remain ignorant of the link that binds them together. He is One, He is Three; He is man, He is God; He is merciful, He is just — all these things I can follow separately, but conjointly they are impossible of understanding.

However, there is this much comfort for me: I have to say to myself that I am not surprised that I do not understand Him. When people ask me how I can explain the existence of evil or sin, I can answer that I do not know, and that, granted there is a God, it is impossible that I should know. It is to be expected that, if God created the world, it would be impossible for the world to understand its Creator; but if the world began itself, then it would understand itself. Consequently, I am content to go through life in trust — conscious and, indeed, proclaiming as part of my belief, that the ways of God ought to be mysteries to me, yet not thereby depressed or losing confidence, but rather keeping tighter hold of the little knowledge of God that has come to me through revelation. It is good for me that, when I go out at night, I do not bump my head against the stars.

∞

The mysteries of life strengthen faith

It is the perpetual platitude of the pious that reason puffs up and faith humbles us; and presumably there is something to be said for this. Reason is quite likely to produce in certain minds a perfectly conceited and foolish attitude as though we were capable of understanding all things. Just because we find that there are certain things that we can understand, we may possibly take it on us to assert that we are going to accept only what we can prove. It is possible that we may take up this dogmatic position and, on the basis of this pure, unprovable prejudice proceed to refuse acceptance of divine revelation.

Fortunately, man is unable to remain obsessed by any such foolishness for long, but such an attitude is really common in the early stages of human development in the natural sciences. It was the snobbish attitude of the mentally *nouveaux riches*, the people who had just come into a fortune and pretended to despise others whose wealth was less showy, although much more valuable.

But the terrible thing is that reason quite soon finds out, not its wonderful power, but its utter hopelessness when up against the problems of life. It discovers, not how much but how little it knows of the ways of God and man. It is oppressed by its limitations. It finds that the influence of the body upon it is considerable. This delicate instrument, whereby reason had hoped to discover the whole meaning of life, is at the mercy of all the elements. The slightest ache or pain robs reason of its keenness; weariness makes its movements impossible or fantastic; a serious bodily derangement can reduce it to absolute incapacity. Instead of reason being the plummet by which the depth of the universe is to be sounded, reason is discovered to be so faulty as to render any of its soundings suspiciously incorrect.

On the other hand, the whole effect of faith is the exact opposite. So eager are we made by the wonders about God that revelation brings to us, that we are reduced to disregarding the limits of our creaturehood. There is nothing sacred from our touch. The very sanctuary of God is invaded, and we speculate almost irreverently on the doings of God in His Heaven.

Open any book of theology, and you will be amazed at the hardiness of the theologians who seem to dogmatize about all sorts of things of which they are almost quite ignorant. There is nothing that they are not willing to tackle and decide. Every possible point will be settled without any admission or any confession that all the while they are depending upon very slight grounds of argument.

All this is not to destroy our confidence in the writings of theologians, but merely to say that the temper of reason and faith is really the very opposite of the popular conception. The effect of reason on anyone who is really intelligent is, by itself, to make one conscious of the little knowledge that the human race has amassed. It is to reduce us to a state of hopelessness; whereas faith is so illuminating that the chief danger is lest we ignore the vast difficulties that there are to be found in life. Place the believer and unbeliever side by side, and ask which is the more conscious of the limitations of human endeavor. Ordinarily it is the agnostic who sees the real problems of life. It is not that they are not apparent to us, but faith is so inspiriting that we forget all about them. It is the Christian who is the optimist, the agnostic who is the pessimist.

For faith, then, the very infirmities of nature — weakness, sleep, weariness, and so forth — that make reason so aghast, make faith, curiously enough, more active. Every obstacle to faith becomes its defense, and every enemy a new recruit. The physical sciences have given to Catholics a much more splendid vision of faith and God than they had before, enabling them to see the wonders of God in greater profusion. Every advance of the enemy only serves to show how intimate and how natural is the supernatural.

An older generation startled us by telling us that all other religions contained in fragments what the Catholic Church held in a complete form, but we found on examination that this was one more reason for acknowledging the truth of revelation. If the Christian Faith were really divine, then surely man must feel deeply the needs that it comes to supply, and, in consequence, will feebly and brokenly grope his way toward them. Because I can find every single doctrine of the Church taught by some religion or other, and because I can find them gathered together nowhere else than in her, then surely I am convinced that she has obtained, by the swift light of God, what they painfully and falteringly have partly discovered. Surely, then, this should give me a greater realization of the importance of my soul.

It is indeed depressing to find that my reason is so at the mercy of the world, yet is it reassuring to find the world, in turn, at the mercy of my faith. Even the sorrows of existence, the triumph of evil, the apparent impunity that is guaranteed to crime, the early deaths of those who most promise good, find in faith an easy acceptance. We strive for their amelioration, but we are not troubled by their evidence. The despair with which my reason confronts the whole of life is turned into a rapture of entire sympathy with the power, wisdom, and love of God.

⚮

Base your values and judgments on faith

It has been said now for some time that all our sports have been spoiled by professionalism. Boxing, for example, has been accused of no longer following the old lines; the earlier method was, on the whole, a series of head attacks; whereas the newer style is in-fighting, which, without being either illegal or even unsportsman-like, is yet, on principles, different from the tactics employed by the earlier generation of fighters.

But it is not so much the manner of fighting that has changed as the idea that lies behind it, the purpose for which the combatants engaged. Formerly it is asserted that they fought for the victory. It used to be considered that the entertainment was for the benefit of the spectators, but at present it is simply to produce the earliest knock-out. The new fashion is much more efficient, and the most efficient must always be adopted.

So, again, the whole recent legislation for social matters has been largely conducted along the same lines. No thought is given to what the people want, or whether, indeed, they have any right to expect to be asked what they want, but only to what is the most efficient way of treating them. Houses are not built in accordance with any preconceived ideas that the people might have who are to live in them, but solely the ideas of those who are to build them.

Again, the question of what is called eugenics is resolvable simply into the same thing. The feeble-minded are to be segregated because they are inefficient. Not one thought is given to the consideration as to whether they have any rights as human beings, but only as to whether they are efficient, in the strictly material sense.

The national life of the modern world is being worked out purely along lines of efficiency. It is true that there is certainly need for the consideration of efficiency, but the trouble is that too much is centered on that single idea to the exclusion of every other. For example, there is the principle also of freedom, an idea that has been far more productive of good in the history of man. A nation that has aimed consistently at freedom has, on the whole, done more for the ultimate good of the world than have those races that have given themselves over to the worship of mere efficiency.

No doubt there are dangers for those who aim too exclusively at liberty. There is such a thing as the dissolution of the bonds of public morality and, therefore, of public discipline. But it is unquestionable that the harm done has been, on the whole, less than that brought about by the extreme promulgation of the efficiency ideal.

It is repeated over and over again by many of the modern philosophers that no nation can afford to lag behind in the struggle for progress. This is true, but do they not very often limit the idea of progress to the merely material consideration of manufacture or trade? Is it not, on the other hand, quite arguable that a nation that is on a lower plane in matters purely material, may yet on the whole question be far more representative of true culture? Just because a poor but religious population cannot make its commerce pay, is it, therefore, to be supposed to have done less for the world than some spick-and-span people that has little else to show for its achievements than terrible slaughter and the invention of destructive forces?

Base your values and judgments on faith

Now, all this is not merely to be applied to the national, but to the individual, life. It is there far more dangerous, because far more likely to be carried to extremes. Thus, is it quite possible that I find myself judging life and life's affairs by the vulgar material standard that may well happen to prevail in the circles in which my business is cast. Have I not found myself adopting their standard even when it is most opposed to the principles of faith? I judge, that is to say, not by eternity, but by time. Poverty is looked upon as a disgrace by half the world, which yet lifts hardly a finger to insist upon its abolition. Yes, probably I am generous enough with my charity. But if poverty is so disgraceful a thing that I will not welcome its victims to my doors, is it not time that I did something far more radical, did something to get at the social causes of this extreme destitution, which no follower of Christ could ever allow to exist if he could well help it?

Sickness and failure are, I am always professing in my prayer-book, signs that God loves me, yet how oddly I treat these pledges of love. I say that faith is dearer to me than life, yet, on the whole, life seems to get the better of faith on most points in which they come into conflict. Am I not, when all is said and done, rather a hypocrite in my idealistic profession of the value of spiritual things compared with the actual tenor of my life, which hardly suggests any such tremendous resolve? Now, the value that I put upon things must be just that value that faith teaches me. Faith is to be the standard of judgment, and according to its dictates am I to settle my choice in life.

Part 9

∞

The Church

∞

The Catholic Church
contains the fullness of truth

All men who think about religion would quite easily agree that
once they were really convinced that a doctrine had been revealed
by God, they would have no difficulty in accepting it. It does not
matter how impossible a thing might sound, or how contradictory
it might appear to the other revelations from God; so long as there
could be absolute certainty that God had actually revealed it, we
would be bound to believe it. For God is the sovereign truth. He
can neither deceive nor be deceived. Consequently, whatever He
says we may be certain does represent truth.

But the trouble is not this. We would accept whatever God
said. The difficulty is to discover what He has said, or, rather, to be
convinced that the doctrines put forward as His by the religions of
the world do really stand for His teaching. Presumably every creed
that has been imposed on the human spirit since the world began,
even if it was the faith of only one soul, would have been accepted
only because that soul was assured that it was the revealed word of
God. If I am convinced that God has revealed anything, I must accept it; but how am I to find out what He has revealed? All religions come to me, and each tells me that theirs is the true church
of God, or that there is no church at all. Each, that is, gives an

entirely different list of the articles to which it demands my assent, yet each claims that it alone represents the real teaching of God, as revealed in Christ. No doubt some, in these times, would not in theory exclude other religions from a share in divine inspiration, but the incessant war that they wage on each other shows that, in practice, they hardly recognize the claims of the others.

Now, for purposes of convenience, we can divide all the religions of the world into three classes: those that, when asked for the supreme rule for discovering what God has revealed, would present the inquirer with a book; those that would tell him to look within, at his conscience; and those that would tell him to look without, at some external authority. The first set (Evangelicals and Mohamedans) are really reducible to the second (nonconformists and agnostics), for the interpretation of the book with them lies finally with the conscience. Hence, we have two main divisions: those that say, "Look within, to conscience" and those that say, "Look without, to authority."

Now, the first set cannot be right, if it is granted that there is such a thing at all as truth, for if the conscience is the real test of truth, how is it that conscientious men differ? If I am to look into my own heart to find out whether Christ is God, or whether divorce and remarriage is allowed, and if my decision (as these people imply) will really be the true answer, how comes it that there are any differences at all in the world?

But if they answer that they do not mean that it is right in itself, but that it is right for me to follow my conscience, then our obvious answer is that, in this case, if they do not pretend to be able to find truth at all, what is the use of their calling themselves a religion? Surely they have no business to pretend to teach what they do not know to be right. It is presumptuous in the extreme, as well as very wicked, for a preacher to endeavor to tell people what he is not sure is true. He ought to leave them to their own consciences and not dare to interfere with the direct inspiration of God.

The Catholic Church contains the fullness of truth

Now, it is not intended to be controversial, but to let me see what exactly I mean to myself when I proclaim my belief in the authority of the Church. It means that I am convinced that she is the divine representative of God on earth, and that when she announces to me any doctrine concerning faith or morals, then I am bound to accept it — not because I understand it or approve of it, but because it is the very revelation of God. For if there is such a thing as truth to be gotten on earth (and our Lord evidently thought so when He commanded the Apostles to teach[81]), then I can be certain that nowhere else is it obtainable than within the borders of the Catholic Church. Other religions may retain fragments of truth, but the Catholic Church alone has the whole truth.

I must, of course, convince myself by every means in my power that she does stand for the Church that Christ came to found — that grew up in the days of the Apostles and has lasted as a living and deciding voice for so many centuries. I have first to be convinced of that, and then I believe quite simply whatever after that she tells me is the Faith once delivered to the saints. To follow his conscience is all that is demanded of any man, but each is obliged to find out where the truth is, so that through the truth he may reach God.

For me, then, by the Divine Mercy, the way of truth has been made manifest, and I must, therefore, be thankful for the wonderful favor shown to me. And my best way of showing my gratitude is by seeking always to see in the Creed the actual story of God, as told me by Himself. I must look on the Church as just His mouthpiece. There is compulsion in truth, and from it no one may swerve. But if there is compulsion, there is also liberty, for it is only the truth than can make us free.

---

[81] Matt. 28:19.

The Pope asserts the truths of the Faith

That the Church is infallible is clear to everyone who reflects on the teaching and purpose of Christ. For if our Lord came to establish a body of teachers who might yet teach as His doctrine what was really in contradiction to it, then man could hardly be expected to gain any benefit from it, nor indeed to be certain when he had actually obtained it, or, when obtained, whether it would be of any advantage to him to have done so. The new gospel delivered by the Apostles to an unbelieving world was obviously a gospel on which much depended for the betterment of the children of men, since it required the death of God-made-man to establish it as a kingdom. All the years of teaching devoted by our Lord to the training of the Twelve would seem to have been futile, unless on it rested the supposition that truth was obtainable and that these were the men whom Christ Himself deputed to preach it.

The meaning, therefore, of the New Testament is that a definite message had come into the world — so important, that the words of Moses were not to be esteemed as of greater authority, and that the Law itself no longer compelled. The Apostles, too, were conscious of the enormous claim they were making in continuing the very work of our Lord, for, remembering His promise to send the Paraclete to take His place, they promulgated their decrees at the Council of Jerusalem with the tremendous prologue: "It hath seemed good to the Holy Spirit and to us."[82] They assert, therefore, that they and the Holy Spirit are, as it were, conjoined forces, whose purpose was to teach the world the truth of God. For this office of teaching, then, it is essential that there should be an infallible teacher.

But the need for infallibility of teaching did not cease with the Apostles. In a sense, it might seem that during their lifetime the need was less, for obviously the early converts would have been content to accept the decisions of those who had lived with the Master, had been trained by Him, and, by their personal familiarity with His modes of expression and even the very inflection of His voice, had been able to give authoritative interpretations to the simple teaching that alone would at first be considered necessary.

But as time went on and all who had actually known our Lord had died, and as, too, the restless mind of man was perpetually asking for new decisions upon new points of moral perplexity, and new interpretations or explanations of the being and actions of God, there must have appeared the need for an infallibility that would be living and final. An appeal to the past is always a secret appeal to the prejudice of the present, for into the past each reads his own interpretation, unless there is some final court that has power to declare what the past itself intended.

In the early centuries we find that councils were called together and debated the points at issue, and then announced what the tradition of the people of God was; but this method depended largely upon local conditions, and there were people who hurried through councils to prevent the opposing party from arriving in time to vote. Hence, it became clear that even the decisions of the council were required to be ratified by some other authority before they would be accepted by the Church as a whole.

---

[82] Acts 15:28.

Thus, partly by necessity, partly because our Lord had so laid it down in the general supremacy bequeathed to St. Peter, and partly because there was no one else who could perform the office, the Pope, or Bishop of Rome, began to be recognized by the faithful as the mouthpiece of the infallible Church. Even in the lifetime of St. John, the Christians appealed to the successor of St. Peter to settle a disputed election to the bishopric of Corinth. Then, as the centuries went on and the means of communication became so much easier, the need and possibility of quick appeal to Rome meant the increase of central authority. Finally, the infallibility of the Pope was declared an article of faith at the Council of the Vatican in 1870. What Tradition had always approved, the Church now declared to be the immemorial belief of the faithful of Christ, not as to His every utterance, as some had contended, but only (a) when, as shepherd and teacher of all Christians, (b) he defined (c) a doctrine concerning faith or morals (d) to be held by the whole Church. If any of these four conditions is unfulfilled, then, although the decision may be true and valid, it is not to be held binding on the conscience.

The extreme defenders of an exaggerated infallibility had to bow to the wise and just definition of Pope Pius IX, while those, too, who judged it to be inopportune lived to thank God for the divine prudence and economy wherewith His heavenly plan had worked through the ages.

I must therefore not allow myself to be led astray by any feelings of irritability against those decisions of the Holy See which seem to me to conflict with principles of common sense. I have to remember that the voice of the Pope is the voice of the age-long Tradition of the Christian people, and that the Pope has no power to make new dogmas, but only to declare what was the Faith once delivered to the saints.

Truth leads to genuine freedom

It is a common comparison to contrast the Church with the great empires of the world, and to note the vastness of design in each. We cannot help but be struck by the hordes of people that these secular empires contain, differing in race, in religion, in traditions, in culture, in their manner of life, and in its expression in language, in art, in dress. Yet, compatible with this huge difference, not merely in external but also in internal and essential ways of existence, there is a unity that appears to transcend the natural divisions of human nature.

In a famous essay, Lord Macaulay pointed out how, out of all the ancient European states, the papacy alone survives, and with a vigor and a freshness that seem to show no signs of real decay. He is, therefore, himself looking at the Church as he would have looked at the nations with their secular governments. Indeed, from a human point of view, there is much likeness between the two great empires numbering many millions and bridging over many gulfs of thought and habit.

But there is this contrast to be insisted on also: the empires of the world have survived or lived long only by adopting the greatest freedom in their several parts. When a number of divergent races are gathered into a unit, it is essential, if they are to continue to hold together, that allowance should be made for these very differences; and local ideas are permitted to color the political forms and beliefs of the sister-peoples. No despotic empire of any magnitude has ever for long dominated Europe or Christian civilization. The spirit of our Lord makes tyranny impossible, or rather, drives to revolution the oppressed.

Now, in the sphere of religion, the opposite principle is to be noted. For if any empire is held together longest by allowing as much freedom as possible to the separate units, a religion that gives up or diminishes its dogmatic position — which allows "comprehensiveness" to be the mark of its formularies — has no staying power at all. The more vague religion becomes, the less does it appeal to the children of men.

It will be found, for example, that in every civilized state, the churches that are the widest in their beliefs, that, to all intents and purposes, make no demands upon their adherents, are those that most bewail a decreasing membership. The contrast is therefore very evident. To give life to an empire, encourage mental freedom; to give life to a religion, insist strongly upon authority in the faith.

Really, when it is examined, there is nothing strange in this; for the principle of politics is the principle of compromise. Every politician knows perfectly well that he will never be able to get quite all he wants; nor, indeed, is he perfectly certain that what he wants is really the best thing for the country, but he judges that, on the whole, his side is in the right. But the believer is seeking truth and, in consequence, does not wish to be put off with the nearest or next best, for there is no next best to truth; it is either right or wrong. It is impossible to work a compromise on the divinity of our Lord or on the question of divorce; one or the other must be the teaching of Christ, and religion presumes that it is important to find out which is His teaching. The contrast between the state and the Church is therefore a contrast in essential purpose. The state gives us the next best; the Church gives us truth.

I must, therefore, be very careful not to allow my mind, brought up in the midst of the modern political forms of thought, to apply them to the region of the soul. It is so easy to say to myself that the insistence of the Church on certain dogmas, and her repudiation of this and that, is uncalled for and opposed to the spirit of the age. It really has nothing to do with the spirit of the age, for that spirit has no power over the range of fact; it cannot affect the reality of truth. It would be as reasonable to denounce the theorems of Euclid as no longer harmonizing with the ideas of a "generation that knows not how to obey." We should answer at once that truth, objective truth, is always one and is dependent upon the intelligence, not of man, but of God. Freedom, then, should be the principle of politics, but truth the principle of faith.

Naturally, of course, there is wisdom in permitting local customs to enter into the discipline and regulations of Christian life, but no local traditions or prejudices can affect by one hair's breadth the gospel of God; rather, the gospel must affect and utterly change the customs and prejudices of all of us. In politics, I aim at freedom, and probably I end by obtaining truth; in religion, I aim at truth and end by obtaining freedom. I try to advocate among my fellow citizens that form of government which allows the individual the greatest amount of liberty compatible with ordered and stable government, and I find in the end that I have gotten that form of government that is most ideal. But in religion, I choose deliberately that form which most authoritatively claims to teach me truth, and in the end, I find that as a result, I am most free, for only "the truth shall make you free."[83]

---

[83] John 8:32.

∞

The Church is holy

It must seem at first to be very like spiritual presumption and very unlike the spirit of Christ for any one church to claim, as against other religious bodies, the exclusive note of holiness. It would seem perfectly absurd, because contradictory, for the Catholic Church, for example, to boast that it was also more humble than any other church; yet surely this is really the case with any religion that claims to be holier than others. Is it not the very central idea of holiness that the possessor of it should know himself to be only a sinner? Might it not almost be made a principle of moral life to say that only those who know their own sinfulness are the least sinful? And does it not really prove the overweening pride of the Church that she sets herself, like the Pharisee, in the Temple of God and proclaims to all the world what wonderful things she has done?

This certainly is the idea that other people seem to get, and perhaps at times it is what we are ourselves very much troubled about. On the one hand, then, we find that the Church claims to be holy, and on the other, that the very statement of the claim seems to be its own refutation, for the holiest are just those least likely to realize, still less to speak about, their holiness.

Secondly, we notice in ourselves and others of our own Faith that the Creed has very little influence on the observance of the

Commandments, and that even the sacraments do not make us in actual life very different from those in the midst of whom we live. Thus, we see on every side of us people who have none of our advantages and yet who are better than we are; so that we Catholics appear to differ in nothing from our fellows, except that they hold certain intellectual propositions which we repudiate and which have very little connection with the rest of their lives.

To all this we can say first that our Lord Himself boasted of His sinlessness: "Which of you will convict me of sin?"[84] although, of course, this is no answer at all, for we are human, and He divine. He can declare truthfully what we never can, for even the presence of the saints in her does not make the Church holy in the sense of being without sin.

What, then, do we mean when we claim holiness as one of the notes of the Church? We mean that, under the Redemption of Christ, she is the source whence comes our holiness, and that she has to offer to all who wish the helps to holiness that each most requires. There is no one whose desires for intimate union with God she cannot satisfy.

Other religions contain many examples of those who follow the footsteps of Christ, but their religion as such, their chapel, is not the means of this achievement. We feel simply that God leads them along His own chosen path. But with us, it is the whole wonderful economy of the Church that is put at our disposal. For each, there is provided the means most efficient for salvation and perfection. For those who feel called to the life of solitude, for those whom God has chosen to fulfill the honorable state of marriage or to continue His work of instructing the young in the ways of the gospel, for those who desire means of laboring for others or for themselves, or for Him, there are the many orders and confraternities with their several purposes and pious prayers. We must not try

---

[84] John 8:46.

to join them all, but realize simply that all these different means exist in order to enable us individually to reach the state of holiness designed for us by God.

When, then, I say that the Church is preeminently holy, I do not mean that I am a saint, but I do mean that, if I want to be a saint, in the Catholic Church there are held out to me numerous aids to spur me on to the perfect love of God. There are the daily Masses, the many sacraments, the daily visit to the Blessed Eucharist, the countless confraternities and guilds that are willing and eager to satisfy every ideal that can ever have come into my mind; or, indeed, if that which I wish to see established does not yet exist, there is no reason I should not myself begin it.

Saints without number, among whom I can surely find those whose lives most appeal to me as the way in which I, too, could be brought to serve God best, are to be found in the list of her canonized children, who are canonized so that they may be an example to me in my labors. So, by this doctrine, I profess belief in an ever-increasing number of blessed souls who, here or in the other world, unite with me in the grand work of following in the footsteps of Christ. Like a huge army with even pace, and with the impetus that comes from a great movement, I feel that with them the way is made easier; that the long, weary journey seems shorter, and the help that each affords the other adds to the general goodness of all. I am surrounded by this influence, which should overcome that feeling of loneliness that causes so much discouragement to human hearts. My own character and temperament require my own special mode for getting to God, but the grace of God is poured out so prodigally in the Church that I have never any need for bewailing my inability to adopt other people's ways. The Church is so great that somewhere I can find that which makes appeal to me, and I shall be led along my own path to Him.

∞

The Church is catholic

The Church that Christ came to found was to teach truth. By that single sentence alone can be proved all the prerogatives that Catholics claim for their Church, for to teach truth in matters of such moment requires the gift of inerrancy — that is, the gift of teaching without error the truths that are necessary for salvation — and the gift of indefectibility — that is, the gift of teaching without ceasing until the end of all the world. To deliver the message of Christ means to preach as one having authority, to tell men how by doctrine they are to arrive at the same life that He had lived.

But not merely has this Church to appeal with authority and without ceasing until the end of time; she has also to deliver the glad tidings to the whole race. If the Catholic Church is indeed the Church of Christ, she cannot be a national church; she cannot entertain so narrow a view of her mission. If there is one thing more than another that our Lord was most insistent upon in His lifetime, it was that His religion was not intended for one people only, but for all the world. The Pharisees hunted Him to death chiefly for the reason that He entirely repudiated the restriction of the kingdom of God to only those souls who could boast of descent from Abraham. He scandalized them over and over again by His appeal to a wider audience than those merely who worshiped upon the Temple-Mount. All their creeds He came to fulfill, to include them in this new Faith, this grain of mustard seed, this leaven, which should affect the whole race of man. He broke through all the divisions of language, or birth, or previous prejudice, and would gather into one all the children of men.

Now, it is just this that the Catholic Church has been able to achieve. She has gone out into the world and deliberately invited all to the new Faith of Christ. At first, there was some discussion, as we learn from the Scriptures, and it was necessary that the first Pope (St. Peter) should be convinced by a vision before he would agree to allow those converted from paganism the full fellowship of the Christian name;[85] but thence onward, all nations found a home within her. She has traveled the whole world over, not as the Church of a nation (for so to label oneself is to repudiate the teaching of our Lord), but as the Catholic Church. She is the Church of all peoples, of all times, of all the ages of man. She has gone to strange countries, not simply to settle there for the benefit of passing merchants, but to take her place in the life of the nations.

Then, within the limits of each people, she affects the individuals as well. She is the Church for the children, the Church for the poor, the Church for the old, the Church for the young. The learned find her dogmas wonderful as the flashing brightness of the radiance of God; the simple discover that her doctrine and her practices make life intelligible, even if not comprehensible. For each, whatever his state or age or capacity, she has her way of good, for she is catholic in every sense of that wide-meaning word: nothing escapes her.

And, even more splendid still, she has gathered together all that is best in all the religions of the world. There is no practice of hers and no belief that cannot be found elsewhere, yet nowhere else are they all put together and formed by the swift revelation of God

[85] Acts 10.

into a picture, toward a portion of which each people has groped its way since ever the world began.

The Church is catholic. To that Church I myself belong. Catholic, then, must be the whole temper of my mind. There must be in me none of that narrowness which would limit the spirit of God to one single fashion, nor would grudge my neighbor his own way of achieving the purpose of his existence. The liberty I claim for myself I should gladly concede to others; for, after all, the Church is large enough to include all. If every nation under Heaven can find protection under her shadow, who am I to dictate to my brother how he should serve God? There is the obvious limit of the Catholic Faith; beyond that, indeed, there is salvation for the children of men, for the simple reason that God does not bind Himself to give grace only in one way.

God, however, wills that all men should come to the knowledge of the truth, and it is the duty of a Christian to bring as many as possible within that fold of Christ. Within the Church, there is also the dogmatic teaching that none may with safety deny. She is the teacher from God, and to whom else can we turn?

But apart from these fixed truths, there are paths and bypaths that each can follow for himself. Yet the self-centered spirit of man is too easily persuaded that it alone has found the perfect way, not realizing that the way of one need not be the way of another; for it is in the power of God to lead me individually to Himself by a path singled out from all eternity that I, and I alone, shall take. My past is as the past of none other, and my future must be unique as well.

Let me, then, be broad-minded enough not to question or be scandalized in my brother. His conscience is lit up by the glory of God, and that should be enough for me. The silly parochialism that would reduce all to one dead level has no part or lot in the kingdom of God. I must not grudge others their own way, nor seek to drive them into my own, for Catholicism means the freedom of the children of God.

∞

The Church is apostolic

The Church that Christ came to found was to teach truth. For that precise object was it established, and by that ultimate end, it is clear, all her institutions are to be justified or repudiated. Her infallibility, her indefectibility, her holiness, and her catholicism are defended by that simple and primary fact. To it also can we trace that note of apostolicity which, since the fifth century, it has become traditional to demand for the true Church of Christ.

For consider what she has to do to justify her claim to be the true Church of Christ. Not only has she to prove that all that He taught she also teaches, or that she can make good her boast that there is none other than she that so closely clings to the doctrines that He set out to preach — clings to them in spite of every age-long endeavor to assert their incompatibility with contemporary movements (for she has felt that to be up-to-date is little required by that which is not of time but of eternity).

But over and above this, she has also to prove that she bears His commission. That is to say, it is not enough to show that you hold the doctrines taught by our Lord, but it is also necessary to show that you have His permission to represent Him. There must be some sort of official recognition; otherwise we might be entertaining false Christs and false prophets. Consequently, we have a right to demand from the Church that she should show her connection with the apostolic band to whom Christ gave the sacred commission to preach His Gospel to every living creature. We have a right to ask her to show how she has descended from that first generation that was of God and taught by God Himself. She must, in other words, trace her line back to the Apostles.

Now, this must not be taken to mean that she has to prove historically that each link in the chain is intact; not, indeed, because this cannot be done, because we have not the time, the learning, or the opportunity for accurately testing this documentary evidence. Already in the fifth century, St. Augustine wrote to refute those who would set aside the Catholic Church as not representative of the teaching of Christ, by quoting at length the long list of popes stretching from his own time to the days of St. Peter, who first ruled the Church from Rome. And, of course, from the date of St. Augustine in the fifth century to our own, it is not difficult to gather from public records the actual names. But really this requires more knowledge and more leisure than can be expected from any of us.

It might not, indeed, take much time simply to compile the list, but it would take a good deal to be certain of each pontiff, whether he did actually follow in the steps of the preceding popes, and whether he did actually connect his own generation to the one that had gone before. But it is necessary all the same that we should be able to see how this direct lineage can be traced back to the apostolic age.

Perhaps the simplest way of all is to take the negative side, and explain that there is no evidence that we can see or have ever heard of to prove that, at any one time, the succession ceased. In other religions that boast the Christian name, we can state at what definite date they came into existence; we can tell almost the very day when the world first saw them or knew them as religious establishments.

Now, if our blessed Lord did come to found a Church, it must have been intended to be continuous; but there is one only Church that can even pretend to make this claim. Therefore, we have a right to suppose without further proof that it alone is the Church of Christ.

I belong, then, to this Church and can thus claim kinship with the Apostles. I should not look upon this as mere spiritual snobbery, a craving to find myself well-connected; it has a far deeper significance than that. But there is this lesson to be learned even from that view of it. The bearer of a noble name must surely take care that nothing base is ever attached to that of which he is but the trustee. He must see to it that no act of his ever reflects evil upon that which was delivered to him not only unsullied, but even glorious. Mindful, therefore, of the apostolic kinship that is mine, I must be careful that so high an honor is not made ridiculous by its association with my own disgrace.

Moreover, there is this also to be said: that not merely should the sense of high lineage keep me from evil, by associating me with those greater than myself, but the sense of greatness is the best incentive to greatness. When I realize what God has done for me, it shows me more the value of my own life, and in consequence, I shall take more pains over my soul. If I thought that God did not much care whether I followed Him or not, that He was too occupied with the vastness of the universe to spare much time for the single units that compose it, I would indeed be little worthy of blame in making no attempts to love or serve Him. But when I see by what myriad chains He has bound me to Himself — when I realize that even after He had ascended to His Father, our Lord still wished to keep me close to Himself in the Church, and that this closeness is symbolized by the bond of apostolic union carefully preserved — then I love Him, for He evidently is at pains to gain my love.

∞

The Church is one

The Church that Christ came to found was to teach truth. From this central idea, it is possible to show that, in consequence, the Church of Christ must be holy, or else the purpose of truth is vain (moreover, the Master asked His Father to sanctify His children in truth[86]).

It must be catholic, for it is the very glory of truth that it knows no boundaries, or divisions of intelligence or of language or of race. It must be apostolic, for it has not only to show its possession of truth, but that it was commissioned by Christ also to teach that truth. And, finally, it can be shown that, for the selfsame reason, the Church that Christ came to found must be one and the same all the world over.

Once, indeed, it is granted that to teach truth is the proper purpose of the Church, then the unity of the Church is self-evident. For if it is certain that there can be no boundaries to the limit of the empire of truth, if there can be no language or race or age that can escape its power, then assuredly it must be one and undivided also. If it is to reach over all the world, then over all the world it must be one. If it has to break down the artificial or natural

[86] John 17:17.

partitions raised up by man's division of the earth, it can do this only at the expense of being the same everywhere.

Truth may be many-sided, as the philosophers of the last generation loved to explain, but it can afford to be many-sided only because it means only one thing from one point of view. But truth as truth must be one and the same always. If it is true that Christ is God, this does not mean that He is not also man; but it does mean that He must be recognized as God always and everywhere. In His death, He died simply as man, for God as God could not die; yet for all that, we must say that it was God who died. Because He is God, He is God always. Hence, the Church of Christ that is really faithful to His name will always preach the same doctrine.

Here, then, oddly enough, or rather, quite rightly, we come on the ordinary accusation against the Catholic Church — namely, that she never will change. Her opponents, whose name and whose quarrel is legion, at least agree in this, that it is characteristic of Catholicism to be found the same in all the world. In every place where she has set up her altars, she comes with one single Faith, and she demands its acceptance by all her children. There cannot be one teaching for those who are clever, and one for those who are rich, and one for those who are in revolt against the conditions of their life. For all, there must be some one message that comes out of eternity, from the lips of God, who dwelleth in eternity, and therefore which will be above all the restless ebb and flow of changing time. Centuries may vary in their ideas of what is graver and what is lesser evil. Men may have one custom today and another tomorrow. They may declare that a rate of wage which troubled no man's conscience in the generation that is gone would be scandalous to the next. But through it all, there must be one only truth. The traditions may alter, but the truth remains.

This, then, is just what the Church has always clung to. When, for example, a new question comes to be discussed, it is her way to find out what has been the teaching of the past upon it, or rather upon some similar aspect of truth, so convinced is she that she must hold fast to that which was, for since it was true yesterday, it is true today as well. In whatever land she is found, she teaches the same doctrine; and in her faith, her sacraments, and her head, she is one and the same the whole world over.

It is this that should give me a truer notion of my Faith. There is always the temptation — especially when I mix, as indeed I cannot help doing, with people who have no fixed teaching at all — to wish that I could alter some of the things I have learned as a child. I seem to see that it would make for the spread of the Church if I could only throw over one point or another, go back upon this doctrine or that, explain away some decision of some pope in some bygone age. The dead weight of the past seems to lie heavy on the Church.

Of course, if the thing in question is merely some disciplinary matter, I may advocate and work for its being set aside; or if a doctrine is merely propounded without the decisive voice of the Shepherd and Teacher of the flock, I may hope that the straitness of the teaching may be modified. But if the question concerns some definite matter that has been decided by the infallible decree of the Vicar of Christ, then I can only bow my intelligence. I am of eternity; I am of truth. Eternity cannot change; nor can truth be other than it always is. The Church is one because she teaches the eternal truth of Christ, and I must submit myself loyally to that unity, without which I would find myself in the midst of the chaos and confusion that is of man, but cannot be of God.

Always, then, I must bring myself back to the spirit of our blessed Lord when He prayed for the unity of His disciples and of all who would, through their word, believe in Him, that upon us all should descend the very oneness of God. I am one in faith with Catholics over all the world. Let me endeavor by holding fast to truth to bring others, too, into that one fold, conscious that unity built on any other foundation than truth cannot survive.

Part 10

∞

Prayer

∾

God is present even in
the ordinary things of life

The much-denounced and much-praised word *mysticism* has a real practical value for Catholics. It describes not so much a system or a doctrine as a definite attitude toward life. The ordinary pious person, or indeed people who are far from pious and yet are much affected by the beauty of nature or of things and individuals in the world, are wont to say that these lift up their minds to God. They are so impressed by the loveliness of that which appears, that they are led to suppose that there must be a loveliness infinitely greater to account for that transient beauty, glimpses of which are vouchsafed them here on earth: "How beauteous must His beauties be who framed the glories of the day."

Nor is it simply the sight of the beautiful things that God has made that produce this impression on the mind. The handicrafts of man are also wonderful and make those who have in them any sense of the meaning of life exclaim in surprise at the amazing marvels of God's power; for whatever is in the creature must be even more excellently in the Creator. Hence, all this wonderful increase in the scientific inventions of man does not, in any sense, make our faith stagger. Or perhaps it does make it stagger, not as though God could not be, or need not be, but at the more wonderful manifestations of His glory. If He who framed the glories of the day must be so beautiful Himself, then He, too, who gave man the power to do these marvelous things must be infinitely more marvelous Himself. From nature, from man's works, and still more from the wonders of man's own personality, his self-sacrifice, his humility, the fierceness and consuming fire of his love, we are led step by step to a more splendid appreciation of the meaning of our worship of God.

Now, all this is very beautiful and is often called mysticism, but mysticism it certainly is not. The real meaning of mysticism is much more important, much more helpful, deeper, and more revolutionary.

Take, for example, the things that make us say at once that they are mystical. We read the story of St. Francis,[87] and we hear of how he called the wolf of Gubbio, which was doing so much harm to the inhabitants, "Brother Wolf"; how, to him, death was a sister, and the sun a brother; how, in fact, the moon and the stars and Christ our Lord were all his kinsfolk. We say at once that St. Francis had a mystical vision of life.

Or, again, when we find St. Catherine of Siena receiving the head of a condemned man into her arms in order that she might comfort him in his last hours, and speaking at once when she found her white garments colored with his blood in such a way as to make it difficult to distinguish whether she is referring to the Blood of Christ or the blood of the poor dead criminal, we cannot help seeing that she, too, has attained the mystical vision.

The same sort of thing is to be found in the sayings and doings of every mystic. We may not be able to say quite what they have that makes them mystics, but we can recognize the mystical element as soon as we have heard of it.

---

[87] St. Francis of Assisi (1182-1226), founder of the Franciscan Order.

God is present even in the ordinary things of life

What, then, really is it? Perhaps the easiest way of expressing what is with great difficulty put into human language is to say that the vision of the mystic makes him or her see that the whole of the universe is one. Thus, St. Francis was not lifted up to God by the thought of earthly things in the sense that he forgot earth in looking at Heaven; but he was able (and this is surely the whole meaning of mysticism) to get such a vision of Heaven as allowed earth also its place in the same plane. A mystic is not one who sees God in nature, but one for whom God and nature fit into one plane.

It is just this vision that is so essential in human life.

The chief bother that exists for most of us is that everything seems so disconnected; there appears to be no plan of things, no design in them at all, but every dreary moment of our day is connected with the next simply because we happen to be continuous through it all. There is the sight of nature and the wonderful works of man, the sudden gleam of genius and the slow-plodding ways of honest toil, the kindly side of man's strange character, his self-sacrifice, his illogical generosity.

Then, too, come the mysteries of God's kingdom as we learn them from the Church — the overwhelming truths that stand out against the skyline — the Trinity, the Incarnation, the Redemption, the indwelling of the Spirit of God.

Now, the difficulty is for me to see that all these are not separate, but one. To unite the petty details of our daily lives to the tremendous being of God seems an impossible proposal, but, to the mystic, all things are possible — not because he lowers God to the level of the ordinary things of life, but because he suddenly sees these glow with a divine transfiguration and can never again look upon anything in human life as common or unclean. I must train myself to realize, for example, that the Incarnation is not simply that Christ our Lord became man, although that itself is full enough of wonder, but that, by so being, tabernacled in the flesh, He lifted up all created things to Himself, and became a brother to all the world. I must pray very earnestly to see the connection be-tween all things that are, to be conscious of the action of God working through earth and Heaven, the experiences of life and the very being of the divine Three in One.

∞

God does not desire your perfection, but your attempts to attain perfection

Faith is the basis of life, and charity is its crown; but hope is its greatest need. Most of the difficulties of life come because man is so prone to lose heart. His distractions in prayer suggest to him that he was not meant for such high acts. His weekly tale of sins at Confession seems to imply by its almost identical repetition that it is useless for him to continue his efforts at "a firm purpose of amendment." His faltering attempts at perfection disconcert him from any very persistent or long-continued service. His cold and listless Communions take away his feelings of devotion and lead him to fancy that it would be better not to go at all than to go with so little seeming effect. This joylessness in the sacraments does far more harm than that, for it makes him close the very gates through which alone help can come to him.

The whole of life tends to depress a man who is at all conscious of his capacities, his responsibilities, and his failures. Is he, then, a great sinner? Not at all. Has he lost his faith and love? Most certainly not. What, then, is wanting to him? Hope.

He has given up hope; he is disheartened; he is too discouraged to go on. He is very human; oh yes, but he is very foolish also, for when hope has gone, all is over. Failure counts for nothing. Defeat, disappointment — these matter nothing at all, so long as hope sits patiently, stirring the embers, watching and tending the fire, coaxing the flame, never despairing and never leaving the wind to work its will. That the clouds should come up over the sky, or that darkness should encircle the earth, brings no real terrors, for we are sure that the dawn will come out again and that the sun will break through with its golden glory.

Now, hope frankly starts by acknowledging the certainty of trouble. It implies that life is hard, implies indeed that a perfect life (that is, a life without fault) is impossible for man. That is to say, the first thing for me to do is to realize quite simply and quite definitely that I shall never overcome one single fault, at least in the sense that I shall never be able to find myself free from temptations. I may improve; please God I shall! I may lessen the number of my sins by narrowing the occasions of them. I may so far clear myself that the old fault has ceased even to be repeated; for the goodness of God may achieve all these things.

But at any rate, I must never expect that this will be done for me so completely as to prevent forever any struggle in my life. The sins that troubled my boyhood will haunt my steps until my gray hairs.

As a child, I knew I was naughty and thought that grown-up people did nothing wrong. Now that I am grown up, I look upon children as the innocent followers of Christ. But now the certainty that I must face is that always I shall be a wrongdoer. I must reconcile myself quite determinedly to this prospect, not buoy myself up with false hopes of a time when I can rest securely upon my oars. Life is always a pull upstream. The terrible thing is when people expect to find things ultimately easy and discover them to be continuously very hard. The shock is too much for them; they lose heart and can never recover.

This, then, is the first point I must get into my mind, and it should need little to make it sure. I am a failure from the beginning, and shall be a failure to the end; at the best, says our Master, an "unprofitable servant."[88] I can never be perfect.

The next point, when that first has been fairly faced, is more reassuring. I can never be perfect; nor does God want me to be perfect. He does not expect perfection from me, for the very simple reason that He knows He would not get it. He knows man, for He made man; He knows exactly the limits of his power. Only the Heavenly Father is or can be perfect. It is foolish of me, then, to be discouraged because my prayers are full of distractions, my Communions cold, and my confessions always the same. God does not ask from me perfection in any of these ways.

Rather, it would fill me with wonder if, for any length of time, these things went wholly well. I would at once grow suspicious. God does not ask from me perfect prayers or perfect sacraments. He does not ask me even to overcome my temper or my want of charity or my untruthfulness. He does not ask these things, for He knows He could not get them from me.

What, then, does He ask? That I should *try* to overcome them, only that and nothing more — that I should try, day after day, despite failure, repeated and certain, to overcome these obstacles to my union with Him. For goodness consists not in the love of God, but in the attempts to love Him. If, then, I fail, let me not be discouraged, but, realizing my own weakness and confident only in God's strength, let me go on striving my best, for my business in life is really little else than to continue to fail without losing courage or lessening effort. The phrase of St. Catherine should ring always in my ear: "God doth not ask a perfect work, but infinite desire."

[88] Luke 17:10.

∞

Grace should draw you closer to God

Grace is the free gift of God. It can be merited only because God has made it meritable. The very possibility of its acceptance is itself a grace that no merit can acquire. It is the gift of God, which is given to us only to draw us on to God Himself. Its reason lies in the Beatific Vision, for its only purpose is to lead us to that. God, in effect, created man for the joy of Heaven. Of Hell it is distinctly affirmed by Christ our Lord that it was made for the Devil and his angels, whereas of Heaven He declares that it is the kingdom prepared for men. This, of course, should not be taken as implying that Heaven exists for man only, or primarily, since its essential act is merely the contemplation of the Eternal Beauty, the ravishing vision of Power, Wisdom, Love in perfect harmony, the adequate knowledge of the ever-blessed Three-in-One. But all that we really mean is that God created man for the ultimate enjoyment of Himself.

Each individual whom God calls into the world has his destined place in the economy of the divine plan. That place is the direct result of God's own decree, so that the good are predestined to the happiness of eternal life. This decree of God is the first act, if one can suppose a first act in that which knows no sequence; so, by a subsequent act of God's Providence, men's lives are arranged for their final reward or failure.

Grace, therefore, is ordained to nothing else than the ultimate purpose of man's creation. It is the free help of God whereby each of us achieves His final predestination. Man was intended from the first to be raised to a supernatural order; that is, God created Adam so that he should know his Maker, not in the mere material sense in which our natural human wit can discern His traces in the physical and intellectual universe, but with that ineffable intuition resulting in a participation by us in the divine nature. For Scripture insists, with a monotony that is almost wearisome, that the effect of grace is to make us the very mates of God: "All who do justice are born of God";[89] "All who are born of God do not sin, for the generation of God preserveth them";[90] "The Father gave it to us that we should be called and should be the children of God."[91] It is in this sense that the Fathers understand these texts of Scripture and the famous words of St. Peter, wherein he expressly describes the effect of the promises of God as making us "partakers of the divine nature."[92] St. Cyril of Alexandria[93] especially declares that by grace there shines in our soul "the mark of the substance of God."

This grace, therefore, is ordained to glory. God created us for Himself and has held out to us His helping hand to reach to the heights of that contemplation. Grace, in other words, is the means whereby we are made conscious of that other world and enabled eventually to attain it, not by our natural powers, but by God's free gift.

I must, therefore, realize that this grace lies entirely in His hands. The knowledge of the wonderful heights to which I can climb must necessarily enlarge considerably the sense of my own

[89] Cf. 1 John 4:7.
[90] Cf. 1 John 3:9.
[91] 1 John 3:1.
[92] 2 Pet. 1:4.
[93] St. Cyril of Alexandria (c. 376-444), bishop and Doctor.

dignity. The fact that I am made a partaker of the divine nature should influence me to respond to the place to which I am called. It should add to my view of the world, of others' souls, of the infinite reverence due even to the most sordid and most miserable child of the human race. We are all, by this grace, partakers one with another in the very substance of God.

But while, in this way, giving me a nobler appreciation of my vocation as a human being, and extending my importance in my own spiritual estimation, I must remember that it is all His doing and none of my own. He has, indeed, permitted me to merit certain graces, which for all my merit yet remain His gifts; but certain others can never be the wage of goodness, only an added gratuity due to His generous condescension to my poverty.

But the chief view I must take of it all is the consciousness that I am made for Him. Consequently, every time I realize He has been helping me, I must redouble my efforts to reach Him. Each grace is not to be rested in, but made a stepping-stone to the next grace. The grace of faith, for example, is but the beginning of life, not its end. It is but an illumination whereby I am made conscious that He calls me higher; and the daily blessings of health, friends, work, the beauty of nature, and arts and crafts have to be viewed as daily given helps to reach His side.

∽

Prayer depends on faith

Prayer has been defined to be the raising up of the mind and heart to God; but it would be more descriptive, and perhaps more accurate, to say that it is the raising up of the heart, through the mind, to God, for it is a commonplace of conversion that knowledge precedes love. It is true, of course, that the opposite statement would be equally valid, for I cannot know anyone until I am in love (that is, in sympathy) with him. But although this is so, I must still begin by having some rudimentary knowledge of the existence of that which I love; that is to say, I must at least know of a thing before I can love it. Since, then, prayer means getting into communication with God, it is clear that I must always, consciously or not, get into my mind some truth about God.

Let us suppose a mother is praying to God to save her son from peril. She really has convinced herself (either deliberately or simply without realizing what she is doing) of two quite definite things: first, that God is certainly able to help her; and, secondly, that He can be affected by her loneliness and desolation of heart. In other words, she is holding to two dogmatic truths: the omnipotence and the mercy of God.

And whenever we analyze prayer, our own or another's, we shall find that at the back of it lies some truth about God that we or they have accepted; and it is only because of that particular truth that we turn to that particular prayer. Thus, again, we often praise God because of His greatness; that is, we first believe Him to be great and then praise Him for it: but belief, in any case, comes first. Unless I believed in His mercy or His power or His justice or His beauty, or one or another of His many attributes, I would never turn to Him at all.

Notice that, in all this, the word *belief* is used, for our real knowledge of God as He is in Himself comes to us only by faith. Reason can (says the Council of the Vatican) prove the existence of God; but it is at least possible that *my* reason never has proven it. My reason may never feel convinced by its own reasoning. In any case, the real knowledge of God as a supernatural power, with the full heights and depths of His divine life, cannot obviously be attained to by the reason, except insofar as it is illumined by supernatural light.

And it is just this supernatural light that we call faith. It is a vision. No doubt it is true, as Cardinal Newman[94] has admirably phrased it, that the act of faith is partly an act of will. There must be the wish to believe at the back of me, a movement of the grace of God. All the arguments in the world cannot prove the supernatural status of the Church, for arguments are obviously rational, whereas the supernatural transcends reason. Ultimately, therefore, the mind that says, "I believe" does so because its reason shows that the Church is eminently credible; and its will takes the one further step ("the leap in the dark") and, under the direct interference of God, completes the act by asserting, "I *must* believe."

Yet in spite of the fact that this act of will is essential, the gift of faith is still, in its purpose and in its effect, an enlightenment, an apocalypse, a revelation. This vision is an entrance into the kingdom

[94] Ven. John Henry Cardinal Newman (1801-1890), noted writer and convert to the Catholic Church.

of truth, for it tells us about God and the soul, this life and the afterlife. We become as little children in implicit obedience and gain also the clear sight of a child. Prayer, then, is based on the knowledge of God, therefore on revelation, therefore on faith.

Consequently, when I look at my prayers, I must see what part faith or the Creed plays in them. I must get my faith quite clear, or at least as clear as I can, before I can settle down to pray. Before the Crib, or before the Tabernacle, I must begin by making myself conscious of what exactly I believe. I must go over in my mind the significance of the Incarnation: Why did Christ come? What purpose had He in coming? What was He going to effect? What motive had He in coming? I fix upon one single point and try to see really what I know about it. He came, for example, to redeem me. Yes, but what does *redemption* mean? It is a common word, frequently on my lips; do I realize what it implies? And so on.

This is the only way to pray. Perhaps I begin at once in prayer by thanking or asking or praising; then I find I have nothing more to say. I am used up. Really I have begun all wrong; I have begun in the middle. Let me start always by some act of faith, and then go on quite slowly.

Notice the liturgical prayers of the Church. They begin generally in some such fashion as this: "O God, who by the life, death, and Resurrection of Jesus Christ . . ." — that is they begin from some dogmatic truth. So, again, our Lord's own prayer, "Our Father, who art in Heaven." This, too, is a piece of information that faith alone makes known to me. If I leave faith aside, no wonder my prayers are dull, monotonous, a bore to me.

But, then, shall I have to learn all about my Faith? Certainly. I must go back to my catechism. I shall find prayer growing easier as my knowledge of God increases. The two run parallel, prayer and faith. The absence of either, or their disuse, paralyzes the practice of the other.

∞

Prayer raises the heart to God

The first act of prayer is knowledge; the second is love. For I must always remember that the ultimate purpose of prayer, as of all spiritual life, is to get into union with God. For that end was I created, and to that end I must turn all and every supernatural enlightenment. Love is always the end of acquaintanceship with that which is perfect. I know my friends with a deep and true knowledge, and the knowledge does not remain as though in some separate compartment, having no influence upon life. I know their kindness, generosity, and loyalty, and this makes my love itself, without any deliberate act on my part, increase also very considerably — just as, again, the more I see the beauty of a thing or a person, the more I am attracted by it.

The word *attracted* is very appropriate, for it shows what has happened: the thing or person, in consequence of the increasing evidence of its beauty, actually draws me to it; it does not come into me, but leads me to it. Thus, theologians who describe the Beatific Vision of eternal bliss tell us that the real act of possession is an act of intellect; but that once we have seen God with our minds, we cannot help loving Him. Really, no doubt, the reason is that the division of mind from heart is purely artificial; they are both mere functions of the same indivisible soul, which, when once it knows what is lovable, loves it by the same energy. The very appearance of beauty produces its own effect. In prayer, then, we begin by contemplating some fixed mystery or truth, and our heart then burns within us.

In other words, prayer is not an abstract science or art, but a handicraft of life. It is no use for me to set out in order, however elaborately, article after article of belief. The Medievals said, "God taketh not delight in logic" — that is, there is no prayer, no union with God, in merely tabulating our knowledge of Him and describing it accurately, and remembering it in great detail. All that would be possible without prayer; prayer means that the heart, too, has been touched. The psalmist sang, "From my heart broke the good word"; and again, "A flame burst forth."[95]

It is not prayer, therefore, when I merely weave theological patterns out of the truths of Faith; but it is prayer when, contemplating God as revealed to me, I find Him to be so lovable that my heart longs for His company and for the return of His sympathy. Nor should this be difficult. Any scene in the life of my Divine Master, as recorded in the Gospels, must, as I study it, make more and more evident to me His mercy, His gentleness with sinners who are conscious of their sin, His meekness and humbleness of heart; and as these become more and more evident, surely my love will follow.

So also the mere contemplation of any article of the Creed must certainly light up the depths of the mysteries of God at least sufficiently to let us see how really beautiful they must be. The mind explores all these wonderful things only to draw the heart more deeply after it. The mind lights up the loveliness within, and the heart is aflame with the vision disclosed. No one can gaze for long at something that is genuinely beautiful without being caught up in the rapture that the spell of its loveliness must cast.

[95] Cf. Ps. 44:2; 38:4 (RSV = Ps. 45:1; 39:3).

While, then, I recognize that faith in prayer is intended to lead me on to love, this does not mean that I must wait for a great flame to burst forth. This is, indeed, a matter about which I must be most careful, for I may discourage myself or be led astray by delaying for too long or rushing too impetuously along. By *love, rapture,* and *ablaze*, nothing more is meant than an inclination to follow God's Commandments and live as faith prescribes. It has nothing to do with feelings, emotions. It does not mean that I do not pray if I do not feel love for God in the same way as I feel love for my friends, or that I must go on working out the particular mystery or article of belief until my whole being is stirred and raised to a white-heat of devotion.

I am only a beggar and cannot be a chooser; I must be content with the crumbs that fall from the table of God. No physical delight or appreciation of God's nearness to me is needed, nor is it in any way a sign that my prayer is fruitful; for this may depend rather upon digestion than upon the love of God: in fact, the very absence of it may make prayer, bravely persisted in, all the more pleasing in the sight of the Most High. Here, then, the upraising of heart that should follow upon the heels of faith may be unfelt, even unconscious. It is shown rather in the day's work than in the moment's emotions. "If you love me, keep my commandments. . . . Not he that saith to me, 'Lord, Lord!' but he that doth the will of my Father, shall enter into the kingdom of Heaven."[96] These are the proofs of our genuineness in prayer.

Anyway, I must be satisfied with what is given to me, nor should I seek to say much. The prayer in the Garden was but the repetition between long silences of one single petition. By faith, then, is God's beauty unveiled, and the vision of this beauty sets my heart on fire with love.

[96] John 14:15; cf. Matt. 7:21.

≪∞≫

Talk to God as you would to a friend

The whole doctrine of prayer, from its practical standpoint, can be summed up by saying that it is talking to God as a friend talks with a friend. That is, indeed, the best test of my prayers. Should I venture to talk to anyone I was fond of in the way I talk to God? We read in Scripture of God walking and talking with Adam in the cool of the evening, and we say to ourselves, "That is perfect prayer." What does it matter in what shape God appeared, or whether He appeared at all? At least imagination grasps what the sacred author intended.

Or, again, when we find it written of Enoch that "he walked with God till God took him,"[97] we say, again, that our ideal of prayer could not be better described.

Or lastly, for the quotations could be multiplied to any extent, when we first come across this wonderful sentence, are we not immediately conscious of what is meant: "God spoke to Moses, face-to-face, as a man is wont to speak to his friend"?[98] Now, here we have, in a very brief epitome, all that, from a practical point of view, we need to know about prayer. It is simply the converse

[97] Cf. Gen. 5:22, 24.
[98] Exod. 33:11.

between my soul and God, to be carried on in precisely the same fashion of language and the same pregnant silences that characterize my own talks with my friends. These must be the models by which I individually test the value and the sincerity of my prayers. Nothing else will do, nor will anything else for long hold or attract me. Prayers will ultimately bore me unless I carefully follow out these directions.

First, then, the matter of prayer is originated by the mind out of the articles of Faith, and the result is that the heart leaps up to love God in consequence, and this love itself is expressed in the simple language and silences of friendship.

Now, this "talking as with a friend" involves certain consequences. It involves a view of prayer that should make it very much easier for me. For example, prayer must be perfectly natural. I must speak to God in my own language, or else I cannot hope to pray frequently or well. I may ape the thoughts and style of another, but only for a while, since I soon wear his garments threadbare or show occasionally the real clothing that is beneath.

My conversation with friends is perfectly easy. I have no character to keep up with them; they know me too well to be taken in by what I do not mean and will not be at all impressed by any pose. So with them I lay all that aside, and appear as they know me to be. I say exactly what I think in the language that is most spontaneous and natural to me. Let me see, then, that the same naturalness is to be seen in my prayers. If my temperament is emotional, my prayers should be emotional; but if by temperament I am very matter-of-fact, what good would there be in my attempting to use the rapturous language of ecstasy?

The sooner I learn that I cannot fit myself into another's prayers, the better for my own peace of soul. They will either be too large or too small; in any case, they will only hamper my movements. Just as ready-made boots do not fit, so neither do ready-made prayers: the former blister the feet; the latter blister the soul.

Talk to God as you would to a friend

My prayers should therefore be my own, and I should ask only for what I honestly want. It is a mockery to ask God to take me to Himself if I cannot really say that I want to go; and it is a lie to speak of myself as the greatest sinner in the world if I know that I certainly am not.

Quite honestly, then, I will speak to God in prayer as a friend speaks with a friend. That at least will be my ideal, and I shall do nothing deliberately that conflicts with it. Am I, therefore, to cast aside all my prayer-books? Not at all. It is true that, as far as possible, I should endeavor to do without them, for surely my needs, my reasons for thankfulness, and the motives that I have for praising God should supply me with abundance of material for talking to Him. But undoubtedly, from time to time, I do find myself strangely silent; perhaps I am really only very tired. Still, it is helpful always to have a book, provided that we realize it to be merely a model and not the only way.

Yet even here, at these times when our hearts can say nothing from sheer weariness, or from whatever other cause, we should still keep to our test and use the privilege of friendship. For surely one chief way in which friends differ from acquaintances is that we can be silent with friends, but allow no pause in the conversation when we are with an acquaintance; should this last happen, we grow uncomfortable and cast about for something to talk about, but to be in the friend's presence is joy enough. Conscious of each other, we are content; walking side by side, we may say never a word, "make" no conversation; or sit, as on either side of the fireplace sit old cronies, speaking not at all, yet happy. For silence expresses things too large to be packed into language; and out of the fullness of the heart the mouth most often cannot speak. Hence, when I come to Communion, or make a visit to my Friend and find I have nothing to say, let me say nothing, be silent, wait for Him to speak, and at least be glad that I am near Him.

∞

Do not let distractions
discourage you from praying

It is a constant source of annoyance to find how full of distractions our best prayers become. Hardly have I settled down to my devotions, made the Sign of the Cross, and put myself in the presence of God, than I begin to find myself overwhelmed by endless thoughts that have no connection with my prayers. I suddenly wake to discover that my mind has been wandering along, considering all the businesses of my life, my anxieties, my hopes and ambitions. As soon as I am conscious of this, I go back to my prayers and endeavor once again to get into conversation with God. Nor shall I find, unless I am rather unusual, that even now I am really any safer than when I began; probably the whole time I am on my knees, my mind is practically occupied with the troublesome task of disengaging itself from thoughts it has no desire to consider.

At Mass or Holy Communion, it is possible that I have longer intervals of devout contemplation, but even during these sacred moments, souls who are really longing to love God with fervor and generosity are not seldom absolutely overborne by the inrush of distractions.

All this is troublesome and distressing to me, but that is all; it is troublesome and distressing, but not sinful, for sin implies a

Do not let distractions discourage you from praying

determination and deliberation that are here obviously absent. The only harmful result can be when I am so wearied by my incessant struggles, so impatient at the apparent emptiness of all my prayers, that I finally, in sheer disgust, give up the whole attempt, in the thought that I was not meant by God for this kind of exercise.

Now, although it is exceedingly troublesome to have to wage war thus endlessly throughout all my praying time, it is certainly not at all to be unexpected. From a purely natural point of view, from the physical aspect of it, it seems certain that once I put myself in a state of quietness and have no very definite movement to catch and hold my attention, all the deeper and noisier interests of my life will at once spring into renewed activity. I have silenced the outward clash and clamor of existence, and the persistent inward battle cries are bound to make themselves heard. I may have paid no attention to them, but they were there all the time — much as I lose the consciousness of the ticking of the clock, and only the ensuing silence reminds me that all the time it was really heard, but not attended to. Much in the same fashion, merely entering into church or kneeling quietly in my room, I am in reality allowing the repeating echo of my anxieties to be heard; all the interests of the day and the deeper mental impressions have been stored by that subconscious memory, which never forgets.

There is, then, nothing unexpected in all this, for it is the release of perfectly natural energies. And, what is more important, there is nothing sinful, for sin implies willfulness. Now, it is clear that whatever direct willfulness there is, whatever will there is, consists in the effort with which I endeavor to get back to my prayers; for the whole trouble of distractions is that they come of themselves, and involve no effort whatever. Distractions, therefore, are not ordinarily sinful, and only become so when, grown conscious of their presence, we deliberately pursue them.

Why, then, do distractions come to us from the evil one, if they are not sinful? To this we may best make answer by saying that they do not all come from the evil one, but arise quite simply from purely natural reasons such as we have already described. And they can be only indirectly traced to the Devil in the sense that the weakness of our mind is due to the effects of sin, original and actual sin. But, of course, every way of assault comes to the hands of the spirits of evil; and these may quite easily make use of distractions that are not in themselves sinful, for the effect of all these troublesome interruptions of prayer on souls timid and impatient is to make them inclined to give up prayer. They are a great source of discouragement, and whatever tends to depress the human spirit is the very best ally that the Devil can have. He counts on all this, and hopes that my impatience under them may do me a great deal of harm and spoil my efforts at a close union with God. My meditations, grown dull with distractions, will be omitted, my prayers become more seldom; and the food of my soul being denied it, my soul must starve.

I must, therefore, be patient under the cross and continue my devotions unfailingly; all the more persistently because of my very distractions, for my need of God's strength is greater. One good way of getting rid of distractions is, as soon as I am aware of them, to pray for that person or matter which causes them; if, despite this, the same trouble continues, I must resign myself to the good hands of God, and not lose hope in my efforts after faith and love.

∞

Learn to pray by
meditating on the Our Father

One day the Apostles made this request to our Lord: "Teach us how to pray."[99] Now, so many questions must have been put to Him that have not been recorded, that we are very grateful that this has been set down, for it gives us His whole answer.

But before coming to His words, let us just notice this: the Apostles do not ask Him to be taught prayers, but prayer. They do not say, "Teach us some prayers," but, "Teach us how to pray," which is obviously of infinitely more importance. It was just this view of things that our Lord Himself insisted on, for He does not reply to them by telling them to use a particular form of prayer. His words were, "*Thus* shalt thou pray," not, "*This* is what you must pray." That is, He simply confirms their own attitude, implied in their very particular question; He answers them that the particular words He was using were meant merely as a model.

Prayers may be most beautiful and most touching, but they are useless unless they are really intended. To repeat words is not all that is meant by prayer. The Apostles had numberless prayers in the Sacred Scriptures, such as David and the prophets had composed

[99] Cf. Luke 11:1.

under the inspiration of God; but they felt it was not prayers, but the attitude of the soul in prayer, that was most important to discover. Therefore, their request was not, "Teach us a new prayer," but, "Teach us how to pray." And our Lord's answer endorsed their supposition; not "This," but "Thus, shalt thou pray"; not "in these words," but "in this fashion."

This distinction is of great importance for us to realize. Our Lord never intended that we should merely learn by heart the Our Father and recite it day and night. No doubt it is very beautiful and very simple, and can be meant quite easily by anyone who cares to use it. But that is not the purpose (although it is one purpose) of His gift of it to us. He evidently desires that we should take it to pieces, study its composition, and make it the model of our conversation with Him and the Father.

Obviously, it is impossible for this to be done in this book, for it would require a great number of meditations to work through the whole and find the meaning of each carefully (because divinely) intended phrase. Moreover, the real benefit would be lost, for the true value would be appreciated only when we had done it for ourselves. I must study it carefully, petition by petition, noting the distinct meaning of the words, the arrangement of the order, and the gradual development of the ideas of fatherhood, and so forth.

But this much may perhaps be set down, on the understanding that we may use another's remarks on condition that we judge and reject them if they do not touch the personal note that dominates the harmony of our own lives. First, then, it is worthy of comment to observe how easy and conversational the Lord's Prayer is. There are no appeals to God, as though He required forms of address different from anyone else. Indeed, this prayer is little else than a series of remarks made by a child to his Father. The very want of connection between each petition, the staccato notes that mark off phrase from phrase, seem to suggest that it should be said very slowly, pausing after each group of notes to let their meaning and harmony echo to the base of the soul.

Then, again, it is also worthy of comment that the child does not at once think of himself or his needs, but turns instinctively to the excellence and greatness of his Father: "Hallowed be Thy Name." Without request or word of thanks, he raises his voice in praise, desirous only that this praise should ever more increase until the valleys of earth echo as gloriously with His greatness as do the hills of the heavenly country. Only when this is done does he turn to his own needs and venture to plead for their contentment; and even so, he makes no request for luxuries or high spiritual favors. Bread only does he require, his urgent, instant, daily need; and he does not soar above such an unromantic view of the life of the soul as supposes it only not to be led into temptation, but delivered from evil.

Lord, teach me also how to pray!

∝o

Contemplation means
watching and listening for God's voice

The form of prayer known as contemplation will no doubt sound too ideal, too far up in the clouds to be of any practical use to the ordinary individual. It has been so shut out from our ordinary notions of the sanctity required from men and women that the result has been that it is relegated in most people's mind to the cloisters. Contemplation! Oh yes, monks and nuns may contemplate, but not layfolk! That is the tyranny of a prejudice which is based on a misconception; for contemplation is an essential to all those who would live godly in Christ Jesus.

Prayer is too often robbed of all its effects, is reduced to hard-and-fast rules, is mapped out and labeled and regimented until it hardly seems at all to be the language of the heart. It becomes instead (and the elaborate instructions of so many books on mental prayer amply bear out this view) a highly artificial science, where notices meet us at every step, burly policemen in the guise of theologians bar our passage, and definite and well-ordered paths, macadamized and straight and uninteresting, stretch out in military fashion to the skyline. All adventure has gone, all the personal touches, and all the contemplation. We are too worried and harassed to think of God. The instructions are so detailed and insistent that we forget what we are trying to learn. As a consequence, we get bored, and so, no doubt, does God.

But to contemplate is perfectly simple; it is to gaze. The Egyptian statues seem crystallized in contemplation: they sit so silently after the fashion of the changeless East, with their hands upon their knees and their eyes fixed at a dead level, gazing far out into the even desert. The statues of Buddha, too, despite their gesture and their corpulence, and the self-satisfied air they usually suggest, have about them the sense of restfulness. They are still and contemplative. Even the writhing figure of the Crucified, stripped of all accidental dignity and composure, yet, by its hushed and brooding inertness, speaks of deep-souled peace. And we are sure that the prayer of our Master on the hillside by the lake or in the garden of Mount Olivet, for all its agony and its oppression at the near thought of death, was the still prayer of contemplation, the gazing with questioning yet patient eyes upon the infinite being of God.

This surely is prayer — an upraising of the heart through the mind, a speech with God such as friend with friend, or such as lover has with beloved when the mere sight and presence is enough to make glad the heart. It is prayer; but surely it is a far easier and more natural form than the overbusy and irritating attitude I try to take up toward my soul. " Martha, Martha, one thing alone is necessary; Mary has chosen the better part."[100]

To achieve this, I must begin by faith. It is only by true knowledge that I shall be led to gaze on God; it is only by an accurate acquaintance with Eternal Truth and Beauty that I shall be able to appreciate all that contemplation means. My mind, lit up by the truth of Revelation which the Church has taught me, is fixed upon some mystery or portion of a mystery. I try to think out the deep meaning of it, then reach the further end of all my knowledge, and wait before the Truth.

[100] Cf. Luke 10:42.

It will appear to me at first dimly, looming out from the darkness, where my own ignorance must leave it. Slowly, as I gaze, the details, unguessed, unnoticed, will appear, emerging against the more shadowed background. Across the distance, steals, perhaps, the fragrance of God; I can even hear the whisper of His voice. Gradually I find that there are inner meanings to all these sanctities of God, which come only to those who patiently await the unfolding of the seed of the kingdom.

All this is contemplation: not preludes, nor composition, nor colloquies, but the bare, naked truth, clearing in outline to the soul that is content to watch in silence at the feet of Christ. By faith, then, I learn from the Church the truths of God. These I understand in the sense in which she explains them. Then, with deep trust, I watch and listen for the voice of God.

∞

Silence enables you to hear God

Silence is no less necessary for those out of the cloister than for those within. For monks and nuns, it must, of course, be more rigorous, more material, if such an expression can be allowed for that of which the essence is the absence of matter; but for those who live in, but not of, the world, it must be no less faithfully kept. Nay, rather, because of the very rush and tumult of life, the need for it in the souls of those whose business it is to pass their days close to the humming and whirling machinery of existence is far more pressing and urgent.

Even physically, for such as have their time fully occupied, crowded with incident and crossed with the lives of so many others, there seems a recognized need for a break from time to time for perfect rest. The necessity of a sabbath, or day of rest, betokens how human nature cries for a lessening of the tension at least every now and then. We men whose lives are filled up with such activities that the whole being is riveted in fixed attention on our work, require moments, not simply of relaxation for amusement but also for mere and sheer silence. To be serious is even easier than to be amused and requires far less effort than to be amusing; hence, our very pleasures take their tithe of our energy and do not of themselves recreate the soul. For this recreation, as for creation itself, silence must precede speech; and out of the stillness alone, as of old, can leap the word.[101]

The soul, then, like the body, has need of silence, which is the necessary condition for recollection and contemplation. Such a silence as this means also the actual cessation of all distracting sights, sounds, and perceptions. It supposes as part of its essence a really physical silence (a contradiction in words, but not in ideas) as required for a few minutes daily, or at least from time to time during the week, for silence is the mother of thought. To talk is to expound, and to expound requires premeditated matter, and to meditate requires silence.

Am I not conscious very often how much I need this silence? Does it flash in upon me during my conversation that I am frequently making use of expressions and arguments that I cannot really justify and that do not seem fully to contain and bear out the construction I put upon them? I must admit that a very great deal that I pretend to take for granted has only a vague significance, hazy and incomplete. There is much that I dread being questioned about. Does not my soul loathe many of my crowded and jaded hours? My vapid and empty conversation — my endless gossip, the baldness of my ideas, the imitative nature of my remarks, the dull and platitudinous moralizing in which I so frequently indulge at the expense of others — repeatedly show, even from a human point of view, the need I have of thought, and therefore first of silence. Otherwise we become mere gramophones, grinding out the records composed by the labors of others.

I must be silent, therefore, that I may speak. But this, after all, is the lowest reason that can be urged; there is at least one other that is more commanding. I must be silent indeed so that I may speak, but silent also so that I may listen. If I am always talking, how can I hear what others are saying? Above all, how can I hear

[101] Cf. Wisd. 18:15.

the voice of God? He will make no effort to out-shout my own words, nor the clamor of life that I deliberately pursue: His is the still, small voice that is heard only when the whirlwind has passed.[102]

Now, it is of supreme importance to me to hear what God has to say, far more important than His hearing what I have to say. And just as, in prayer, it may well happen that I reproach God with never giving me His whispered counsel or comfort and yet never with my own persistent speech allow Him opportunity to get in a word edgeways, so it may well happen in life that I make no efforts to catch His voice. It is the still waters that are ruffled by the slightest breath of wind, and it is only the silent souls that hear the slightest whisper of God.

Yet the loss of all this to me! What marvelous opportunities perhaps came in my way, what needed advice, wisdom, and love were thrown away upon me! For I was so disturbed, fussy, noisy, that the Divine Word passed me by unheeded, deafened by the tumult of earthly things. Let me learn silence in my life, for God does not shout.

---

[102] 3 Kings 19:12-13 (RSV = 1 Kings 19:12-13).

∞

Music reflects the harmony of creation

The origin of music in historical times has always been traced to religion. There are endless myths in every form of primitive folklore that connect the two together and make the first musician a saint, a hero, or a god. Over this art, above all others, has been cast the romantic spell of divine worship, and this bears out the legend: that the earliest emergence of music is connected with ritual and associated with sacrifice. The tom-toms of the savage races, beaten to drown the cries of the victims, are thus reserved for the service of the gods, while their connection with war and military attacks is due only to the notion that battle is merely a vaster sacrifice than any other, and that the slaughter of men appeases the anger of God.

So, again, all the other arts have clustered around the sanctuary and the shrine, and have developed themselves in adorning these hallowed places. Painting, architecture, literature, and dancing have grown up under the shadow of religion; and in their exercise we recognize something of a divine inspiration. The idea seems to have been that, because God required none of the necessaries of life, He could be worshiped only with superfluities. The place where His glory dwelt was not really supposed to be a lodging-place, but only a local site where the majesty of His presence might, from time to time, make its appearance visible. It was beautified and made "lovely" because it had no need to be made comfortable: man builds his home for convenience, but his temple for honor. So, too, in its development of sacred music. Following the same historical idea, Christianity introduced a mystical origin to the organ when it placed St. Cecilia[103] as its inventor.

Nor is it to be wondered at that music should have come especially under the influence of religion. In the purpose of faith, or rather, in the structure of its machinery, there is an extraordinary parallel between it and the science of harmony, for music is, in a very marked way, a unification of distinct sounds.

The idea that underlies it is, quite simply, that there are seven separate notes that complete the tones of the voice, although, by means of arrangement, these may be variously sounded at a high or low pitch. Starting, therefore, from these seven, it arranges them in a definite order, but in endless combinations. It starts, that is to say, with difference, and achieves unity; out of seven it welds together harmony, and out of diversity constructs a chord. It is forever marrying what God has put asunder. It glories, not in the splintered colors of the rainbow, but in their perfect and harmonious concentration in pure white light.

Science, on the other hand, works by contrary principles: it deliberately sets out to find difference. Where the amateur sees only mere repetition and specimens monotonously alike, the specialist takes a positive delight in discovering new species and minute points of difference. His business is always to distinguish, to separate, to label. He has his knife forever ready to dissect. He plans for his museums his long line of cases that stretch out endlessly, and builds new wings in huge palaces to house his ever-increasing number of varieties. The type of mind that science generates is

[103] St. Cecilia, second- or third-century martyr and patron saint of musicians.

always inclined to grow less and less fond of the arts. Even when harmony continues to appeal, it is most often because it notes the differences that are united, not the unity of the differences.

Now, it is just here that music finds in religion its old ally, for the purpose of religion is to gather together all the isolated phenomena of the universe and fit them into a single scheme. It takes up the broken pieces of a shattered world and places them, as a child does his puzzle, to form a perfect picture. It gathers up the fragments that remain to fill to overflowing the baskets of the soul's food. For religion, which insists absolutely on the unity of God, preaches also in consequence the unity of the world. There is no chance in life, no haphazard; but all is directed by a Supreme Providence toward a supreme goal. All human life, whether the individuals or the whole race or the continued details of individual experience, is not a separate accident, but part merely of a larger scheme: for Divine Power, Wisdom, and Love created the world and order it.

Religion, therefore, fronts the world, and facing also its manifold differences and variations, yet sees it as the seamless garment of God. It takes up from the single standpoint of the Divine Maker and Controller of all things such an attitude to life, that joy and pain, failure and success, good hope and ill, find themselves one in Christ.

Music, then, makes appeal to me by preaching its gospel that out of variety and difference is achieved the harmony of creation. It mirrors for me the world, and I see God in the center of the orchestra of the universe, beating time and keeping together every form of music. "Even that vulgar and tavern music which makes one man merry and another mad, strikes in me," said old Sir Thomas Browne, "a deep fit of devotion and a profound contemplation of the First Composer."

∞

The Liturgy unites all
members of the Church

It is the work of Christ to complete, through the direct teaching of the Holy Spirit, His preached Gospel. Scripture thus in the main tells us what to do, but not how to do it. Scripture gives us the sacraments, but the Church adds their formularies, prayers, and setting. Scripture most often shows us the spirit; the Church describes the body in which that spirit is lodged. Thus it is that she is denounced by her enemies as something formal, whereas she is but the outward and visible sign of an inward, invisible grace. Because her children are not souls merely, but men, she has to give them not God only or some gifts divine, but all that is sacred tabernacled in its incarnation.

So, too, prayer must be a natural, spontaneous act. It must be the free talk between friends, between God and myself. Nor, indeed, is there anything on earth so free as prayer; even the air is only "a chartered libertine." To taste of the joy of life, to feel its rush of pleasure in the springtime, to know all that is meant in the sheer ecstasy of existence, to take delight in some flower or fruit, to be alive in the sunshine, to experience the relief when duty has been done, or the pleasurable sensation when we have been generous, or to have found once again a friend — all this is perfect prayer, prayer unspoken, but fully expressed. But prayer must be of endless variety to suit our endless need. Sometimes it must be formless, for our whole sensations cannot be formally represented; but sometimes also it must take on forms — the stiff, brocaded dignity of life; for these, too, are human, no less worthy of God because they are wholly the work of man. Those who wish to pray always without form often end by praying not at all.

There are, then, certain formal prayers that are also required by the nature of man; the Psalms, the Canticles, and the Our Father represent the Scriptural use of this kind of prayer, and the lives of good and holy men have very frequently closed with verses of these upon their lips. Savonarola[104] and St. Francis sang the Psalms; and as He chanted the twenty-first psalm, the Master on the Cross bowed His head and died. There can be, therefore, no objection to the mere fact of formal prayers.

Acting, then, on the inspiration of the same Spirit through whom the Scriptures themselves became the Word of God, the Church composed her Liturgy. In this, as in the biblical prayers, it is worthy of note that the main method is the prayer of praise. It is this precisely that suffers least from being formalized, since we praise God, not for what is in us and therefore changing, but for what is in Him and therefore unchanged. Hence, these can have, without any danger, the impersonal touch that formal prayer must always exhibit. In the Gloria, we have a very good example of what is meant.

This language can be common to the wide world; and since the Liturgy of the Church is intended exactly for the devotion of a congregation, it must be composed to suit the mass rather than the individual. It is always, therefore, general rather than particular and, consequently, has practically no danger of becoming stilted. For this reason, accordingly, the Liturgy of the Church is the one

---

[104] Girolamo Savonarola (1452-1498), Italian Dominican reformer.

exception to the rule that prayer, in order to be really meant, should be spontaneous. This, while on the whole true for the individual, is false for mankind generally.

We should, therefore, although there is no compulsion in the matter, be eager to follow the Liturgy, by understanding its own words. We become, in this way, united to the Church Catholic of all tongues, ages, and climes. We find our faith becoming stronger and less timid when it feels itself one with such countless numbers. The sense of isolation, of dwelling as strangers in a foreign land, is lost when we grow conscious at Mass or Benediction or at the reception of any of the sacraments, that we are bridging over all times and places. All the world over, what we see and hear and are saying is being witnessed by others besides ourselves. We are not lonely travelers toiling after some lost trail, but a huge army, whose uniform and whose battle songs are the traditions of our race. We enter into the inheritance of all the saints.

All that is best in literature, art, and religion is swept up and gathered into one — the wonder of the Mass, the depth of the Psalms, the night prayer of Compline, the radiance of the office of Prime, the consoling tenderness of the Office for the Dead. Here Hebrew, Greek, and Latin are like three solemn kings who bring their gifts to Christ. Out of all nations have come the creators and preservers of the Liturgy, and these bring with them the spirit and the genius of their own peoples. All find there some lot or part in the magnificent yet simple services, the curious, often now unmeaning rubrics that speak as relics of bygone cultures and civilizations, the cumbersome classicalism of Byzantium, the decadent paradox of Carthage, the fantastic interpretations of Alexandria. Yet not only the past is mirrored there, but the present: "French lucidity and German depth, the ordered liberty of England, the flaming heart of Spain."

Part 11

∞

Studying your Faith

∞

Learn how to read the Scriptures

Although, for a Catholic, there is much other teaching than can be found in the Scriptures, these are the written Word of God. He is their author, in the sense that He inspired the thoughts and fashioned them into language, while He adapted to His purposes the personal and contemporary circumstances of the human scribe.

But it is obvious that there are many passages, indeed whole chapters, that seem to have nothing to say that is likely to be at all helpful to us. We can read through descriptions of the tabernacle, with the detailed injunctions as to how every part of it is to be constructed, and yet feel, when all is finished, that we have learned nothing at all that can be said to carry warmth to our souls. So, again, the long lists of warring captives and the settled estates of the several tribes leave us cold. Yet we are bidden to search the Scriptures, for there is to be discovered the enlightenment that God wishes to shed upon His people.

The trouble probably comes because we make the mistake of supposing the Bible to be a book. It is not a book, but a literature. Each separate portion has to be understood in the light of its own meaning, and we cannot, therefore, suppose that each chapter or each book will be equally illuminating or even illuminating at all. Although all must be treated with reverence, not all need be read.

In fact, we may suppose that, as each part of the Bible has its different human author, with his own different style and different message, so each part will also appeal differently to different souls. Merely to take the various commentaries written by various hands is to see clearly the totally different concept that each writer brings to his study of the Scriptures.

We have, therefore, to single out the particular part from which we can manage to learn most. Solidly to read through the whole text would not be conducive to much profit, and, since the Scriptures were written for our instruction, it would be foolish to continue what experience tells us will give us no benefit. For the majority, therefore, it will be the New Testament that will be the most frequently and hopefully used.

I must try to understand the purpose for which each book was written, the audience for which it was intended, and the point of view that governed the selection of certain portions of the sacred history and the omission of other portions. For this, again, there are various introductions and aids to the study of the Bible.

I must study carefully, if I really wish to make the Bible my own; not, indeed, in detail, but the main lines of the writer's intentions, what he chiefly wishes to prove or to emphasize. This must precede my meditation, if my meditation is to be intelligent. It means some trouble on my part, but once I have taken the pains to understand even a little, I shall find that the interest will grow and that there will follow constant food for my soul.

I should read just enough to provide myself with a thought for the day, in no hurry to get to the end of the incident or parable, but calmly stopping at some sentence or phrase that brings with it a sudden illumination.

Then I can afford to put aside all other books of meditation and prayer and cleave to the Word of God, consulting, from time to time, some work of doctrinal exposition, lest my own interpretation err in any way.

Learn how to read the Scriptures

But the staple food shall be the New Testament, for there is none that can be better for my soul. No better advice, no more healing comfort, no more piercing devotion can be found than in the life of the Master. It may take me long to find that volume alone sufficient for my spiritual life, but that should be the ideal toward which I climb.

∞

God speaks to you in the Scriptures

The Scriptures are the inspired Word of God, the written testimony left to man of the nature of God's being and of His Providence in the governance of the world. In the Old Testament, we have the record of His dealings with the human race, particularly of His action toward the Hebrew people, and of His gradual unfolding to them, by successive revelations, His unity, power, wisdom, and love. By details of historical fact, which, in some cases, are intermixed with doctrinal meaning, we learn the story of Creation, of the Fall, of the chastisements that in consequence hardened men's lot on earth, of the Deluge, of the call of Abraham, and of the prophetic announcement of the Messiah to come, the expected of the nations.

Now, it is possible that the knowledge of some of those historical facts may have been learned by the sacred authors from contemporary documents, the baked-clay cylinders or inscriptions of which the last generations made such wonderful discovery. Certainly at times we have definite references given by the writers in the Scriptures to court chronicles, on which, obviously, their own accounts are based; and one such writer describes his volume as the laborious abbreviation of the records of his time.

There is, then, nothing harmful in saying that biblical inspiration does not mean that the ideas or materials for the construction of the works were infused directly by God. They may or may not have been. But at any rate, it would be quite sufficient if God simply illumined the judgment of the inspired writer as to which facts he was to single out for record, and which particular version of them he was in the main to follow. He may at times have been really little else than an editor of another's work; as Baruch may be the inspired writer of the Lamentations of Jeremiah. The inspired writer is moved in his intelligence to judge, and in his will to cause to be set down, the exact wording that God desired.

In the New Testament, God made a full and new revelation of Himself. It was no longer the gradual process that had been a real addition in revelation, but an immediate and full revelation that should yet contain seeds of truth whose development might take centuries for their full growth. The shrine of this revelation was twofold: the living tradition of the Church and the New Testament. Between them, every fragment of the teaching of Christ has been preserved for the race. Neither alone suffices, but they need to be supplemented by each other.

And here, again, it is necessary to notice that scriptural inspiration does not necessitate the infusion of fresh knowledge into the mind of the writer solely by the direct intervention of God. Much of the Gospels was known personally to the writers; and they may even have made some use of a primitive record, written or orally preserved among the Christians. At any rate, there is much in the Scriptures that, while being inspired, need not be revealed.

Thus, when St. Paul says that he left his cloak at Troas,[105] did God reveal this to him while he sat and composed or dictated his epistle? We do not know whether it was revealed or not. Of this only are we certain, that it need not have been. It would certainly have sufficed had St. Paul remembered merely by natural memory, perhaps even at the prompting of a fellow laborer, where he had

[105] 2 Tim. 4:13.

last had his cloak. There would have come a light into his judgment illuminating him as to what to set down, and an impulse in the will causing him to set it down in writing. And that is all that is meant by inspiration. So, again, the rising or setting of the sun is not taught as a revealed dogma, but the writer was inspired by God to use that particular expression.

But for our purposes, it is necessary only to realize that the Bible is intended as a literature of moral and doctrinal teaching. It is a literature and not a single book; that is to say, it is made up of parts that, to be understood, must be interpreted in the sense in which they were written. It would be foolish to take poetry as literally as prose, nor should I be surprised if, in a professed abridgment, statements should occur seemingly contradictory, since the space was not sufficiently ample to allow for a full explanation. Therefore, it is of the first importance that I should find the purpose that lay behind the author's mind and his object in composing, or the circumstances that inclined him to insert this and omit that.

Secondly, not only have I to realize the intention of the human author, but I have also to bear in mind that the Divine Author had His own vaster designs in the composition of the work. He saw before Him all those people and occasions whence comfort, or help, or perplexity were to arise; and for them, for me, the whole was issued. Just as I can say that God died for me, so as truly can I say that for me, too, for my instruction, were the whole Scriptures composed; for my moral and doctrinal enlightenment were these several books inspired; in them am I to find the teaching my soul needs. Particularly is this true of the New Testament, wherein I can see the record of that perfect life that is to be the model of my own. In language simple and full of force, which has formed the meditation and consolation of numberless souls, this life has made men and women devoted to their fellows. Above all, it should lift me up to a union with Him where I can be buried in His love.

Make time for spiritual reading

I cannot hope to keep my soul alive unless I continually give it the food that it needs. Read I certainly do, at all times and in all places. And the purpose of all this reading must be not merely to fill in certain barren moments of the day (although this also has become a convincing reason for much reading), but to furnish myself with information and with the principles whereby to judge the various movements, policies, and gospels that are preached by others or practiced by myself.

What, then, is the ordinary matter that comes into my hands for this purpose? Presumably it is very largely that form of literature which can be grouped under the heading of journalism, whether newspapers, periodicals, or such novels as follow simple lines and require little mental activity for their comprehension. I buy the newspaper that advocates the political principles that appear to me the most expedient. I accept its account of what happens in the national life and read the story of my country from the point of view that it has taken up and with the interpretation that it supplies.

Now, this is not blind and unreasoning obedience, for I have chosen my paper to begin with in order to suit my politics. Yet there is this peril attached: that imperceptibly the atmosphere of my reading begins to influence me on points on which I was not originally at one with my party. I notice others becoming the slaves of their press. Unconsciously I am probably moving in the same direction.

Is this wrong? It is not so much wrong as foolish, and not so much foolish as (if I so continue) inevitable. For if I limit my reading to one particular view of life, it is certain that I shall get narrowed in my thoughts and visions. I am living in the provincial circle of my family ideas and cannot rise to criticize them or even measure and control them. This is obviously full of danger, for I am, in effect, handing over (indirectly) my conscience to another's keeping and making no use of any other lights that may possibly be shed upon fact and fancies.

Must I, therefore, force myself to read what is written by the side opposite to me in temper, in policy, and in principle? To do so would probably be stimulating, but it is not necessary, for there is another way that is simpler and more effective, and that is to resort to the principles upon which the whole of life must be faced by Christians. I should recall to myself those views of conduct which are part of the Christian inheritance, and learn to measure things by the values that Christian Tradition puts on them. In other words, I shall find my soul kept freer and fresher by a systematic reading of spiritual books. It is by this literature that I shall be prevented from accepting too readily and too wholeheartedly the political and social programs of my leaders. I shall realize that there are definite standards of judgment that otherwise I may carelessly forget or pass over as of small consideration.

Perhaps I feel inclined to cry out that spiritual reading is dull and uninteresting. It is so just because I so rarely indulge in it. The whole tendency of my day is toward things that are material. I have very probably to work for my living, or at least have much to occupy my time, various little duties and cares that absorb my energy and my interest. Consequently, I get more and more immersed in things that are merely earthly, and I find it increasingly difficult to lift myself out of the clinging embrace of these necessary but lower interests.

Now, the very fact that I experience this difficulty makes all the more essential my attention to the spiritual life; for if I am wholly steeped in things temporal, there can be little wonder that I lose my relish (an appropriate word) for things eternal. I must, therefore, seriously consider how much of my time is given to taking in a store of spiritual thoughts, the solid and sublime principles to which I can cling in all my perplexities of thought or action.

Do I have by me a book that I find helpful? I should not force myself to peruse volumes that make no appeal and have no sympathetic views to attract me; but I should take some book, such as describes a character that appears to me real, living, and, although immensely above my own, of some kindred significance. Taking such a biography or any other work that depicts the spiritual side of life, that talks of the soul and God and the things of God, let me think over it and follow it. It will at least give me a chance. Novels, papers, and so forth may be necessary at times, but they cannot be necessary all the time.

∞

Follow a method in your reading

It is generally obvious that we cannot hope to retain our faith unless we habitually practice spiritual reading. The whole trend of everything we read (and nowadays we read everything) is not, perhaps, opposed to the existence of the supernatural world, but certainly ignores it. Literature, therefore, on the whole, while it appeals to the nobler needs of man as a natural fact in the universe, neglects all those finer emotions of the soul that depend for their origin and their encouragement on actual doctrines requiring authoritative interpretation. These obviously are entirely at the mercy of the writer, who, with a fine disregard for all infallibility save his own, lays down as the conclusions of modern science whatever first principles his temperament inclines him to accept. Of course, modern science "concludes" nothing at all that in any way encroaches on morality or religion, for in these two regions, it remains in the hesitating attitude of expectancy.

But the result of these self-elected pontiffs is to impress those whose intelligences are even less active than their own with the finality of all modern teaching. The definitions of these popes gain credence by sheer repetition; and since the whole literary world is alive with them, there is a grave danger of our drifting heedlessly into the ranks of their adherents. For, although spiritual reading is really essential to us, it cannot form the only reading in which we indulge; nor, indeed, would it be healthful for most of us to ignore contemporary literature, however tainted, nor contemporary journalism, however noisily material.

First, however, it is essential that we should settle with ourselves the method of our reading. This is probably very much haphazard, based on no system, without any critical acumen, and, therefore, reaping hardly any of the immense benefit that might easily be gathered from the literary harvest. In a letter to a young man who had sought his advice, Lacordaire writes: "By reading as you do at random, without aim or order, you are losing valuable time, and, what is more, you are getting yourself out of the way of real work, which is a great misfortune for the mind." It is this rebuke that we must perpetually, in the interests of our soul and of the more spiritual faculties of our mind, put to ourselves as necessary to perfection. We browse in all the fields; but we browse so carelessly that we have nothing left with which to "chew the cud."

We ought, on the other hand, when we approach any classic, for example, to have some notion of the author's antecedents, to be able to appreciate life's problems from the particular angle from which he saw them, and to notice how his hopes or his perplexities developed or grew less; in other lesser books, with flippant novels and "light" articles, there is also a great deal to be found if we have the patience to look for it; but it will not disclose itself without some difficulty, at any rate, at the commencement. Only with the sweat of our brow will the bread of mind and body be earned and deserved. In the kingdom of the pen there are no "idle rich."

There is, secondly, the actual material of our reading, the matter as well as the method. Here, of course, advice is cheap and probably impertinent, certainly useless. Some have bidden us feed on nothing but "the food of giants"; but this is wholly impossible, for who are the giants? Is my neighbor their judge? Then he must have measured the others and found them to be wanting; and if it is given to him to decide, why not to me? His experience has been greater? Then at least give me a chance to extend my own.

Perhaps the only advice that is worth giving (for it will assuredly be acted on whether given or not) is to read just what we honestly feel inclined to read. Of course, books that our conscience revolts from should certainly be laid aside; but apart from this moral censorship, it would appear that hardly any lists can be drawn up by others that will be so serviceable as the lists we draw up for ourselves. Let me put down only those books that, from my interest in author or subject, or from what reviews or quotations I have read, do really make an appeal to me.

Probably the amount of my reading and its variety will never harm me, so long as I have some sort of method. If I can be deliberate in my method, the matter may well be left to look after itself. Such a wide selection is now open to me that I should be able to benefit myself by the richer experience of others, and the glimpses they afford of beauties that I must train my eyes to find. Thus can I harvest the full fields of past and present; otherwise I shall live beyond my intellectual means, venturing upon work that requires more than my capital allows. My thoughts and counsel will grow more glib but less efficacious, for I shall have used up my store of experience, and we do not further need to be reminded of our duty in submitting to the ruling of legitimate authority banning certain books or classes of books.

∾

Use the gift of reason to study the Faith

As the intellect is man's highest natural faculty, its exercise should be his chief concern. The distinction we make between human and brute nature depends for its expression on the difference between intelligence and instinct; on the employment, on the one hand, of the reasoning faculty, and the following, on the other, of a spontaneous suggestion, which is *ex hypothesi* uncontrolled.

In fact, we may even more briefly explain this difference by noting to what extent self-control enters in. Man has this particular power; the animal has not, for to control instinct is the work of deliberation, and deliberation itself supposes reason. A man is so much higher, therefore, in the scale of his humanity according as he is able to have complete dominion over himself. The perfect man alone has the full lordship of himself. This, no doubt, is finally achieved by his will; but the will itself must be subject to the reason.

Consequently, since man is man in virtue of his reason, he has the declared duty of exercising and training that reason. It is his essential faculty, his proper distinguishing mark, the very condition of his free will; his responsibility for its stewardship is accordingly his most important burden. And because, left to itself, it tends to lose its force or grow out of its healthy form, man is morally obliged to study as best he can; he cannot afford to allow his highest talent to lie idle. It is incumbent on me, then, because I am a creature; it is part of the law of my nature to exercise by study the faculty of my reason, to sharpen it by use, to develop its keenness. Every human faculty unused gets atrophied, and reason, as we know, is as subject to this process of deterioration as any other. Because I am a man, I must study; not read necessarily, but think.

Now, again, it is equally obvious that a certain value in my study will be due to the actual thing studied. It cannot be a matter of indifference to me what I eat, for not only should I consider the pleasure of my palate, but I should take into account my state of health, the season of the year, my immediate needs, and ten thousand other things. Since I must feed my mind, too, I must take care that the food is of such a nature as will benefit my reason, for alas, my mind as easily as my body may be hurt by poison. It is necessary for me, therefore, not only to exercise my intelligence, but to exercise it on fitting material.

It may be stated generally that everything that tends to refinement of thought tends also to the perfection of the mind. Whatever science or art may make most appeal, along whatever line we choose to develop in some one art or science, so long as we are serious and thorough, we can hardly go astray. It is true that "culture" may yet fall into brutality, and, turned to base uses, become a thing abhorred by God and man; but long before that, it has ceased to be "culture." It has somehow taken up principles opposed to the teaching of Christ, to the moral enactments of His gospel. It has ceased, in other words, to be culture at all. For culture need imply no learning, no power of quotation, no incisive criticism; it means only the appreciation of the higher, finer, nobler side of life. That is why, in its truest and deepest sense, it is a safeguard against sin, for its whole tendency is to set the soul above merely gross or sensual or petty temptations. The chief point, then, is that the material on which we choose to sharpen our intelligence must be of such a kind as shall not spoil its keenness or its cleanness.

Yet although, on the whole, study opposes sin, it is patent from experience that scholars have often been narrow, vain, and even bestial. But that is more often due, not to scholarship, but to pedantry; not to the education that they should have received, but to the information that alone was given them. They learned to distinguish between material essences, but the fine temper of literature perpetually eluded them. The age of specialism, with all its wonderful results, makes this also even more likely. Each in his narrow groove forever laid is tempted to ignore every other science but his own. The author of the monograph may be also the monomaniac; he is so steeped in his own particular material that its taste and aroma clings to him even when he mixes with other men. He has "the fixed idea"; whereas sanity is one of the chief ingredients of sanctity.

I must, then, above all and through all, keep hold of faith; for that, since it deals with God, deals with the highest and most universal cause. It lifts man up out of his petty little circle and makes him survey with Catholic vision the whole wide world. It lessens the estimate that he may have of his own stock of learning as though it contained the treasures of the world. The study of God would have preserved scholars against those petty ambitions and faults that have ruined them. It would have given a touch of immortality to the fleeting achievements of man.

My reason, then, because of my dignity as a human soul, must be put to its highest use. I cannot let it run idly, but I need not read much. It will be enough if I think, especially if I think of God.

Educating yourself in the Faith
means applying its truths in your life

To educate is, as the Latin origin of the word implies, to draw out; it does not mean to pour in. Education and information are not the same things, nor should they ever be confused. To acquire knowledge means merely to absorb into our mental store a large amount of facts. Even to retain such a knowledge, with the facts set in the right order and related to each other as causes or effects or occasions, may signify nothing more than a wonderful power of memory. It may be, indeed, a means of education. Thus, people are often described as being well educated, when they are merely well informed. To have read enormously and to be able to quote bits of classical authors may or may not be helps to education; in themselves, these things are certainly not education.

We cannot say of a man that his historical education has been completed when he has acquired a large list of dates and names, and can even draw maps; nor would the knowledge of a single period necessarily imply education. Even to have collected all this material, and to have fanned the imagination into flame with the grandeur and humor of the detailed past, and to have made the reason follow a whole chain of causes and effects in the prolonged account of some movement in history, do not constitute historical education, unless there has been produced in the mind a corresponding reaction. For education is not to pour in, but to draw out.

Education, then, to be worthy of the name, means that I have found in my soul all sorts of unexplored regions, tendencies, principles, yearnings, instincts, and desires, hitherto unrealized and undeveloped. They lay there, dumbly felt, beating vainly against the bars of my soul, but utterly unable to give an account of themselves or to express themselves intelligently. They had found no language, were obscure; but by dint of training, I find the meaning of myself and so of all the world. The huge, clumsy progress of the race, which we set out in scientific order under the name of history, may help me; the intricacies of translation, the beauties of art; but these are of no use until something within me has responded to their call. Thus, Socrates went about asking questions, getting his hearers to understand their own thoughts and to take the trouble to search the meaning of the words most frequently on their lips.

Hence, too, religious education must be something after that fashion, if it is to justify its own name. Lists of Hebrew kings, lists even of Commandments, Beatitudes, deadly sins, and sacraments, are not education in themselves. The knowledge of them may make us learned in our Faith, which is a good thing in itself; but a true religious education must be discovered in the heart and developed, not poured into it from outside. Frequently in Catholic schools, the children who get the prizes are not the ones who most live their Faith afterward. Hence, to repeat, education, religious or otherwise, is deeper than mere information.

I must, therefore, realize that religious education has no age limits. I cannot suppose that, because I have passed from school or college, my education has thereby finished. The principles, the direct guiding lines of life, ought to have been taught me from a consideration of myself. But that is merely the beginning of miracles. From that, I must set out through all my days developing what is within me, trying to grasp the meaning of the motions of my soul.

Thus, my education will cease only with life — if, indeed, it will cease even then: shall I not through all eternity be discovering with unending surprise the depths and heights of my own created nature? The Beatific Vision means surely a more intimate knowledge, not of God only, but, in consequence, of myself also.

This education of mine must be effected by reading, by writing (at least for my own benefit, and for making my ideas more clear), by conversation, and above all by contemplation. To find the meaning of faith, I must look within; the truth of the doctrine and its most accurate expression I shall learn from the Church, but its value I must learn from myself. I must examine under the light of infallible authority my own longings, hopes, and aspirations, and find them answered or explained in the Creed. I must not only absorb the articles of the Faith and be able to repeat them, but must discover them hinted at and suggested by my own human nature. For the light of God "enlighteneth every man that cometh into the world"[106] — not, indeed, as though Catholic doctrine could be achieved by mere natural knowledge, but because my soul itself has been supernaturalized.

[106] John 1:9.

Part 12

∞

Self-discipline

∽

Christianity calls for self-denial

It seems a pity that ordinarily both the defense and the rejection of fasting are based on the simple lines of health. No doubt these should control the amount of fasting, for we have to take care of our bodies as things given to us by God. But fasting is not prescribed because it is good for our health (although it may be), nor is it to be rejected because it is bad for our health (although that also may be a perfectly proved result). These considerations must affect, and affect seriously, our practice of fasting, but fasting itself is based upon a far higher law — namely, the principle of penance preached by our Lord.

It must never be forgotten that the revelation of Christ did not come to us in order to enable us to lead happier lives in every way; our pathway may or may not be smooth. But in any case, it is foolish to suppose that religion has as its object to make us healthy, to keep us fit, and to do all the other wonderful things that the so-called "muscular Christian" perpetually promises. No doubt it is perfectly true that a good-living man is likely to be in a very fit state of health, but the trouble is when this fit state of health is made the test of a good life, for following on this line comes the axiom that everything that is detrimental to us must be at once given up. The half-truth that lies behind this saying is really obvious, but it cannot be formulated so roughly. Rather, we should remember that, in our following of Christ, we are taught that the daily cross is a mark both of our love and of His; and the daily cross must surely be something that demands a sacrifice from us. To surrender to God something that costs us nothing can hardly be said to be after the model of Christ.

We have, therefore, to deny ourselves with a denial hardly less effective or brutal than Peter's denial of Christ. Now, I am constituted of body and soul, and of both I must pay tithes to the Lord. Both must feel the effects of this denial, for I cannot be said to deny myself unless it is something so thorough and effective that my whole being makes its sacrifice. Undoubtedly the soul is of even greater value than the body, and, of the two, its sacrifices are the more pleasing to God, for its self-seeking is more harmful than the other. The sins of the flesh never received from our Lord so severe a castigation as sins of the spirit, no doubt because they are less dishonorable, profaning a less worthy vessel. It was the failings of the Pharisee — cant, hypocrisy, and pride — that were far more the subjects of our Lord's displeasure; the ruin they effected was greater and seemed unlikely to be detected by those who suffered from them.

Yet the soul alone can hardly represent the man, and just as body as well as soul must worship God in genuflections and prostrations, so must body as well as soul deny itself for Christ. The parallel of sacrifice and worship is indeed complete, for both oblige only when possible. And this is the key to our attitude on fasting: a conscious recognition of the due mortification to which my whole being must submit. No one part of me must escape, and so for the body we have the whole series of penances that are grouped under the heading of fasting, the acts of self-denial that bring under subjection all the wayward and restless desires of the flesh.

Assuredly there are times and conditions of life when fasting becomes impossible. And the Church herself allows for this fact by her own principle of fixing the age limit before which no one is bound and after which the obligation ceases. She implies, at least, that certain forms of bodily self-denial are at certain times of life imprudent; indeed, the whole tendency of all the commandments of the Church is only to impose them when possible. It follows, therefore, that, once it can be ascertained that it is morally impossible for me to fast, for me the personal obligation at once ceases. Yet even so, it must be insisted upon that the reason to be alleged for this dispensation from fasting is not that the body suffers, but that it suffers in such a way as to prevent other duties from being performed; the mere fact that physically I feel weakened is no bar at all. The following headache and so forth are certainly to be expected; and, indeed, it would seem as though these very things were the reason for the fasting being prescribed. But the sufficient motive for being dispensed by the circumstances of the case can only be that my physical weakness will not allow me to fulfill certain other obligations incumbent on me.

It is, then, simply a question; not that fasting puts me to inconvenience — that is what it is intended to do — but it puts me to such inconvenience that other things that it is my duty to perform cannot be properly done. It is the recognition of the crossing of one law by a higher law, the duty of the particular form of self-denial being forbidden by the duty of a certain way of life. Hence, really I have to renounce fasting, not for reasons of health, but for the more perfect following of Christ.

Let love underlie your self-denial

The self-denial of Christ has been made a law for His children. We cannot call ourselves His followers unless we make up our minds to follow, and to follow means quite definitely to take up our cross. Hence, penance becomes a necessity of the Christian life. The whole New Testament rings with this idea. The Gospels show it in action from the Incarnation to the Passion and death. And the letters of St. Paul formulate that example in words that are still striking and arresting. There the Cross is exalted with a vehemence of language that is astonishing in its freshness, and the Crucified Figure is, as indeed he asserts, the central thesis of all his exhortations.

In the acts of the early martyrs, and in the Liturgy of the Church, it is not at all infrequent to find the term *athlete* applied to those who fought so strenuously for an incorruptible crown. Perhaps the idea of employing such a word came from the persistent metaphor of the same St. Paul; he is always turning to the great public games for his comparisons of the New Dispensation. Time after time, he speaks of the training necessary for the fight, of the splendid lure that the prize gives to everyone entering the lists, of the stern necessity for all who so enter not to play with their rivals in halfhearted fashion as though idly beating against the nonresisting air, of the steadfastness and courage required, and of the ultimate reward, itself exceeding great.

Through the Middle Ages, the same metaphor lingered at least as a literary habit. Nor is the notion at all fantastic, for we can quite readily suppose that the whole of life can be divided between the training and the race, the long days of preparation interspersed with intermittent struggle.

Now, it is just under the idea of training that the true concept of mortification is to be found. It is not the end of life, but the means of achieving the end of life. It is not sought for in itself, but because it is necessary in order to attain that faith and hope and love which it is the purpose of our creation to secure. Hence, to those who are at all perplexed over the limits that prudence should set to austerity, it is simpler to make answer that it is essential in itself, but that the particular form it takes must depend entirely on our personal circumstances.

Necessary to the Christian in some way, mortification or austerity may exist in varying forms and degrees, which must be gauged to be prudent or not according to the extent they help us or hinder the fulfillment of the Christian ideal. Its whole justification is that it comes as a preparation, leading up to greater things. It is, in fact, merely the training for the athletic arena of the New Law; and just as it is possible, by choosing a foolish system, or by exaggerating the limits laid down, or by not paying them sufficient attention, to unfit the body and mind for a contest in the games, so also, because I mortify myself unwisely, too much or too little, the whole effect of my labors may be to unfit me altogether for an exact following of Christ.

Now, it may not unfairly be said that the limits of training begin where the needs of life end, and the needs of life end when training begins. Training, therefore, is busied with what is above the margin of decent livelihood. Supervision is to be exercised only over the luxuries, not the essentials.

Hence, I can at once find a ready rule by which to measure my mortifications. I can mortify myself in things of the flesh and things of the spirit only just so far as the things I curtail are not necessary. Once I come upon what is needful to my life (not to life in general, but to *my* life), then I have reached the extreme boundary of penance, and further I need not go. It is, then, very largely a personal matter dependent on my health and work; consequently, it is extremely variable, and I must be prepared to speed up and slack off according as my needs determine. Consequently no one is so fit to judge these for me as I am for myself; indeed, others can judge only according to the information and evidence I myself provide.

Hence, when I put my case to others, I have probably already prejudged it for myself, and they can hardly do more than ratify my own opinion; thus I do not gain any real confirmation by referring the matter to them because I suppose myself to be biased. I cannot help describing my state as I judge it to be. But in the whole trouble of it, I must remember that beneath it all must be love.

The life of Christ — above all, His death — can find no rational solution except in love, for in suffering as such, God can take no pleasure. But love that denies itself for love, is love such as we know it to be, and such as our hearts have found to be a law of their own movements. The self-denial, then, that is commanded us is incomplete without that final call, "Follow me." It is that perfect form that beckons and gives heart and life to all creation's toil. The putting away of my own will profits me nothing without charity, and charity suffers all things.

Christ gives meaning to suffering

God sends us suffering because He loves us; we accept suffering because we love Him. Love is the only answer that can be made to suffering; it is the only explanation of suffering save that of the Christian Scientist, who denies that suffering really exists. Either it has no real meaning, or its meaning is love.

One set of pagan philosophers, with very noble ideals and with the desire of lifting human nature above itself, tried to make man impervious to suffering. It taught that suffering was stoically to be borne with, for everything that was disagreeable to man was virtuous. The Epicureans, on the other hand, taught man to escape from suffering, saying that it was degrading and debasing to him, since everything pleasurable was alone worthy of the name of virtue.

The Christian alone teaches that suffering is to be embraced. This idea is based upon the fatherhood of God and the story of the Incarnation, for it supposes that the father only allows such suffering to come to each child as shall be for his own good. Naturally, God could have prevented it altogether, but in His wise Providence, He has not done so; consequently, we are driven to assert as the ground claim of faith that it can only exist because Wisdom and Love and Power are one. We are really as children whom the world's toys have led astray, and who, when scratched or hurt in our play, run back for comfort to His arms. It is not, therefore, simply as a punishment that we should look on suffering, for such a view of it will add more troubles than it can answer. Suffering is also the very expression of love; almost the only language that adequately describes its feelings.

Love, then, which can alone explain suffering when it comes, can also alone give us the strength to accept it joyfully, for life is tolerable only when it is permeated with love. There are hardships for everyone; do what we will, we cannot escape them. Yet it is not the troubles of life, but the way we bear them, that makes life tolerable or not. To repine, complain, or cry out only digs the pointhead deeper into the flesh. It is the fretting against imprisonment that makes imprisonment the terrible torture that it is; the trouble is not that the walls are small, but that the mind is too big and, in its desires, schemes out beyond the narrow borders of its cell. The anchorite was contented in his tower, but the prisoner essayed night by night to escape; their conditions were the same, but their hopes and desires were different.

The whole secret, then, of life is to adapt our desires to our conditions. Love puts into bondage as many victims as hate; but those whom love's chains bind are glad of their lot. It is just so that our whole relation to God leads us to be tranquil in trouble, to be glad even in sufferings. We are told, indeed, that God punishes with suffering all workers of iniquity. But those also whom God loveth He chasteneth, and for us, who try, fitfully indeed yet honestly, to love, we can feel sure that it is only the strength of His embrace that we feel. Love, then, alone will help us to understand life and its sorrows. As children in perfect trust and hope, we must rely on Him so that even our pain is from Him and will lead us to Him.

Of course, the full realization of this is the attitude of the saints; for they seem to have achieved that same state of soul to which St. Paul confessed that he had reached: "For which cause I take pleasure in my infirmities."[107] Of one saint we are told that he considered himself neglected by God on any day in which no suffering came to him; it was as though for the moment He had withdrawn His caressing hand. We are told of another that she began to be afraid that she had fallen from God's grace whenever her sufferings ceased.

Now these "hard sayings" of the heroes of Christ seem too high for us even to attempt to practice; to love suffering and rejoice in it seems more than we dare even ask for. Yet there is this to be considered: that our blessed Lord Himself found it perfectly compatible to shrink from suffering and yet to be resigned to the will of God. His whole frame sweated blood when faced with the loneliness of sin and of death, yet He could be still in absolute union with His Father, so that the combination of the two is not necessarily impossible. To shrink from suffering and yet to love seems a contradiction, yet it was not only achieved by our Lord, but confessed to by the saints.

God, then, for us is the Master of Love, and His chosen ones are those who have learned deepest in His school. Sorrow, then, far from opposing love, is its perfect expression, so that, without it, love would pine away in silence. It is caused by Love and can be made tolerable only by Love. It is, above all, in the Sacrament of Love, which we receive with a *Domine, non sum dignus*[108] in our heart, that we shall obtain the strength and courage to bear life's troubles with a serene heart. For it is the Crucified who alone explains the Crucifixion.

[107] Cf. 2 Cor. 12:5.
[108] "Lord, I am not worthy."

Part 13

∞

Forming yourself

∞

You must form your conscience

Catholics, just because of all their efforts to secure Catholic education and a Catholic atmosphere for their children, must admit that conscience can be changed, trained, and developed. We protest that it is possible for the consciences of children brought up under non-Catholic principles and with non-Catholic ways of regarding life and its obligations to become distorted and even destroyed. All the promptings that are right and normal and that should be almost instinctive may become hopelessly obscured, and their fine delicacy so blunted as no longer to produce that feeling of shame and moral reprehension that should at least follow an evil deed.

No doubt there are certain principles that are so fundamental and elementary that it is very difficult to imagine them wholly inoperative.

Such, for example, is the rudimentary idea that a man should do to others only what he would wish them to do to him. In varying forms, this idea seems to be of universal acceptance; but other subsidiary notions can certainly become obliterated by custom or ignorance.

St. Paul uses a most expressive word to describe the effect made by sin upon the conscience, for he speaks of sinners as having their consciences "seared";[109] that is, the delicacy and responsiveness to evil suggestion have been lost through a hardening of the soul's perceptive faculty, comparable to the loss of all feeling produced by a burn, which hardens the skin and deadens its perceptive power. Thus, by everything that we proclaim, we show that we Catholics regard the conscience as something not definite or stationary, but easily affected and capable of education and refinement.

Conscience, therefore, is subject to influence; hence, it cannot be a mere collection of principles. Sometimes in our conversation we speak of a man of conscience as "a man of principle," as though the two things were necessarily the same, whereas they are quite distinct. Principles are unchanging, whereas conscience is alive. Conscience is more accurately what the poets have always described it to be: a voice, not in the sense that it is a voice external to us, but that it is the inarticulate expression of our whole being. Perhaps we have had the notion that conscience was the voice of God whispering in our ears, a voice that tells us of things of which we are ignorant, an instructive suggestion, much as revelation is.

But conscience is nothing of the kind. It is the voice simply of ourselves, although based upon certain rudimentary principles such as we have already described. It is, if you like, a faculty, like the musical faculty, that must, first of all, be inherent before it can be cultivated, but which assuredly requires cultivation. Left to itself, it might go off into all sorts of wrong paths. It needs to be taken in hand by someone who has both judgment and taste, by whom it may be fashioned to its best purpose. Conscience is always changing, always fluid, so that we do things today that our conscience is silent about, whereas tomorrow it may furiously upbraid us for even thinking of them.

I must, then, obviously train my conscience, for of itself, except in the very simplest things, it will not necessarily act aright. There

---

[109] 1 Tim. 4:2.

are souls, indeed, who are naturally Christian, but how few, and these not on every point!

Now, to train my conscience, I have need of some definite principles by means of which I can be certain that I am on the right path. What are these? There are three such sources: the principles of the natural law, such as justice, truthfulness, and so forth dictate; the principles of the supernatural law, laid down in faith and morals by the Church as representing the teaching power that Christ left to continue His work; and the actual life of our Lord, which takes in concrete form the abstract principles that the others profess. In the first two, we see simply how life should be lived; in the last, we can see it actually lived.

These separate sources, if properly studied, will give us the main ways of achieving a properly regulated conscience, for the real trouble of conscience is that we are responsible for conscience itself. It is not enough for me to say that my conscience lets me do this or that, since the further point can quite properly be put: Has my conscience any right to do it? Certainly it is possible to have a false conscience, and it is possible also that this falseness of conscience may be my own fault entirely. The question, then, is not so simple as it sounds, for conscience is not the external voice of God whispering to me, but is really just the voice of my whole being; it is not separate from me, but only myself.

To see, therefore, whether or not my own conscience is correct, I must make frequent meditation on the Faith and on the Gospels, and on that code of moral life which I find accepted even by those who make no pretense to be following the teaching of Christ. Only when I have done this shall I really know whether my conscience is healthy or scrupulous, whether lax or too personal, or whether it follows the lines laid down by our blessed Lord and continued, after His design, by the Church. Conscience is above all, but that is only because it has been formed after the fashion of Christ.

∞

A properly formed conscience is infallible

Conscience is a voice springing from the whole being. It is partly a judgment on principles, as when my conscience tells me that such-and-such a principle is wrong, and partly an application of principles, as when, in the ordinary round of events, I reject a temptation to do something because my conscience informs me that this would not be right, would not accord with certain principles that my Faith has taught me to accept. On the whole, and chiefly, it concerns the application of principles rather than the mere selection of principles, for these are selected by the reason or the instinct, or the light of revealed truth.

In the voice of conscience, then, we notice the idea of moral obligation of moral insistence; the root idea of it is "I must." This voice of conscience, then, we certainly have to obey, for it is the sole personal command that reaches us. Even authority could not be accepted nor its ordinances respected unless it had been backed by the full majesty of conscience. Conscience must sit in judgment on the claims of authority before investing it with the sanction of the moral law. A Catholic has first to convince himself of the divine mission of the Church, and be sure that she represents the teaching body that our Lord came on earth to found, before he can allow her to make with effect any demands upon his allegiance.

Either deliberately or by implication, he has to be made sure of his ground by conscience. So, again, in every action in which the moral obligation that we summarize under the name of duty is felt and attended to, I have to convince myself of the authority of conscience, and I have to put conscience in judgment over the claims that are made upon me.

But while, in this way, I am completely under the dominion of my conscience, I have to remember that, in consequence, I cannot move until my conscience is sure. I may not act until my conscience is really determined; I cannot act, that is, when my conscience is in doubt. The reason for this principle is that, were I to do so, I would in effect be saying to myself, "I don't know whether this is right or wrong, but I am going to do it anyway." Obviously, this would be altogether a disrespectful attitude toward God, a complete disregard for the law of God.

Yet on the other hand, it is surely very difficult to make up one's mind determinedly on all the points that have to be settled by conscience. Surely, at least on the spur of the moment, it is almost impossible to be certain. Often I have to admit that I am not quite sure, but that I think a certain thing is allowed. And here am I doing wrong, for I am acting on a doubtful conscience? No. Why? Because really and practically my conscience has been made certain.

What has happened is that I have put myself into some such position as this: I have said I must act from a sure conscience, but in this particular matter, I am not quite certain what is right. However, it seems to me that under the circumstances, I have enough to justify my doing it, for I do really think it to be allowable. Hence, I have done the best I could under the circumstances, for if I were certain that the thing I was going to do were wrong, I would, of course, not have done it. But as I must act somehow, and as this does not appear to me to be actually wrong, I am justified in going through with it. In this way, by a reflex act, by getting, as it were, behind my conscience, I have in reality made my conscience sure and can proceed to act on it.

I have, then, just to do my best, for my conscience is infallible; that is to say, if I make up my mind seriously that a certain thing is right, it becomes right for me. My conscience is not infallible, of course, in the sense that whatever I think right is right in itself, but only that it is right for me. Suppose, for example, that when I am quite a boy, I think that I have a vocation to the priesthood, or at least I think it possible that God may have destined me to be a priest; and suppose, further, that, after considering it carefully — praying, asking advice, and looking at my capabilities, my gifts, and my circumstances — I come to the conclusion that I have no such vocation. What is to happen if I find out afterward that God did intend me really to have been a priest?

Nothing will happen at all, and God Himself will applaud my action in giving up the idea of the priesthood, for I am conscious that God can ask me only to do my best. He cannot expect from me absolute perfection, for He knows (since He made man) that all that I can do is unprofitable. All that He can with any right expect is that I should try to do the right thing. But I have tried; I have prayed, sought counsel, and considered the matter; then I have acted as I honestly judged best, and I must trouble myself no more about it. Even when other people tell me what they think I ought to do, even when the priest gives me advice in the confessional (unless I have been rendered abnormal and incapable by scruples), I must finally remember that with me and my conscience lies the ultimate responsibility of it. I may not plead their words in my excuse, for my soul is my own. Guided by conscience, which itself has been trained by faith and the moral law and by the example of Christ's life as I find it in the Gospels, I have to steer my own way.

∞

Conscience must yield
to the authority of the Faith

It is the teaching of the Church that I must always follow my conscience. I can never try to shelter myself behind authority and say that, although my conscience objects, I have a right to put it aside and follow authority blindly. Put in this way, I am certainly wrong, for in that case, I would be using authority to break up conscience; I would be using that of which the whole basis is an appeal to conscience (for the idea of duty that is contained in the idea of submission to authority is part of the very fundamental of conscience) in order to violate conscience.

Yet, on the other hand, is it not true that authority once proved divine must be obeyed, that authority can even instruct conscience, teach it principles of right and wrong, such as, left to itself, it might never find out at all? This contradiction is sometimes, perhaps, a puzzle to me as a Catholic. How am I to deal with the situation when my conscience and the authority of the Church, whose divine mission I accept, come into conflict?

This puzzle, which, of course, is absolutely simple for Catholics when they once start to examine the matter, is altogether a scandal for non-Catholics. Forgetful of the fact that, during the whole of her rule, the Church has been the champion of conscience against tyranny of the state, or tyranny of superstition, non-Catholics are in haste to suppose that conscience and authority are in opposition, whereas they are necessary for each other; it is impossible to find the one safeguarded without the other. Wherever authority has broken down, I shall find that, in effect, conscience has also been overridden, and where authority has been upheld, it has but confirmed the rights of conscience.

But I must begin by recognizing the distinction that, on the whole, conscience is rather concerned with the application of principles than with the settling of principles. Our Lord came to teach truth, and consequently, I am sure that in His creed I shall find what I want to guide me through life.

But where I shall fail is that I shall from time to time be uncertain as to where or how these wide principles are to be adopted in my ordinary life. How far does self-sacrifice become an evil? When exactly am I obliged to consider my own good name? When shall I scourge with ropes the buyers and sellers in the holy places, and when meekly submit to their authority?

Here, then, it is clear that, in this matter, there will be little possibility for opposition, for the conscience does not concern itself with principles, and the authority of Faith concerns itself with little else. Faith says to me that I must not kill, and conscience has to settle which sort of killing is really murder; the two spheres are thus, on the whole, divided.

Yet it is certainly possible for them actually to come into conflict. Thus, I can suppose that my Faith tells me of an everlasting place of torture called Hell, while my conscience tells me that I cannot believe that God would be so cruel. What is to happen? First, am I certain that this is of Faith? Yes, I am certain. Then why does my conscience object? Because it cannot square such a place or condition with God's mercy. Then I look back at my conscience and say: Well, first of all, our Lord uses the phrase "everlasting fire," and if we follow His words, we cannot go wrong. Then, the

Conscience must yield to the authority of the Faith

Church has never said that she quite knows what the punishment really consists of, nor can we really have any very accurate concept of eternity. Lastly, at the most, all I can say is that my conscience does not quite see how divine mercy and eternal punishment fit in, but I cannot honestly say that they do not fit in. Thus, the only point that conscience blocks is merely a personal difficulty in seeing how things that Faith tells me are compatible can really be so.

Thus it is in every case. Conscience may stick at the explanation, but it has to leave the principles alone. My conscience itself is a growing thing, quite capable of training and cultivation. For years, I may consider certain things allowable and come to find them forbidden only later in life. Many a practice that a boy has thought in no sense wrong, later years have shown him to have been, indeed, full of evil. Or, again, I have, perhaps, not realized many of the social evils to be quite so terrible as they actually are, for all through my life, I must teach my conscience ever greater refinement, keeping it well informed of the decisions of the Church, being careful, lest it should grow heedless or too accustomed to evil, and therefore no longer angry at injustice.

Whatever the voice of conscience dictates, I must fearlessly follow. But I have also to be sure that conscience itself is properly taught the correct view of life, comparing its acts from time to time with the authoritative decisions of the Faith and with the familiar example of the life of Christ. I must in this way take care that I do not yield to authority in those matters where authority has no right to interfere, nor, on the other hand, erect into a principle of conscience what is really nothing other than some foolish fancy of my own intelligence.

∞

Try to discern the causes of your sins

The reason we fail so often in our attempts to overcome our faults is that we start quite the wrong way around. Usually our efforts are directed to the task of overcoming evil, a dull and spiritless endeavor. As a result, our eyes are trained to look on the less pleasant side of our character, to the discouraging occupation of counting up the number of times we have done wrong. What can come from this but an unhopeful vision of life? We look back on the past day or year, and it is measured for us simply by the sins we have committed. No doubt it is very important to be conscious of our shortcomings, for otherwise we shall grow into the fashion of the Pharisee and be self-complacent sinners. But, on the other hand, a too-exclusive view of our falls from grace will absolutely paralyze all our efforts, and we shall be so numbed by despair as to be unable to proceed.

But worst of all is that we call this unedifying process an "examination of conscience." Surely this is to confuse all sorts of ideas. If I examine my conscience, do I really expect to find only evil in it? Have I not a right to peer about and see whether there is some good there as well? Is it fair to myself to suppose that I have never done anything well? Surely this will necessarily be the result of concentrating on what I have done wrong without keeping equally before my eyes what little real good, of course under God's grace, there has been in my life.

In any case, I have no business to call it an examination of conscience, for conscience is not simply composed of evil, is not indeed anything at all of that fashion. To examine my conscience, I must actually review my whole being, good and ill alike; it must be thoroughly undertaken and not lightly rushed through. Do not very many of the terrible scruples that grow so easily out of modern spiritual training arise from this practice of scrutinizing too closely the evil and avoiding the good in ourselves?

Conscience is simply my whole nature articulate. It is the voice, changing and never stationary, that results from my Faith, my actual way of living, from my ideals, and so forth; hence, the better and finer my state of soul, the more refined and delicate my conscience will become. As I advance up the scale of creation toward the perfect figure of our Master, I necessarily look more and more askance at wrongdoing and feel a terrible hatred for all injustice. But as I get more and more hardened in sin, naturally my conscience becomes less and less susceptible to the prompting of any higher ideal; indeed, no prompting at all comes from within, for it has no longer any meaning to me.

If, then, I am to examine my conscience, I must surely go right behind all the merely apparent actions of good and evil and see the causes of my deeds. It is not examining my conscience to know that I am uncharitable, untruthful, impatient, or impure. I want to know why I fall, or what makes me fall. The sin is a sin, but when I have learned that much, I cannot hope to make progress unless I can also find out the reason for it.

A general would be a foolish fellow who was content to count up merely the number of times he had been defeated, and considered that he had done all he ought to do when he had published the statistics of his losses. A government that gave an accurate list of its defeats at by-elections, and left the matter there, would hardly be thought to have done anything except to discourage its supporters.

In every case, it is necessary to find the failures, but still more important to discover their causes; and for this, it is essential to go over the whole ground, to discuss both good and evil, and not to be content with a bare enumeration, but to probe more deeply into the ultimate reasons for things. Yet does it not happen that I speak of an examination of conscience when I have hurriedly, in my night prayers, gone through my sins during the day?

What, then, have I to do? I must examine my conscience; that is, I must look at myself as nearly as I can as God sees me. I must not be as that foolish man of whom St. James tells us that he saw himself in the mirror and then went off and forgot what manner of man he was.[110] Perhaps I am even more foolish and never even look at the mirror to see what I am like.

To change the metaphor, I stand on the brink of my own soul, shivering and never daring to sound its depths, for fear that I should find much that I would have to change. But I must face myself and count up the evil and the good, and not be content with the enumeration. I must look for the causes of things. Thus, surely many a child has been confessing his sins of untruthfulness and never realized that his real trouble was cowardice. Night by night, he had examined his "conscience" in the sense of finding out what he had done wrong; but he had not been taught to discover the causes of his troubles, with the result that he never improved. Had he been properly instructed, he would have found that he was not really untruthful, had no desire to tell a lie, but was simply terrified into lying because he feared the consequences. Thus, he should have set to work not on the virtue of truth, but on the virtue of courage. He has never improved, because he never knew what caused his untruthfulness.

[110] James 1:23-24.

∞

Nurture the good in you,
rather than only trying to avoid sins

Undoubtedly my first step to achieve holiness or goodness is to discover my predominant fault. This requires some looking for, since it may possibly be hidden underneath a good many other sins that have concealed it. Thus, it may well be that the fault I have most frequently to confess is not really my predominant fault, but only the result of it, while the real sin skulks away and refuses to come to the surface. Impurity may be caused by other things, such as love of ease, selfishness, even pride. Often it happens that we are wrestling with the wrong enemy, not getting hold of the source of his strength, but fighting frontal attacks against an ugly mask. All the time, the cause of our failures will be quite undisturbed and in possession of the field.

First, then, I have very carefully to examine my conscience. I must go very thoroughly to work and sift the whole of my actions with some trouble. Just as I find that, week after week, my list for Confession is practically always the same, so in all probability I shall find that whenever I examine my conscience, the results are pretty much alike; hence, there will be no need for me to make this examination very often; once it is done thoroughly, that will be sufficient for some months. Nor should I fancy that it is helpful to look every now and then to see how things are going on, or, indeed, busy myself overmuch with whether it is going on at all: for, first, it is a foolish gardener who persistently digs up his bulbs to see if they are sprouting, and, secondly, I shall find it extremely difficult, even when I have dug up my soul, to know whether I am progressing or not, for it must surely happen that when I am at my best, I shall see only more clearly than ever in how much I have failed. So that the worse I see myself to be, the better, perhaps, I shall really be.

Hence, I must beware of making purely negative resolutions, for then I shall simply look back at the past as measured by failure. If I make up my mind to avoid this or that, the result will be that I shall have no other standard of judgment in moments of spiritual stock-taking than the occasions on which I have broken my resolutions. The final result of this will be that I shall exclaim in disgust that I should never have made any resolutions at all — a perfectly logical conclusion.

The more cheerful and helpful way is to reverse this procedure. Already I have found out what my predominant fault is, for I have made a thorough and careful examination of conscience. Then, when I am certain, or at least as certain as I can be, I must concentrate not on the sin, but on the corresponding virtue. My resolutions now will not be to avoid this or that, but to increase or develop this or that. I shall not finally measure my past by a series of faults, but by the number of times, few perhaps but nonetheless real, when I have actually managed to achieve success.

The gardener who spent all his time digging up the weeds and never thought very much of strengthening his plants would produce a very tidy but depressing garden. He would have hurt his back by stooping, and never stood upright to enjoy the beauty of his garden. But a good gardener knows well that if he will only do his best for the flowers, they will derive goodness from the soil and so leave less from which the weeds can get the nourishment they need. Weeding must be done; but the first thing is the flowers. So, in my soul, all my energies should first be spent upon encouraging my poor feeble virtues to grow strong, and then, by their very strength, they will cause the sins to diminish. I have, therefore, not to make my resolutions to avoid this or that, but to improve in this or that.

Let me suppose that I have found out that my chief failing is uncharitableness. My resolution will be to take up as strongly as I can a charitable judging of my fellows. I should not simply try to avoid the temptation when it comes, but rather make positive efforts to increase what little store of charity I have. I must start with my thoughts and gradually get into the way of trying to find a good motive for everything I see. St. Catherine of Siena, in a humorous moment, told our Lord that if He had only given her an opportunity for it, she would have discovered an excuse for the Devil himself.

We cannot, indeed, say that right is wrong or wrong right, but we can, while denouncing a fault, suppose that the motive was good, for the motive forever eludes us. Often, when I went out of my way to help someone, they saw not the motive that I had, but only its result, and were annoyed; and as others have misjudged me, so it is possible that I misjudge others. In this way, I shall find that it is not difficult, after a while, to think kindly of everyone, and to think kindly will end in speaking and acting kindly.

I must, that is, develop the virtue corresponding to my predominant sin rather than look to the sin itself, develop my charity so that I have no longer any temptation to judge unkindly, so that gossip will not please me; encourage in my heart so great a love for purity that foul thoughts will not remain with me, and foul conversation will bore me; seek truth and justice, so that lying and the defrauding of my neighbor revolt me.

∞

Detachment allows your soul true freedom

Before setting out to mold our characters, our souls must be in perfect freedom. I cannot address myself to such an undertaking until I am unhampered in my movements. In order to achieve anything that requires much effort, it is essential for me to avoid everything that prevents action, even though in other ways it might be useful, and might, indeed, later be ultimately repossessed.

Thus, in a case in some sort parallel, a battleship going into action clears its decks of every obstacle. Things that have their use at other times, that will again become useful, are for the moment altogether sacrificed in the immediate and compelling interests that dominate the situation. Danger of fire from shell, and danger also to the free movement across the deck that might at any moment become essential to the safety of all concerned, are sufficiently pressing to force the destruction of everything, however useful, that might possibly impede this freedom. Or again, for the same thing is observable whenever there is any occasion for swift and determined action, in military operations, liberty and mobility of attack are themselves so absolutely of life-or-death necessity, that houses, industrial centers, and cultivated plains may have to be ruthlessly harried, and great national loss inflicted on his own dominions by the general, in the interests of final victory.

Or, in a more homely illustration, a man going to work vigorously, or even going in for sport, rolls up his sleeves.

Now, something of the same kind of thing is necessary in the work of forming our characters. I must have perfect and unhampered liberty of soul if I am to work at all easily. In a certain sense, this is also the final result of the whole spiritual life: that it produces a detachment in the soul and effects a real freedom that marks off the saint from the sinner. The great-souled lovers of God need nothing else upon earth than God's constant presence. They have attained that liberty that was promised to the sons of God, so that neither life nor death nor any other creature can separate them from their Friend. The attainment of this in part is essential for the beginning of the spiritual life.

Before the Fall, the soul of Adam must have been especially beautiful from this very freedom. The whole harmony of passions, will, and reason united in acting with solemn and pleasing smoothness; nothing disturbed, no discord broke in upon the matchless symphony. It was as though a perfect piece of machinery were working without friction, and with such absolute adjustment and nice balance as hardly to suggest the possibility of any untoward accident dislocating the mechanism. Then there befell the terrible sin of disobedience whereby "came death into the world and all our woe." Thenceforward, the only possible remedy was, under the grace of God, to be achieved by man's own energy.

Freedom must be grasped; it is never given. It is something to be fought for, something that is bought only at a great price; indeed, for some, it is death alone that frees the soul from all the tanglements of existence. There must be nothing to hamper or clog the free movement of the will or the reason, nothing to obscure or ruffle the one, nor to blunt the energy of the other. As with the boxer whose every limb is, by training and practice, brought into immediate subjection to the mind, so that the rippling muscle moves under the silken texture of the skin at the slightest instinctive prompting of the intelligence, so must every emotion and passion obey the will in the light of reason.

Now, although it is true that this perfect adjustment and nice balance can never be completely recovered, yet it is both the basis and the goal of the spiritual life. I cannot go forward until I have effected the subjection of myself; and when finally I overcome and enter into my kingdom, then only shall I have achieved perfect freedom. I must begin with this, and thus I see the necessity of acquiring a spirit of detachment from all things in the sense of subordinating my own will to the will of God, realizing by faith that I cannot escape from it, that whatever happens comes to pass only because God has allowed it in His wisdom and His love. I must frequently meditate upon this divine will.

Then, again, I must try to be perfectly truthful in life; that is, my life should correspond absolutely to my thoughts. Once I start posing or pretending, I become the slave of a pretense. Never shall I be able to free myself until I revert to myself and am not content to act as others expect of me. Compromise, just because it is a lie, cannot be allowed within these limits that circumscribe truth. To be prudent, to be on my guard, yet to keep myself undisturbed, to possess my soul in patience — that is the great secret of life. Especially in these days, when speed enters so enormously into life, when everything is at a rush and hurry, I must take care to be in perfect serenity of mind, lest I add to the disturbance of existence and break in upon my peace of soul and perfect freedom, without which spiritual life is rendered impossible.

Cultivate good habits

Once we have discovered our predominant fault, we have to endeavor to cultivate the virtue most opposed to it. But it is just here that the difficulty begins, for surely I have tried over and over again to compass this and have failed.

What is a virtue? There is this difference between a good action and a virtue: a good action may be quite isolated, whereas a virtue is a definite habit established in the will. So, in the same fashion, a vice is an established habit of wrongdoing. It is possible for me thus to do good, to tell the truth, be charitable, or be patient without really having the virtues of truth or charity or patience.

What, then, do we mean by an established habit? What is a habit? Of course, we have a vague idea that it means we have gotten into a way of doing certain things and have gotten the knack of them; and certainly it is difficult to describe in other words this apparently simple thing. However, we may start by saying that a habit does not incline us to do anything, does not give us a push in its direction; but once we have made up our minds to do it, we find that the fact of the habit enables us to do the thing much more easily, promptly, and without friction.

Thus, suppose I have obtained somehow the habit of being tidy; it is much easier for me to seize hold of a confused mess and put it into order. I have such a horror of untidiness and such a custom of putting everything in its place that it becomes much easier for me to do it than it would be for others who had no habit of the kind. I must realize, however, that having the habit does not make me tidy, but only makes it considerably easier to be tidy. In other words, to make use of the expression of psychologists, a habit does not force the will to act, but enables it to act with greater smoothness.

This will be more apparent, perhaps, if I try to see how a habit is formed. Let me take a material habit, a habit of the body, in order that, by visible things, I may the more clearly understand things invisible.

I am learning to shoot. First, I shall be trained probably at a stationary target. Slowly and deliberately I take my aim for firing, until, in time, I have gotten my eye into the way of it and find I can score a good number of "bulls." Then, perhaps, I am taken out to the moving target, or the clay pigeon, and finally to the actual flying bird. But in the meanwhile, an extraordinary change has taken place. At first, I was very slow and deliberate in taking aim; now I shoot at once, lifting the gun, aiming, firing, all within a few fractions of a second.

Or, again, a very favorite example is the simple dressing in the morning. When I was a child, it was an intensely laborious process, requiring at first constant assistance to pilot me through the vast array of garments with zippers and buttons. If every morning the same efforts had to be made as I had then, my day's work would never get done.

The toddling of a child is strenuous to him, not simply because his limbs are weak, but because the effort at balancing is a tremendous strain upon his energy, which, if he continued all through life, would make all walking intolerable.

It is to be noticed that what has happened in each case is this: from effort I have passed to effortless action — at first, slow and deliberate, with attention required so as to be certain of every step in the process; then a stage when effort slips from the action, and by a sort of instinct swiftly, without thought, as it appears, we do promptly, easily, and without difficulty what we have learned by habit. Habit, therefore, is simply a faculty of our nature whereby, by repeated action, we acquire an ease in movement and so forth that does away with effort.

Now, it is precisely this that we require so incessantly in our spiritual life. For us, the great trouble is the determined efforts that have to be made. We find the struggle so fierce that, in despair, we relinquish the effort altogether. We should remember that, at the beginning, there is bound to be extreme difficulty, extreme deliberation, extreme slowness. It is only gradually that we shall find it possible to lay aside effort and fall into the pleasant lines of habit.

But what a gain to be able to hand over to mere instinct (it is not really that) what had first been so tiring a task. It will be useful for me to think over the three rules that are given, so that, in the formation of the habit of goodness that is most opposed to my besetting sin, I may gradually, positively, set up something really efficient. These rules are:

> • *As far as possible to accumulate circumstances such as will make the forming of the habit least of all interfered with:* to avoid, for example, those places and people whose proximity I find to be, on the whole, tending to make me break it. In simpler words, let me avoid the occasions of sin.

> • *Never to allow exceptions until the habit has been firmly established;* to beware, above all, of that very deceitful excuse "just this once," for that phrase is never accurate: "just this once" leads easily to many other times.

> • *To find every opportunity for exercising these habits.* Do not let me wait for the opportunities to arise, but let me go

out to seek them, for it is clear that, in order to establish these habits by means of repeated act, I need to exercise the acts frequently, and the only way to achieve this is to go out of my way to find these opportunities.

∞

You are responsible for your character, not for your temperament

Many people seem to worry themselves a great deal more over the things that they cannot help than over the things that they can. They are greatly agitated over the color of their hair (for which they are not responsible), and but little over their tempers (for which they are). This want of proportion is doubtless observable in myself. Do I think more of the accidents of birth, fortune, and personal appearance than of the self that I have created? For I myself am responsible for myself. "To be born a gentleman is an accident; to die one is an achievement."

Other things, then, I may not be able to help, but myself I can. As I am at this very moment, as my character is — truthful or untruthful, pure or impure, patient or impatient, slow to wrath or quick-tempered, eager, enthusiastic, energetic, or lazy and dull and wasteful of time — I have no one to thank but myself. Of course, I may blame my temperament and say I was born so. I may accuse the hereditary tendencies or my family, or excuse myself because I have been spoiled or cowed or left to my own devices, or have been deluged with too much religion or starved with too little.

But despite all this, the fact remains that I myself alone am responsible for my own character; for character is an artificial thing that is not born, but made. It is the result of human effort and human guidance, of human wisdom and human folly. I am as I am now to the eye of God because I have so made or marred myself, either deliberately and of set purpose, or else by allowing myself to drift along, and never moving hand or foot to save myself from peril.

But surely there is such a thing as temperament? Surely people really are different from birth? Surely even the physical formation of the body, physical health or the want of it, the whole stream of tendencies inherited or instilled in early childhood, the evils produced by a neglected education or an upbringing that is not Catholic, do most certainly affect my nature and make some difference to me. Have I not, on their account, some justification in excusing myself from being wholly responsible for the evils in my character?

Here I must begin by realizing that I must make a very real distinction between temperament and character. Temperament is natural; I am born with it. Character is artificial, the result of my way of life. I am born with a certain definite temperament, and for this I am not responsible; and on this account, too, I may well suppose that God will make allowances for me. At any rate, this temperament gives me a setoff, a push, in one definite direction: for some are by nature gentle, generous, and obliging, while others as naturally are cross-tempered and easily ruffled.

But this need not settle my character. Of course, if I make no effort to tame any evil tendencies of my nature, then temperament and character will coincide, and my actual life will only mark more deeply and emphasize more pronouncedly the original defect with which I started.

But that is my own affair, for it is possible for me to act in opposition to my temperament and to produce a character that is the reverse of my nature.

St. Thomas, indeed, in a very brief passage, seems to suggest that the worse our natural temperament is, the better for us; nor is it at all difficult to understand his argument. If I have a bad temper by nature, let me, first of all, go down on my knees and thank God for it; for it is surely highly probable that, if I had a good temper, I would be obliging and kind, not from any supernatural motive but from sheer nature. Suppose I was of that comfortable disposition which says yes just because it finds it impossible to say no; surely my acts would hardly ever be supernaturalized.

But, on the other hand, suppose I am so cantankerous that I can be generous and helpful only at the cost of a mighty effort. Then I can be certain that every obliging thing I do is done only from a high motive; it is the very contrary force that stiffens me into goodness. Just as an enemy is the necessary material out of which to fashion victory, so is an evil temperament the foundation on which a strong character is to be built. This character is, of course, nothing else than the group of habits formed around the axis of the will; and these are achieved only by repeated acts, so that it is by deliberate and energetic actions alone that I can react against my own temperament.

But, above all, I must beware of allowing myself to be careless in life, without ambition or ideal or plan; for to drift through existence is at least as dangerous as deliberate evil consciously performed. I am quick, then, by nature, or mean or thronged with impure imaginings. It does not much matter what my own trouble may be, but, instead of bemoaning it, I should set to work, by deliberate and conscious reason, to reform myself under the grace of God, not follow the blind impulses of nature.

Part 14

∞

The sacraments

∞

The sacraments give you strength

The three great virtues, faith, hope, and charity, teach us the true following of Christ. They point out to us, that is, wherein the pathway that He chose can be traced; they tell us what we have to do in order to be saved. By means of faith, we learn what are the mysteries that God has vouchsafed to reveal to our race, and thereby, because truth and knowledge open to us the kingdom of God's love, we are led closer to Him. Thus, hope enables us to see on what grounds future attempts at holiness and the firm purpose of amendment are made possible. We grow confident of the divine mercy and, conscious of our own weakness, place in it all the source of our courage. Thus, there arises the full flower of charity. Faith is taught through the Creed, hope through the voice of prayer, and charity through the Commandments. For, as our Lord more than once insisted, love of God is no emotional experiment to be narrowed to its expression in words, but it must find in acts the sole sure showing of itself: "If you love me, keep my commandments."[111]

But all this is not enough. It is not enough merely to know what the right thing is, although this, too, is essential. I must know how to please God before I set out to please Him. Yet even when I

[111] John 14:15.

do know what He would have me to do, there are still difficulties in the way. To know what is right is one thing; to *do* what is right is another. Here is the unique power of Christ our Lord. It is sometimes said that the whole of Christianity is contained in the Sermon on the Mount. If it may be said reverently, the Sermon on the Mount is the least original side of our Lord; every religious teacher almost has said what was said then. But to this He added another thing; He taught us what to do and, further, gave us the strength to do it. This strength comes through the sacraments.

Just because He was God as well as man, Christ had power over all creation and could help man even in the most intimate portion of his being, within the boundaries of his will. Here the force and value of the sacraments come in; they give us the help of God, by which we are enabled to do that which we know to be right. Divine Himself, He can give us divine strength. He can lay down the commandments and then give us also the sacraments to enable us to keep them.

It does not take us long to find out the need we have of help, and consequently He has given us these seven means of obtaining His aid. These correspond to the various stages of the soul's development and are the recurring helps, chosen with regard to the sevenfold needs of life. Baptism begins our life with its new birth. Then Communion becomes the food of the soul. Confession is the medicine whereby our ailments are removed and our health restored. Confirmation fills up the gaps in our strength that the early dawn of battle discovers to us when we stand upon the threshold and begin to see the long line of foes drawn up against us. Marriage affords us those graces of loyalty and duty required for the exact fulfillment of the marriage contract. Holy Orders confers on the priest those high powers and that high vocation whereby we, too, are made partakers through him of the deep life of the Mystical Body of Christ. And the Anointing of the Sick prepares the soul for its last long journey or gives (if God sees it to be good) health and strength to the body. Thus, all along life's highway stand these helps, from which the power of God is imparted to us and by which we are made partakers of the divine nature.

Now, the way in which these things are communicated to us has been itself a stumbling block to some, for our Lord has chosen to give His grace by means of material things. In every sacrament there is what is called an outward sign, which represents the inward effect on the soul, but also does actually produce that effect. Thus, in Baptism the water, chosen because it shows the purpose of the sacrament in cleansing from sin, itself, through the merits of Christ's Passion, causes the grace to operate on the soul. Again, in Confirmation the oil hallowed by the bishop, by its being applied to the forehead, works in this way also upon the soul, conferring upon it the gift of strength, which in the East is often typified by the produce of the olive.

Now, to many outside the Church, it seems difficult to suppose that matter can so affect the spirit, yet is it not one of the commonest principles of God's dealing? Especially since the Incarnation, He has often made use of the body or the visible appearance of things to show and to cause His works on earth. In the miracles of the New Testament, how often He made use of clay or water or the outstretching of a hand, or nails or spear or a cross. These things are surely in the same fashion, as the blessed Body that He chose for Himself, things of matter, yet, as with our own, the living Temple of the Holy Spirit and, in His case, united hypostatically to the Word of God. The whole tendency of Christian worship and doctrine is to make use of visible things to produce invisible effects. Here, then, also I must realize the material side of the sacraments and see their place in the economy of the divine plan.

But, above all, I must use them for the saving of my soul. They are the channels He has chosen for imparting His grace to me. Without them, I shall surely perish, but with them, I shall become a partaker of His divine nature.

∞

Baptism makes you God's child

It is through the sacrament of Baptism that we are made the children of God. The fall of our first parents bequeathed to us an inheritance that put us at enmity with God, and so affected us that we were unable of ourselves to follow steadfastly the paths of the divine commandments. The Original Sin so upset the harmony of our nature that the perfect kingdom was reduced to a state of anarchy, and it is precisely this state of anarchy that is the Original Sin we inherit. Revolutions, betrayals, and treachery make up the history of my soul — foes within leagued to foes without, plotting to overthrow the rightful government.

In the earlier state of Adam, called by theologians the state of original justice, the powers of the soul were organized in perfect order. The passions, or nonrational faculties, so to call them, obeyed the commands of the will, the will obeyed the reason, and the reason obeyed the infinite reason which is the law of God. Thus was his whole being in absolute harmony, and everything done by him was orderly and right. Then, of course, came the Fall, which disturbed this harmony by discord; for henceforth the emotions or passions strove to dominate the will, which, in turn, dictated to the reason what it should justify or denounce — the inferior powers, that is, assumed the reins of government and lorded it over the man. They obscured his intelligence, so that, through passion, he was no longer able to judge correctly. They disturbed the will to such an extent that St. Paul could accurately describe himself in the paradox, "To will is present with me, but to accomplish that which is good I find not, so that I do not the things that I would."[112]

Then comes the sacrament of Baptism. At once, through the merits of Christ's sacred Passion, we become the children of God. All the enmity that we had incurred by our sinful state falls from us, and we stand openly as the sons of the Most High. Original Sin, as we have spoken of it, can be seen to be, not an act, but rather a state of ill-health to which the soul has succumbed. It is not that we have done anything wrong, but only that we have inherited an evil condition. It is a state, indeed, of positive guilt in which all men share through their inclusion by God's ordinance in the will of Adam.

But we can here consider the effect of Original Sin as a disorder of the soul, wherein the passions dominate the will, and the will overrules the reason, and the reason defies the law of God. We are told that Baptism sets right the effects of Original Sin, but surely, we ask, does not the sad state that St. Paul described still continue even after we have received the sacrament of Baptism? How, then, can it be said that Baptism restores us to the friendship of God?

What really happens is this: although, by Baptism, the whole order and properly regulated harmony of the soul is at once reestablished so that we become even as Adam was before he fell, yet there remains the terrible possibility of further sin. We are not healed of all our tendency to sin, nor of that corrupt desire of our will which turns our thoughts to evil, but we enter into the position of being able to conquer that desire and lead it in the right direction. We are not led back into those golden days of peace, but

[112] Cf. Rom. 7:18-19.

we have now the power in ourselves under God's grace to set up once more on earth the kingdom of the Father.

The value, then, of Baptism is that I am no longer a child of wrath, but that I become a child of God. A seal or mark or character is stamped upon me, whereby I am set apart forever as a son. The very sinful nature whence I was rescued by this saving sacrament is now made, as it were, of the nature of God. I partake of the divine nature. I am lifted up from the depth of my degradation to the height of God Himself. Hence it is that there is so much in the commentaries of the Fathers and early writers on that wonderful mystery of the Incarnation, insofar as it brings Him to earth and lifts earth to Him.

Surely if I could only realize what great things have been done for me, I would never again lose courage or hope. If I could only get myself to understand that God has indeed made me His child, that I am no longer His servant but His son, I would never more put to myself the querulous and foolish question as to what use I am here at all. Sometimes I am tempted, when things spiritual are very dull and seemingly not very successful, to cry out that there is no advantage in my going on or attempting to go on, when I am evidently of so little consequence in the sight of God. He has so much that is more worthy of His attention that I cannot conceive His having the time or the desire to look after me also.

But then I have to say to myself, "I am now His son." I am a son of God by that sacrament that can never be repeated, for it has no need to be repeated, since what was done once has been done for all time. The passions, through prayer and austerity and the power of the sacraments, are to be brought into subjection. The will resigns its sovereignty to the reason, which, in turn, now more closely observes and obeys the will of God. Baptism does not set us right, but, by the high privilege it affords, it gives us the power to set ourselves right.

∞

Confirmation reminds
you to answer God's call now

I will probably acknowledge that, to a very large extent, I have neglected to make use of the sacrament of Confirmation. Of course I have received it, and I know well that it cannot be repeated. How, then, can I be held to blame for neglecting that which I have received just the one time that I can possibly receive it?

To realize this, let me ask myself why it is that it can be received once only. The answer is naturally that thereby I receive a character, or mark, on my soul that can never be effaced. But what does all this mean? It means really that I cannot receive Confirmation more than once for the simple reason that I have no need to repeat it. Once given, it is given for always, because the effects last as long as life lasts. The grace of Communion may refresh me all my days, but the Presence fades. Absolution removes all my sins from me. They are forgiven forever. But if, unhappily, I fall again into sin, again must I approach this saving sacrament.

With Confirmation, on the other hand, the sacramental grace perseveres until the end. Once I have been marked with the grace of Confirmation, I have had set up in my soul a power, a force, that never runs dry or can be drained or even wholly affected by sin. When I do wrong, the grace ceases to work, but it does not cease to exist; so that as soon as I have reconciled myself to God, back again comes the flood that Confirmation, for good and all, established within me. Hence, the value of it does not consist simply in the day of my reception of it, but is to be made use of all the days of my life. The indwelling of the Spirit of God, begun in Baptism, is now made perfect, and the wonderful sevenfold gifts of God are put into my charge, so that with me it lies, whether I have the benefit they can confer or not.

But every sacrament has both an outward sign and an inward grace. What are these in Confirmation? First, the external thing, the material instrument of God's grace to my soul, is the anointing of my forehead by the bishop with the consecrated oil. That is the essential outward sign. And the inward grace? Strength. In the East, oil, which is at once a food and a preservative of the skin, is in frequent use among athletes. It is, indeed, the source of the strength of the toilers and is mentioned in the sacred Scriptures as the symbol of that which it helps to produce. Hence, it is the external representation of that inner strength of which the soul stands in need.

Usually Confirmation is administered to children just when they stand upon the threshold of life and are beginning to feel that there are many difficulties they will have to overcome and endure, just when they are becoming conscious that life grows not easier, but harder. Can I remember that, at that age, I discovered that not everyone quite held with me about the duties owed to God and all that they entailed? I found that the things I held sacred, and the people I had been taught to reverence, were now held up to my ridicule. And the things I had been afraid to do, afraid even to think about, were spoken of and done openly before me without shame. Even my own inclinations began suddenly to become more forcible, and unsuspected instincts and hidden forces I did not yet understand began to be felt and to give pleasure. Thus the full practice of faith, hope, and love also, in turn, grew increasingly difficult to observe. Then I was confirmed; that is, these tendencies were henceforth to be counteracted by the indwelling within me, not merely of grace, but of the very Spirit of God. He Himself was to take charge of my soul.

I have been taught, surely, that the object and effect of this sacrament was to make me strong, that this strengthening of me was to be achieved by the abiding presence of the Holy Spirit, and that this abiding presence was to continue for the whole of my lifetime. As the need endures, so must the remedy endure. This sacrament, therefore, is tremendously alive, nor is it right that I should regard it, as perhaps I have often done in the past, as though it were some childish thing that had to be gotten over while I was quite young. Do I not find sometimes that people look on it much as they look on the measles as a normal heritage of children?

But surely, in my fuller age, the need for divine strength increases rather than diminishes. As a child, I probably thought that I was naughty only because I was a child, but supposed that when I grew up, I would find life easier. Instead, I discovered that I looked back upon my childhood as the innocent time of my life and looked upon my older years as necessarily years of wrongdoing, although perhaps I clung to the salve of conscience that in youth a man might be a little wild, but in his old age had time to become a saint. Thus, it is always yesterday or tomorrow, never today. But Confirmation suddenly reminds me that it is now that God calls, and now that the Holy Spirit makes appeal to me to remember His presence and to make use of it.

Do I, indeed, think of that presence in my times of stress? In the struggles of temptation, do I sufficiently have recourse to that Divine Helper given me? Do the sevenfold gifts really signify anything practical to me? Let me turn in devotion to the Holy Spirit, recite the hymns to Him, and be conscious always of the resident force pent up in my soul.

∞

Confession is the tribunal of mercy

The state has set up courts of justice, the Church courts of mercy. The state, in the name of justice, punishes; the Church, in the name of mercy, forgives. The whole apparatus of the civil law is intended to track down the criminal, to follow the traces of his work, and to discover his identity. It gives him, indeed, every possible means of escape in the sense that it affords him opportunity for proving his innocence or establishing such an explanation of his action as should procure his release. He has an impartial judge who probably has not heard his name ever before mentioned. His jury is presupposed to be altogether uninfluenced by personal motives, so that he can actually challenge and reject every member of it whom he may consider to have a personal antagonism toward him; and his counsel may be offered him at the expense of the state. The whole boast of the law is that it is utterly impartial, the unfaltering judge, the deliberating jury, the legal accuser of the advocates.

But parallel with this, and intended as the result of the whole organization, is the action of justice, a strict rendering to each one of what is his due — punishment to the guilty, acquittal to the innocent. The confession of the criminal would not ordinarily affect his penalty at all, so that the plea of "not guilty" is almost always put forward so as to throw the whole burden of proof on the shoulders of the law.

But the Church has no such ideas, does not at all contemplate the action of justice. To trace the criminal, to confront him with witnesses, to twist his evidence from improbability to sober fact, is to violate the seal of secrecy and to commit a crime so rare that the annals of Church history have to be ransacked to find even a doubtful occurrence of it. There is never any attempt at any such thing. It is a principle laid down for the guidance of priests that the penitents must be believed when they accuse or excuse themselves. Hence, the very personality of the culprit is shrouded in the hushed whisper, the free choice of the confessor, the rigorous suppression of all details of place and name that would be likely to lead to the confessor's knowledge of the people implicated. The penitent may desire to unburden himself to the priest, but the priest himself cannot force him to do so. Even if he does happen to recognize him, he will not remember outside what he has learned within.

This shows the different methods pursued by Church and state, the different purposes of mercy and justice. Perhaps some will declare that Confession does really achieve more justice than do the courts of law, but such is not the intention of the Church. She seeks only after mercy, waiting for the penitent to come so that she may listen and, by God's power, forgive.

Confession, then, is the tribunal of mercy. I go to it, perhaps shrinking from the avowal of my misdeeds, not because I have done anything particularly shameful (although this would almost necessarily add to the effort required), but from the very disinclination of telling another of my hidden faults. It offends my humanity; really it offends my pride, for it is difficult for man to beg for mercy, even from God. It is really that which makes Confession so hard for me; to ask for mercy seems contrary to all the self-respect that makes man rise to the heights of his nature. Had he to stand and receive a punishment in some sort adequate to his failure, it might be easier because more heroic; but to have to beg for forgiveness is an achievement that only Christianity has been able to produce in the nobler souls of her children. To recount my tiresome and petty delinquencies is harder to flesh and blood in some ways than to make avowal of a deliberate act of passion.

Yet it is the mercy of God which alone can bring me to my knees and make me ask for my forgiveness; and this mercy I must regard as a high privilege, something that adds to and in no way lessens the value of human dignity. On Him must my eyes be fixed so that even my sins are remembered, not for my own humiliation, but for His tender love. I go to seek His mercy, not simply because I love Him, but far more because He loves me; not because to err is human, but because to forgive is divine.

∞

Sorrow for sin is the
essential element of Confession

It is to be regretted that the English name for this sacrament is Confession, for it seems to make the essence of the sacrament consist in the mere avowal of sin, whereas that is of lesser consequence than the act of sorrow that precedes and follows it. In other languages, it is sometimes spoken of as the sacrament of penance — that is, of penitence — and this is really a more accurate description of it. But it would be a less difficult doctrine for very many if they could only realize that it is in fact the sacrament of sorrow.

Indeed, sorrow is the whole essence of it, for there are times when the avowal of sin is quite impossible. It happens at times that a man may find himself in a country where he cannot speak the local language, nor the local priest understand his; he cannot, therefore, make his confession.

Or, again, a still more common case is that of a person suddenly struck down by paralysis or apoplexy or some such kindred illness, which does not allow the power of speech. Here it is clearly impossible for a confession to be made. Yet, in each of these instances, the unfortunate man may well desire to have his sins forgiven him. What is he to do? He cannot confess, yet he may approach the sacrament of Confession. How? By asking for absolution, not perhaps in words, but by signs; and, as the priest says the words of absolution, by making an act of contrition or sorrow.

Here, then, it is evident that the whole essential portion of the sacrament is the sorrow, for the sacrament has been fully performed without the telling of the sins. The confession and the satisfaction are necessary, but they are not essential.

Sorrow for sin is the one thing which is of absolute necessity in this sacrament. It is, therefore, the part of the confession on which I must most dwell. Sometimes I am not apt to worry a great deal about my list of sins, taking surprising pains to discover every single fault and the exact number of times I have fallen, and then hurrying over my actual sorrow as of less importance. Of course, I know perfectly well that the sorrow was really the more necessary of the two, but it does happen that I devote perhaps less time to it than to the other.

Here, then, I must see what can be done to set this right — not the persistent torture of the conscience until Confession becomes a thing to be avoided, but rather, dwelling far more effectually upon the sorrow and its motive. Certainly this would make my spiritual life happier, and whatever does that is sheer gain.

I think, therefore, of my sins and then try to realize what they cost our Lord. In the house of the Pharisee, with the sensitiveness of perfect humanity, He numbered up the slights that had been put upon Him.[113] What would He say to me? Nay, what is He saying to me? So many times have I been forgiven, and so many times has that forgiveness been forgotten — all His love wasted! The alabaster box, filled with the most precious ointment, broken across my heart: the fragrance still fills the world with wonder, and I forget. To confess is surely a little thing compared with what I have done that requires forgiveness; to confess is even a satisfaction; it

[113] Luke 7:44-46.

unburdens my soul of its great weight. But beyond confession is the sorrow.

Surely, then, it is not difficult to be sorry for my sins, not difficult to turn as Peter turned when he had looked upon the face of Christ and, going out, wept bitterly. But Judas — had not he, too, tears upon his eyes when he had hurled back the money until it rang upon the marble steps of the Temple, and went out into the night with the consciousness of how he had trangressed against love? Yes, he too "wept bitterly," but where he failed was that sorrow for him did not lead on to love. If he had only gone back to the Master, we would have kept his feast each year as the most blessed of penitents.

My sorrow, then, must make me turn to love Christ more. On the other hand, I must not think that I have to *feel* sorrow. I must not suppose that I have no real contrition because I feel sure that, if the opportunity arose, I would fall again into the same sins; nor imagine myself to be a hypocrite because I am afraid that next week or next month will find me once again telling the same list. For I have to realize that by sorrow I mean that, together with regret for the past, I have also a firm purpose of amendment — that is, a determination that, in the future, I shall try to do better. I have no right to promise that my next confession will find me free from sin, for I am promising what is above my power to perform; but I can promise that I shall try. Failing or successful, I shall at least have made the attempt, and for the rest, God Himself must supply.

My sorrow, then, in Confession is the essential part of it, and to it must be devoted the greater portion of my time. And the sorrow must be supernatural; it must lead on to God. It need not be emotional, but it must include a real determination to do my best to overcome myself. By the pitiful sight of His five wounds, by the generous kindness of the Creator, by His own absolute lovableness, as the supreme and perfect Good, I must fix my will resolutely and forever try to fulfill His service.

∞

Communion gives you
strength for life's difficulties

The types of the Old Testament do not merely foreshadow; they help our understanding of the fulfillment. They foretell and interpret, for God, whose power designed the world, can arrange life and the chances of life so as to portray some future happening.

Now, one of the most splendid types of the Blessed Sacrament was given in the story of Elijah, whom angels fed in the desert. He had passed through a time of adventure and excitement. His challenge to the priests of Baal to prove the authority of their gods by bringing down fire from Heaven to consume the sacrifice had ended in his triumph. The altars had been set up on Carmel, a trench dug about it, and a day set apart.

First, the priests of Baal clamored to their god, while Elijah with terrible mirth mocked their failure. Over the altar they leapt, cutting their flesh with knives. Then, when his turn had come, the prophet poured water over the sacrifice until it ran down and filled up the trench. But at his prayer, God sent fire that burned up altar and sacrifice alike with so fierce a heat that the water in the trench was licked up by the flames.

After so wonderful a proof of God's power, the king, Ahab, submitted, the priests were slaughtered, and, in further token of the divine pleasure, a storm of rain broke on the country that had been three years waterless.

Elijah was wrought up into a state of overconfidence. Consequently, the hostility of the queen, who threatened him with death, drove him to overdepression, until he fled into the desert, where he prayed to die. Then came the angel with food: "Take ye and eat, for ye have yet a long way to go."[114]

Now, this surely is a very true interpretation of the purpose of Holy Communion. It is to give me the courage to persevere. Too often probably to me, as to Elijah, has come the same swift change from presumption to despair. Perhaps I had thought that I had finally quelled some temptation or sin that had long bothered me. A chance sermon or a passage in a book, or the remark of a friend, and at once the old world has come back to me.

Or it may be that it was some trifling but frequent failure that for long distressed me, and then was for a time overcome and driven from power. Always, however, the result was that, however successful for the moment, I found myself ultimately returning whither I had first begun. All the exceptional efforts and fierce resolutions and elaborate addition of prayers, all the feeling of having done great things, ended at best in a respite, which, after all the stress, appeared a complete victory. I thought to myself that the battle in that part of the field had been won, that I could rest now without precautions or guards. Then swiftly has come my fall, although months may at times elapse before my undoing is manifest.

But all the same, the effect in my soul is a quick despair. What is the use of struggle if it is always to end in defeat? I find myself utterly weary, hopeless. The old faults are still there unconquered — at least not slain.

Now, it is just at this moment of discomfiture that I need the voice of God's angel to call me to the Bread and the Wine, for I

[114] Cf. 3 Kings 19:7 (RSV = 1 Kings 19:7).

have always "yet a long way to go." By no means has the end come. For Elijah, the victory of God over Baal, the slaughter of the priests, the downpour of rain, and the fierce run that he made by the side of the king's chariot from Carmel to the royal city of the northern kingdom, had produced a sense of exaltation that was utterly unsound. The nervous excitement was so tense and strained that the least failure at the moment was bound to become as exaggerated as the supposed triumph had been. The opposition of the queen had been forgotten, or its strength underestimated, and as a result, nervous prostration brought him to despair. Instead of triumph, defeat; so off he goes to the desert, where his feelings entirely change. Not now is there any talk of having been more successful than his predecessors, as had evidently been his previous idea, but only, "I am no better than my fathers," and a cry for death.[115]

So with me, the victory, the overconfidence, the despair — whereas the struggle is only just begun, and it would be foolish at the first assault or repulse or reverse (or even after many) to lose heart or run away or submit. Rather, because of my weariness and dismay is my need for the Food more urgent, that in that externally provided help I may walk the rest of my appointed path. Courage is my greatest requirement, and it is here I shall find it. Even if my age is failing and my time on earth to be short, I have need of that Viaticum for the long last journey of the grave.

[115] 3 Kings 19:4 (RSV = 1 Kings 19:4).

∽

In Communion, you
receive the very life of Christ

It is notorious that the taste of blood brings with it a sort of frenzy or madness. We read of animals that have been brought up in captivity and have been perfectly gentle and tame, losing apparently all the ferocity of their nature, until, by some accident, they taste blood. At once they hear "the call of the wild," and the fierce strain of ancestry, so long pent up, breaks out in desperate behavior.

Man, too, in battle seems to revert to an earlier stage of development. The centuries of civilization slip from him, and he is back in a world of "fangs and maw." The long self-control of savage instincts is suddenly forfeited, and the primitive passions, from the tyranny of which he has slowly fought his way to freedom, regain their control. The atrocities in war of which each nation has been accused are the necessary result of arousing the desire to kill. Once the bridle has been loosened, the plunging steed rushes madly on. What is true of a disciplined army is even more true of a mob; it will do the most desperate things, attack the most defenseless people, once its blood has been roused by the sight of blood.

These animal instincts, of which the individual would hardly be conscious, at once assume a power and a directive voice that silences conscience and reduces will and reason to absolute submission. In the records of the French Revolution, there are tales, perfectly sickening, of deeds inhuman in their ferocity. We find proofs of a savagery that would seem to be impossible in Europe, yet was practiced by women of the middle and lower classes who had seen blood flow. They are evidences of the terrible and horrid frenzy that the taste of blood inspires.

So universal has been this experience, that, among many nations, it is forbidden to eat meat from which the blood has not been drawn off. Especially is this true in the hotter climates, so that in the Old Law, God Himself laid down this command that the Jewish people still obey: "But the blood, which is the life, you shall not eat."[116] The old superstition was that the soul resided in the blood, and that if anyone partook of the blood, the soul of the animal passed into the recipient and at once dominated his will and reason. It is almost as though God approved of this teaching, that all the energy of the soul lurked within the blood.

In any case, there is such intimate relationship between soul and body, and they react so forcibly upon each other, that even the food and the drink we use must indirectly affect our thoughts and desires. God, therefore, was at pains to remove all such passionate influences from His chosen people and made them renounce the use of blood. It was because of the frenzy that it was forbidden.

Then came a new commandment, which set aside and deliberately reversed the earlier command. "The blood, which is the life, you shall not eat" is now "Unless you eat the Flesh of the Son of Man and drink His Blood, you shall have no life."[117] One forbids what the other commands. Both apparently bear witness that in the blood remains the life, but one desires that the life should be barred from entrance, and the other commands that it be worthily and reverently received. The opposition is complete, "Thou shalt

[116] Cf. Lev. 17:14.
[117] Cf. John 6:54 (RSV = John 6:53).

not" and "Thou shalt," and the motive of both behests is the same, for the excitement of the blood carries its message to the brain and throngs the mind with thoughts.

The Old Law, we repeat unceasingly, was the rule of fear, but the New Law is the rule of love. The Old Law forbade all such practices as would awake the passions of the soul; the New Law insists upon their active cooperation. The Old Law was a schoolmaster; the New Law is a friend. On the one hand, the tables of stone, on the other, the perfect figure of Christ; hence, the command is opposed, but the reason remains the same. Blood was forbidden, for it inflamed the passions; because it inflames the passions, it is now of obligation upon all; for the blood of an animal makes frenzied the mind, but the Blood of God inebriates the soul.

We approach Communion and partake of this Blood precisely so that it may seize hold of and make captive our love, that it may sweep across our whole being and, in its rush, lift up our soul from attention to other things and absorb it into union with the divine. "But the Blood, which is the Life, thou shalt eat" is the new commandment; and unless we drink it, we shall have no life; whereas He came that we might have life and have it with greater abundance.[118]

It is true that the Church has, in her wisdom, thought good ordinarily to forbid to the laity Communion under both kinds; and it is perhaps the most daring thing that she has ever done, for it seems, on the face of it, in absolute contradiction of our Lord's express commands. But obviously there is no question of doctrine in it, for the blood and body of a living man can never be separated; and although in Mass there is the double consecration to depict the mystical death of Christ, yet where Christ is, He is whole and entire. Consequently when I receive Communion, let me realize that I receive Blood as well as Body, and, with the Blood, the very life of Christ.

[118] John 10:10.

✺

In Communion, you partake in Christ's Sacrifice

The paradox of life was well voiced by Caiphas; it is expedient always that one man should die and that the whole people should not perish.[119] How or why such a law should enter into the world we cannot tell, but the existence of it is unquestionable; over and over again, one single victim has set a people free. The Old Testament enshrined it in the ritual of the Temple-worship and in the religious practices of the Tabernacle. The scapegoat was little else than this mysterious law consecrated and sanctioned by God. Irrational, incapable of guilt, it was driven into the desert, and there, in solitude, atoned for the sins of the whole nation.

This process of vicarious atonement is frequently evident in history, where, over and over again, we find the death of one man, himself most frequently innocent, being required for the abolition of some injustice or the setting free of some people. The story of the hermit who journeyed to Rome to put an end to the gladiatorial games where human life was sacrificed even in Christian times for the amusement of the populace, and who found no other way to achieve his purpose than by throwing himself into the arena

[119] John 11:50.

and thus, by his death, forcing the evil side of such an entertainment on the crowd, is but one instance out of many. The same sort of story or legend can be found in the history of every nation, for, in the attempts made by a people to throw off the yoke of a tyrant, there is always one man who comes forward and, at the risk of his own life, rescues the lives of his people from their oppression.

In the New Testament, the teaching of Christ seems at times to contain little else than this doctrine: that, to save life, life must be lost. It is the one consistent principle that explains all the rest — itself remaining a mystery above all comprehension: one Man dies so that the world may go free. Somehow upon His head are all our sins placed: "He hath borne our iniquities."[120] He took upon Himself the sins of all the world.

Nor should it be overlooked that our Lord did not suffer the loss of life because He despised life. It is not as though He surrendered something, the value of which He underestimated, since to give freely away what is of no consequence to the donor can hardly be considered an act of generosity. He surrendered life just because He put so high a value upon it and realized the responsibilities of it very much more than anyone else has ever done. For Him, all the world was full of beauty. No one ever spoke as He has done of the charm of nature, of field flowers and falling sparrows, or the graceful fascination of childhood. He lived more intimately with the deep joys of sheer life, for in Him was life. He died so that others might live, just because He knew their need of life, certain that life alone could be of any avail for them. He Himself in one place made the comparison of the mother in labor who put herself in peril that she might set free her child. It was the lesson that better the peril of one than the death of all. It is, therefore, He would seem to show, only with the pangs of death that life can at all begin.

[120] Cf. Isa. 53:5, 11.

On Calvary, therefore, this teaching received its highest sanction; but its richest expression, as far as we individually are concerned, is evident in the Blessed Sacrament. Daily can I draw upon this unfailing fountain of sacrifice. Let me look upon daily Mass and Communion as the living gospel of vicarious suffering. Dying daily for me is Christ, here upon the altar. It is the most eloquent missionary venture of all our Lord's life. To have preached it was, indeed, of great avail, nor will the world willingly let His words die.

Men who do not believe Him to be divine have yet taken His parables as the most expressive utterances on the duty of brotherly love. But His example was even more splendid than His words; for the example of the dead is never so potent as the example of the living. He died, but death did not exhaust the scope of his action, for He rose again, and again acted the same principle. He is sacrificed always for the world and, in the Eucharist, puts Himself at the mercy of men.

How can I be selfish in my relation to others once I have received within me this Victim of the world's redemption? How can I be unjust in life or even watch in silence the injustice of others, the oppression of the poor, the spiteful persecution of the rich? If I go every morning to this sublime sacrifice, it must surely have an influence on my day, the influence of having seen God die. I must take home to my life the saying of Caiphas, and prefer that I should lose all rather than that all the world be lost, prefer their success to my failure.

∞

Communion is the sacrament of sweetness

The Blessed Sacrament is often looked upon, as indeed it is, as the sacrament of strength, but one title cannot exhaust the ways of viewing this sublime mystery of God's mercy. There is need always of courage and hopefulness, and the power of persevering, which comes to us in this sacrament. The added greatness that the nearness of God inspires must unfailingly affect us whenever we approach the altar. But sheer forcefulness in religion will not suffice unless sweetness comes as well to temper the rigidity of our will.

There are people, undoubtedly, who have a very welcome influence upon our lives by imparting to us the bracing atmosphere in which they live, the high mountain air, the freshness of soul that comes from those strong characters whose thoughts are always soaring to the high altitudes of faith and principle; but this is not a lasting influence unless it is accompanied by something more. The military genius may be necessary from time to time in the national life, but no military despotism has ever lasted through more than one generation, simply because it is strong and strong only; it is too rigid to accommodate itself to human affairs. The human spirit lives; that is, the human spirit is always changing.

Now, the main feature, the main helpfulness of strength, is just that it does not change at all. It is fixed, and the ramrod is the symbol of its training. A dictatorship was proclaimed in Rome in times of national crisis; it could restore order, but could not act as a permanent form of government. Even the genius of Cromwell could do nothing against the sentiment of the nation; with all his glories, his undoubted success, he could only for his own lifetime secure in military hands the powers of government.

Religion is much more susceptible even than social life to the evil consequences of mere strength. To be strong of will is only one portion of the moral life. It is necessary, but by itself it is short-lived. The fierce and gloomy fanaticism that begins in a flame of enthusiasm will bear down conqueringly upon any obstacle and sweep it out of the path. But its power is only of today. It cannot last until tomorrow; it has no real hold on human nature; it is too inhuman.

One generation, or two generations at most, have been found to accept Puritanism. Just when it is felt by all to be necessary to save the national life from absolute corruption, it has done good; but the final result, unless it is speedily changed, is to drive people to far worse lengths. The interplay of action and reaction is the inevitable consequence. The licentiousness of the Restoration follows upon the whitewashing puritan Commonwealth. The total disregard for Sunday has been produced by the pharisaical observance of it. The militant forms of religion, such as Mohammedanism, have held their place only by proclaiming a general permission for what Christianity repudiates: they have forbidden wine, but degraded women.

A religion, therefore, that attempts to rule by sheer force and to give to its faithful followers nothing more than strength, is not a religion that can last. Oppressive dullness gives way to riotous amusements. The fear of God, which was the motive power of the Old Testament, could not have the hold of the hearts of men that has been obtained by the new commandment of love. The reign of Christ has outstayed the Law and the Prophets.

Communion is the sacrament of sweetness

This, since He had made the human heart, our Lord perfectly understood. The system of the Incarnation was precisely to appeal to that which was most yielding in the nature of man. The little Child in the stable has no rival in the minds of children, and for grown men and women, His winsome robe of childhood does not in vain hold out its little arms. The Boy of Nazareth, the beautiful young man whose appearance on the seashore drew from the disciples of John the question "Where dwellest Thou?"[121] has not ceased from then to now to draw to Him youth and age. His wooing Passion, His charm of person, the fascination of His appearance still attract to Him the love of the generations as they pass. Nor was He content to come that once and then depart, leaving behind but the fragrance of His visit; for He did all things well. To use His own blessed word, He "abides" with us. He is with us all days, even to the consummation of the world.

Now, His return to us on our altars at Mass, at Communion, is not simply that we might worship, but that the need we have of sweetness in religion might be amply supplied. We must approach His presence, gather about Him, for the refreshment of our lives, to break down the hideous monotony of our work, to add the brightness of love to the gray streets and grayer skies. Not holiness alone, but the beauty of holiness, is required to bind our hearts, our whole souls to God. The child, who, with his wistful trust, demands protection, asks for something more than strong defense; he needs also the warm welcome of love. And insofar are we all children, we need the gentleness and mercy of God to be made manifest, or else we shall be too frightened to go on. If religion is to mean much to me, I must approach the altar of the sweetness of God, who gives joy to my youth.[122]

---

[121] John 1:38.
[122] Ps. 42:4 (RSV = Ps. 43:4).

∞

The Mass re-presents
Christ's redeeming Sacrifice

Think of how the Mass is, in a real sense, the center of Catholicism. All the Faith is gathered around it, so that from the mere wording of the Mass, the rest of the Creed could be almost wholly deduced. The divinity of Christ is clear in the wonderful power that is given to the priest to perform this amazing act of worship, or else man could not even have imagined its possibility. So staggering is the doctrine, that when first announced, even by a Preacher who spoke as none other ever spoke, it broke up the little band; and only the implicit trust that the Apostles had in their Master made them continue as His disciples. They stayed only because they had nowhere else to go.

So, if He is God, it can only be because He is the Son of God; nor can He be God only, for the words of consecration tell us of His Body and His Blood. So, again, besides the Trinity, and the Incarnation, we can arrive at the divine motherhood of our Lady and the other mysteries of Faith.

The sacraments also are arranged around this wonderful sacrifice, as the setting around the gem. Baptism prepares us for our part in it; Confirmation strengthens us in our belief in it; Confession makes us worthy of it; Holy Orders ensures for us the continuation of it; Matrimony, says St. Paul, is the symbol of it; and the Anointing of the Sick imparts to us its fruits. For it are our churches built. It is the center of their construction; it unifies all their architectural lines. Without it, the most splendid places of worship seem empty and cold, and with it, however poorly or badly they may appear, they are made alive. Our Faith, our ceremonies, and our lives are grouped around this supreme act of worship.

The reason thus it stands as the most central of all our mysteries is just because it is itself nothing other than Calvary continued. Calvary meant for us the undoing of all our woe and the upbuilding of our lives for the service of God; and in consequence, the Mass being but a prolongation of that "far-off event," it, too, becomes the living reality of that which is most real in all the world. It is not, indeed, a repetition, for the death of God is so unique an event that repetition becomes impossible. Moreover, St. Paul proclaimed that "Christ, being risen from the dead, dieth now no more; death shall no more have dominion over Him."[123]

The Mass, then, is not the repetition but the continuation of Calvary, one with it in essence, although not in appearance, as the Body of Christ on our altars is the same as the body that walked the earth, although it has not the same outward seeming. The priest, by the double act of consecration, slays as by a mystical sword of sacrifice the Divine Victim, for although Body and Blood cannot be severed while life remains, they are represented as distinct in the difference of accidents, and thus is the death of the Lord shown forth until He comes.

This, then, is the reason for the acknowledged supremacy of the Mass, witnessed to by persecutor and persecuted, that it is for us Calvary still continued. And since all our happiness and all our chance of happiness come from that saving redemption, obviously that which is only a continuation of it must necessarily be held in

[123] Rom. 6:9.

deep reverence. It is the eternal testimony of God's love for man, the eternal stimulus to man's love of God.

To encourage my devotion to this tremendous mystery, let me consider what the morning Mass must have meant to the Mother of God. When her Child had been taken from the Cross and laid in the tomb, she was to see Him on earth again after He had risen from the dead; but after the Ascension, she was to see Him no more until that day when she passed to the Day. But at her Mass, when she watched the Beloved Disciple hold up what seemed bread, and when she heard the whispered words of power, she knew Him once again in the breaking of the Bread. Dare we trespass nearer on that sacred intimacy? She saw, as on Calvary, her Son's death.

For St. Peter, St. John, and the rest, how fervent must have been at Mass their reparation for that sad night when they left Him, or denied Him, or stood far off from Him! What comfort, consolation, and encouragement in their missionary ventures, that were ventures of faith indeed!

Let me think of the strength that came to them every morning that they held in their hands the Bread, and knew it, indeed, to become that Body they had seen and handled — for the men and women and troops of little children imprisoned in the catacombs, who found in the Mass, said in the wind-swept passages amid the tombs of the martyred Christians, the grace to meet with patience the trouble that each day brought, who saw in the sacrifice the open door beyond their narrowed lives. However dreary or intolerable in itself, the hour was made glad and cheerful by the savor of this saving rite. Our fathers in the days of persecution risked all for the chance Mass, and the infrequent visit of a priest who might repeat for them the ceremonies of the Upper Room in Jerusalem, and make the loss of lands and life easy compared with the gaining of that "seldom presence."

If I wish to value aright my privilege of the Mass, I must follow intelligently the whole ceremony.

∞

The office of the priest deserves respect

In an analogy that might be drawn up between the life of the soul and social life, Holy Orders would correspond to the various grades of government that are necessary for the well-being of the nation. This sacrament is simply to constitute the hierarchy of priests and bishops, by which Christ our Lord desired His Church to be ruled. Since, then, these were to receive certain powers that were proper to them alone, it was obvious that some sort of ceremonious consecration had to be adopted so that this special and exclusive gift might be recognized as accurately bestowed.

Below the priests are a whole series of lesser ecclesiastical persons: deacons, subdeacons, the four minor orders, and the tonsured clerk; but it is the traditional teaching of the Church that only those who have been ordained to the diaconate, the priesthood, or the episcopate receive the grace of the sacrament. Here, again, we have, as in Baptism and Confirmation, the conferring on the soul of a special character that cannot be repeated for the simple reason that it has no need to be repeated, for the power once conferred remains efficacious for life. Once ordained, there is no need for the service to be repeated, but, morning by morning, Mass can be offered, sins forgiven, the living strengthened for their long last journey. Once a priest, then a priest forever according to the order of Melchisedech.[124] However unworthy or unideal, a consecrated minister of God must remain sacred in his office to my eyes. Nothing can ever remove him from his position, which he holds in the sight of all Heaven, a priest forever.

My attitude toward the priest must therefore always exhibit a consciousness that he stands for something more than merely the official representative of the Church. He has received in a special way the anointing that, in the words of St. Paul, makes him the mediator (because the continuator of the work of Christ through the power of Christ) between God and man. He offers to God the things of the people, and to the people the things of God.

I must therefore put out of my mind his particular personality, or want of it, to forget his social position and my own, and consider him as the representative of God in the things that pertain to the altar. Obviously there will be many things that I shall dislike in his methods and ideals, but where the altar is considered, he is to be treated with the respect that is due to his sacred office. It does not matter who he is; it should be enough for me that he is a priest.

In this way, it is obvious that the Catholic places the priest on a higher post of advantage than do other religious worshipers; yet, on the other hand, Catholics value less than any other the particular gifts of the individual. For them, it hardly matters who is saying Mass, for it is the Mass itself that they go to hear. At the Benediction service, it is again our Lord, not His minister, that concerns those present. Hence, for us, less than in any other religion, the priest does not stand between the soul and God, but is an instrument, as water is the instrument of Baptism, whereby the union of God and man is made effective. Respect, then, for the office of the priesthood is the first lesson that we learn from the sacrament of Holy Orders.

[124] Heb. 5:6.

The office of the priest deserves respect

Not only respect should be shown to him, though, but also a willingness to help him in any way that seems to offer. Of course, there are members of the laity who are already too inclined to interfere in priestly work, just as there are priests who seem determined to stifle every effort of the laity, and who look upon lay-work in a parish as though it were something heterodox. Apart, however, from these extreme cases, it will obviously be of the utmost importance for a priest to have members of his congregation on whom he can rely for the more effective administration of it. There are sure to be clubs for boys, or clubs for working girls, which need the constant attendance of their secretaries and helpers; there are the altar societies, and so forth; above all, there is the Society of St. Vincent de Paul, which may have an untold effect in any congregation. It supplements the work of the priest by being more regular in its visits than he can well afford time to give. It can continue cases that he has once begun, or even begin the visiting of families or individuals where the priest might at first have difficulty in finding an entrance.

Zeal, then, is the other requirement that the priest has a right to look for from us. Says Lacordaire, "The priest is a man anointed by tradition to shed blood, not as the soldier through carnage, not as the magistrate through justice, but as Jesus Christ through love. The priest is a man of sacrifice; by it each day announcing to every soul the primordial truths of life, of death, and of resurrection, and by it each day reconciling Heaven and earth."

It is the Mass that makes the priest possible, the confessional that makes him necessary; but without a laity who have at heart the welfare of their fellow Catholics, who are filled with reverence for his office and zeal for his better accomplishing of it, his time may be reduced to utter distraction. I must realize my duties, examine my past, and make a resolution to offer my services.

∝

The sacrament of Matrimony
has exalted the state of marriage

In the sacrament of Matrimony, our Lord makes sacred the most intimate act of life, wherein two become one flesh. The purpose of the married state He has Himself commanded. Without it, the race would cease to exist, and all the designs of God come to naught; it is consequently essential to the economy of the divine plan. From this, then, we may quite rightly argue that it is a great good. Indeed, God Himself ordained it as a command upon all His creatures that they should increase and multiply, and He has in the New Law made a sacrament to safeguard its interests and to ensure its proper fulfillment.

Marriage itself is an act whereby two are made one in mutual love. All the other ideas that have gathered around the family life have sprung from this as the primal idea. The concept of a family and of even wider relationships, the hoarding of possessions and the encampment or settlement in a house, and the setting up of a sacred hearth around which the family might assemble to ask the protection of its own particular deity have all evolved out of the rudimentary notion that by marriage two have become one. Whatever may be the theories by which we explain the origin of the family — and these theories are as numerous as the professors in

410

universities — we are forced to suppose that the two came to-gether who were before looked upon, as we say, as "single," and that from this they became one: two notes in complete harmony, a union that transcends all difference.

Now, it is perfectly clear from any study of human nature that the whole tendency of individuals, especially when thrown into each other's company, is to separation. The ideas of two tend on the whole to spring apart. The very fact that the other person holds a view is reason sufficient for holding its opposite. Especially is this likely to happen where two are forever facing each other at all times of day, in moments of irritability, in all moods and tempers. The very likeness in taste or temperament or habit is bound to ap-pear at times when it should not, and to produce friction that will lead to serious trouble unless it is treated with a tact that is rare to find and still rarer to find continuously. The effect of a family, which should prove a bond by linking the parents together in a mutual love of at least a third person, in fact turns sometimes to the other result and produces such divergence of views on education and so forth as to produce, rather than peace, ultimate estrangement.

Of course, the answer to all this is that it supposes the absence of love, whereas the idea of marriage is based on love and, apart from love, has no significance. Let love come in, and then the things that might prove a source of difference result, on the whole, in a deeper affection. Difference itself becomes a bond of union. The two souls become complementary to one another; each sup-plies what is lacking to the other.

It is obvious that love does bridge over the chasm and holds souls together. But is not this, too, part of the danger? For although love unites as can nothing else, so long as love is there, what is to happen at those times when love is least powerful — when human charms cease to appeal or, by their satisfaction, have extinguished all desire? Love is strong while it lasts, but who shall guarantee that love will last?

It is just here that the sacrament of marriage enters into its place in the stream of Catholic Tradition. It brings to love the safeguard of a divine protection. It wards off the approach of dullness and boredom by illuminating the whole of family life with the outpouring of love divine. The Spirit of God, in virtue of the Passion of Christ, sets in the soul the power to hold on in spite of every difficulty. It adds to love the wisdom and discernment to allow to each that freshness and spontaneity that is required for the full tale of love.

When pleasure in such a life might make men forget the responsibilities of their high calling, it is the infusion of grace that brings back the vision of earlier days. It is the sacrament that makes the father and mother realize that they have duties to perform to their race, and holds them to the labor and travail whence is born the joy of the world. Abolish this, and in how many cases would not the result be the end of the family, often the end of the national existence?

So highly has the married life been exalted by this sacrament that St. Paul, to whom in many ways the single life evidently made personal appeal, sets it up as the very image of the intimate union that exists between Christ and His Church: so high is it in his eyes that it stands as a great mystery — that is, a shrine of the dwelling of God. For a Catholic, therefore, the married state is itself a high calling from God. The duties therein incurred are of divine origin, blessed by God, and safeguarded by the grace that this attracts; they have become the living symbols of God's union with man. Mutual acceptance means one single law of faithfulness for both, which no amount of custom or tradition can be allowed to impair. Thus does the blood of Christ make holy a calling that is the exact reproduction of the central fact of the Christian revelation, for it takes God to make a family.

∞

The Anointing of the
Sick aids body and soul

The Anointing of the Sick has been in constant use in the Church. From the story of the life of our Lord as told us in the Gospels, we find that the record of miracles achieved was looked upon by Him as a sign that His mission was approved by God. In His answer to the disciples of John the Baptist, He called attention to the wonders that He daily worked among the people: "The blind see, the dumb speak, the deaf hear, the lepers are cleansed, the dead rise again."[125]

In another place, it is written of Him that on account of the unbelief of some of His hearers, He could do no miracle, "except that He healed the bodies of some that were sick."[126] This last was evidently looked upon as so ordinary an event, that even their want of faith could not prevent it. Nor, apparently, does our Lord regard this part of His ministry as something particular to Himself, for He was at pains, when sending out the Apostles in His lifetime, to give them power to heal the sick, and He foretold that, when He had gone, the same powers were to continue in the Church, so

[125] Matt. 11:5.
[126] Mark 6:5.

that things even greater than He had Himself done would be done in His Name.[127]

Nor is it simply in the light of an extraordinary sign, but rather as an ordinary event, that the power of healing is spoken of by Him and by His Apostles; they all seem to take it for granted. In the Acts of the Apostles, this power is exercised with perfect freedom by Peter and John immediately after Pentecost. It is found in every record of the early Church, and no surprise is shown at its continued existence; but rather, the impression is forced upon us that the ceasing of such a power would, indeed, have caused no little wonder.

So common was this gift that it could not even be regarded as an adjunct of sanctity, although it was that also. Not merely was this gift of healing to be committed to those whose nearness to God made them as potent to work good as the hem of the garment of Christ, but to every priest the same power was confided. Thus, the gift of healing became part of the ordinary heritage of the Church. It became a sacrament, and because it thus came into the ritual and ceremonious usage of the Church, it was certain and wise that regulations would be made to safeguard its proper administration.

The conditions that are now exacted are simply, therefore, to be interpreted as growing up around something that, from the very frequency of its repetition, would otherwise be in constant danger of being abused. It is not to be supposed that the Church has forgotten the marvels committed to her for the use of her children. She has never allowed this miraculous power to lapse, or imagined that it was something that failed with the apostolic body. It was to be a persistent sacrament. In the prayers that compose its ritual performance, the idea of healing is repeated over and over again: "By this holy anointing and of His own tender mercy, may the Lord forgive thee whatever sins thou hast committed by thy sight,

[127] John 14:12.

hearing, sense of smell, taste and speech, hands, feet" is the actual phrasing whenever the members of the body are anointed, but the idea running through the whole ceremony is rather the bodily ease that the sacrament is to give. Health to the body, forgiveness to the soul, is the burden of the ritual, and such also is, in a true sense, the burden of the life of Christ.

The care of my life is partly the preparing for my last end. No doubt I best prepare by living as I would be found when death comes to me, but it does not follow that every sickness is unto death, nor should I suppose that it is my business when I am ill to make no effort toward recovery. However great the pain, I should be content to remain here and do my best to use the wonderful body God has given me — resigned to death, but resigned also to life.

Nor should I be like those who imagine that the last sacraments are to be received when there is no more hope; rather, they are to be given as soon as there is any danger at all, and it is to be remembered that they are given precisely so that hope may come, precisely so that I may have the courage to go on struggling for my life. The outward sign is, as in Confirmation, the consecrated oil, and this surely shows that what I most need is strength — courage to face the alternatives of life and death, the long-drawn agony that must precede them both, the tremendous struggle, with my soul already exhausted from illness, to battle my way out to life. The kindness of those about me should nerve me against the weariness of giving in.

For all this, the sacrament is sufficient. It aids my body, it aids my soul. It gives me the grace to accept whatever God has in store for me, but it also is at pains to emphasize the importance of the body and the hope we have that it will be "restored to its former health." Let me, therefore, make use of this sacrament as a preparation for my last end, and as an acknowledgment that even my body and its health are of value in God's sight, so that for it He was willing to institute a special sacrament.

Part 15

∞

Daily virtues

∞

Do not let life's perils daunt you

Boldness or daring is based upon hope, and to enkindle such enthusiasm, that hope must be exceedingly vehement, just as despair is based upon very vehement fear. Yet there is a difference between hope and courage, in that hope fixes its eyes upon the good thing to be achieved, whereas courage is conscious all the while of the immense difficulties that stand in between. Hope considers the overcoming of the obstacles, courage the obstacles to be overcome.

The paths, indeed, may be rough, and the ground hilly, and the boulders that lie in the way may have every appearance of being too huge to be pushed aside ("Who shall roll us back the stone?"[128]), yet hope goes clambering on without much regard for its torn feet. Deliberately it is determined not to look down, but heartens itself for the stiff climb by keeping its eyes fixed on the summit toward which it toils. Not down, but up, do its eyes look. Boldness, courage, and daring are more terrible because more venturesome. Thus, in religion hope keeps its gaze resolutely turned to the grace of God: it repeats over to itself that with God all things are possible and continually reminds itself that it will never be left alone in life, that God is continually watching and aiding.

[128] Mark 16:3.

But the virtue of courage can all the while persist in hoping, and yet be conscious of its own human frailty. It is a sort of hypostatic union that links together the strength of God and the weakness of man. It takes the measure not merely of the summit, but of the hazard that stands between; counts not the crown only, but the peril.

Boldness, leaping at the chance, conscious of the risk, cannot be caused by ignorance. Men do not account him daring who is ignorant of the perils through which he has passed; nor would they say a man was courageous unless they were certain that he had quietly considered the danger, had seen beforehand the venture, counted the cost, yet persevered. Some, indeed, begin great and heroic enterprises in the flush and impetus of enthusiasm, growing slower and slacker as they gradually realize the dangers, perils, and risks. We may call them impetuous, or rash, but hardly daring.

The man who has real courage, daring, may begin perfectly slowly, so much so that others may well judge him to be half-hearted in his work. They see that he has no rush, no swift attempts. He goes on painfully, conscious of his difficulties; yet he goes. He has counted his cost. He has seen beforehand how terribly alone he would find himself. He runs no unnecessary risks; but he goes on unsparingly, relentlessly. He has seen it all, and nothing that subsequently appears will frighten him off. He has long ago passed through that stage. Panic will not affect him, for alone, in the solitude of his own heart, he has already faced the "questing beast." He does not ignore his task, nor put his telescope to his blind eye, but with full vision fronts his peril.

Now, it is just that which must be my attitude toward life, my attitude toward the full responsibilities of my Catholic life. I must face the whole question of it deliberately. I must make quite certain of all that it entails, not dodge things simply because they are dangerous, nor try to shuffle out of my duties on the plea that I was ignorant of my obligations, nor, on the other hand, pretend that Catholic life has no dangers.

Everything that is holy is thereby dangerous. Everything is dangerous in precise proportion to its sacredness. Holy Communion, Faith, and friendship are great gifts, and on that very account are beset with innumerable perils.

Now, it is part of virtue to face all these things with a perfect consciousness of my risk. I must not be content with looking upon the sacraments and so forth as merely helps and comforts. They are all that, thank God, but that does not exhaust their potentialities. The very sanctity of the Ark struck death to the hand put out to save its fall.[129]

Without all these wonderful gifts, I shall fail. It is possible that with them I shall fail also. At least I must be perfectly alive to the possibility. I must, therefore, be wide awake to their peril, yet bold enough not to refuse them on that account. I must accept them with eyes open. St. Paul told his converts that they had to be fools for Christ. I must vehemently persuade myself that for Christ I must also be foolhardy.

---

[129] 2 Kings 6:6-7 (RSV = 2 Sam. 6:6-7).

∞

Use your gifts and talents
to serve God and others

We are continually saying that for the gifts of God committed to us we must render an account. It has been a platitude in political speeches, and in the labor pamphlets of social reformers of every complexion, to declare that we are the stewards of all that we possess, that in real truth we possess nothing, but only administer what God has committed to us. Ordinarily this principle is applied merely to wealth, which is, after all, the most vulgar application of the principle.

No doubt it is of importance that those who hold property should realize that the holding of it involves certain quite definite responsibilities; that no ownership is absolute or without limitations; that what is really superfluous to us is not ours at all, if there are others who stand in need of it. The enjoyment of wealth is no doubt a very obvious way in which these truisms are being ignored; and the results of the more or less modern view of absolute ownership of capital are so apparent and so widespread that naturally people complain about it first.

But there are other and higher faculties, more important possessions or powers, wealth of a nobler kind, that must all be subjected to the same searching criticism. I must look into all the gifts that I have received from God and see how far I have realized that my possession of them is merely such as a steward might have.

We may even advance the principle further and declare that the higher the responsibility, the greater are the claims of others upon us. A poet has spoken from the experience of his saddened life in the line, "The more the gift, the more the suffering." He does but voice the whole record of humanity. Those, for example, whose ears are more delicately attuned to perceive beauties of tone that are lost on others gain pleasure that others cannot feel; yet, at the same time, they have also a distinct and maddening sense of discords of which others have no conception. And so is it with all the gifts of God.

But part of this very pain is also the consciousness that these gifts afforded us by God have to be employed not for our own pleasure, but for the service of our fellows. The higher we are placed, the less do we really belong to ourselves: so that the Son of Man came not to be ministered unto, but to minister, and "the sweetest and strongest" and truest title of the Vicar of Christ is that he is the "Servant of the Servants of God."

We might even quite easily go further and, with reverence, assert that no one is more at the beck and call of creatures than the Creator. He tells us that beneath us are the everlasting arms, and ventures Himself on the simile that He has carried us through life as the mother is wont to carry her little child. In a very real sense, God is the servant of His servants. When they rebel against Him in sin, He goes out to seek for them, hunting for them as the Hound of Heaven, and dies for them again.

How far does this affect me? What are my gifts, and how do I use them — for my sake, or for the sake of those for whom God gave them to me?

First of all, I must face the fact that I have certain definite talents given to me at the entrance of life, or acquired by the continued kindness of God to me. There is no virtue in pretending not to have them, no virtue possible in a deliberate lie. Each has his own talent. For some, it may be a small thing, for others, greater — time, leisure, money, power of sympathy, position of influence, clearness of expression, cheerfulness, wit, beauty, youth's enthusiasm or the wisdom of age, faith or prayer, or skill in some art or craft or game. Politeness to God, gratitude, will make me anxious to know where exactly I have the power of helping others, where my responsibility lies.

Then I must ask myself how I am using this. It is a principle of education that seems most congenial to us to accept, that the only way to train souls is to trust them, that if you want to cure an enmity, you must find some favor that can be done to you by the people who are offended. Now, God has so trusted me. He has given me things to do for Him. Am I doing them? Am I conscious, for example, of my responsibility in being a Catholic, not merely in the uses to which I put my graces and gifts for my own salvation, but as to how I employ them for others? I am a Catholic: am I also an Apostle?

⚬⚬

Living the Faith calls for strength

There is a grave danger in Catholic education, a danger that follows from the very Catholic atmosphere, which, we insist, must surround the early years of childhood. Nor does this peril cease with childhood or with the end of school life, but continues for just so long as we remain within the direct and exclusive influence of Catholicism. For the purpose of education is to train the character of the child; yet it is just possible that the whole time we remained within this Catholic environment, we were making no effort to train ourselves. The whole effect of our surroundings may have been that, instead of guiding us to a healthier state of self-dependence, and realizing our own individual responsibility, we were lapsing into weakness and indecision.

It is true that such a result is a mere possibility, not even a probability. Yet why is it that we see about us so many wrecked souls whose education has been of the best? Why is it that, again and again, boys at school with us, brought up by competent masters and under the strongest religious influences, should, within a few years of their leaving college, have come upon such evil ways? Girls, too, after spending considerable time within a convent school, where the whole atmosphere spoke of purity, faith, and self-sacrifice, have become selfish, creedless, and of evil life. It is no longer possible to deny these facts, for every year brings to our notice further examples of them.

Why should Catholic education so often fail?

We may admit that the evil effect here noticed is due precisely to the Catholic atmosphere, in the sense that the whole danger arises from the greater ease with which goodness is achieved in Catholic surroundings. I may quite easily myself be taking — as many a child, certain later to fail, has taken — the line of least resistance. The good boy loses his faith, and the bad boy turns out best. That is the judgment of the cynic; and it contains just this element of truth: that it is possible that the good boy was good because he found it to be less trouble, whereas the bad boy was bad because he had a will of his own and found he could realize his will only by acting in contravention of all rules and regulations.

Perhaps I can remember at school, or within my family circle, that I was in the habit of fulfilling regularly my religious duties, going to daily Mass, reciting my morning and night prayers, and so forth, not from any sense of duty, but because I found by experience that doing so really worked out as least trouble in the end. If I did everything regularly, no fuss was made; but if I neglected anything, questions were asked and penalties assigned. Is it not quite possible that by my method, or rather motive of action, I got myself into the way of doing whatever caused least trouble? At school, I went to Mass and the sacraments; during the holidays, I stayed away from both: and this for the same reason — it was the easiest thing to do.

All this, to repeat, is the danger to which I am liable just so long as I remain within the direct and exclusive influence of Catholicism. Yet I must have become conscious by this time that religion, to be solid and worthy of the name, requires from me a good deal of strength. Often I hear that it is the weak-willed who take refuge in religion, yet does not my personal experience give the lie to this legend? In my own life, has it been through decision or through laziness that the practices of the Faith have ever grown lax? Surely, for myself, it is the very strenuousness of Catholicism that makes it hard for me to live up to its ideals. It is the very ideals and the demands they make upon my poor human nature that have proven my stumbling block or at least my difficulty. Says Hilaire Belloc, with just that touch of wit that brings home the truth, "To be a good Catholic, one must be a strong man; this is why so many women are good Catholics."

It is the strength of heroism that will alone be wanting to me, if I am not a good Catholic. My prayer should be for strength; to cling to God not by my weakness, but by my strength. I must never be afraid of a deliberate and decisive will. Where authority decides, I must give way. But this, too, requires decision on my part, a resolute act of will based on reason. When authority leaves the course open to me, I shall take my own line, for decision is my need in life. If I decide at all, I shall probably be right. It is "the sluggard who willeth and willeth not."

∞

True freedom comes from submission to God's will

It sounds like a paradox, this phrase of St. James: "the perfect law of liberty."[130] Between law and liberty too often an opposition is set up by those who mistake words for ideas. In reality, they are not opposed, but interrelated; they exist necessarily for each other's sake, for law implies liberty, and liberty requires law. The false idea of liberty has grown out of a false idea of law, for the connection between the two is so close and so essential that any misunderstanding of one will necessitate a misunderstanding of the other.

The wise treatise of St. Thomas Aquinas on law, in the second part of his *Summa Theologica*, fixes as part of the definition of law that it should be according to reason, ultimately according to the divine reason. But reason is also the very basis of liberty. I cannot freely choose unless I can see and set in order what I have to choose and why I choose it. And liberty itself, in its true meaning, can also be described as signifying nothing else than an opportunity given to the will for acting according to reason.

Freedom means simply that I must be able to do my duty, and freedom is always outraged whenever I am prevented from doing

[130] James 1:25.

whatever I ought to do. The purpose, then, of law is to safeguard liberty, and liberty consists in fulfilling law. Liberty has nothing at all to do with privilege; privilege indeed almost always means that other people's liberty is being interfered with. An exemption from a law at least tends to become ordinarily a disregard for law.

When we approach political and social questions, it is still more evident that liberty and law are interrelated. Laws are multiplied, or should be, only that liberties may be increased. Law indeed restrains, but does not thereby oppose, liberty. Law restrains others from interfering with my liberty, and me from interfering with theirs. Hence, an increase in civilization must bring with it a multiplication of laws, for the need becomes more and more insistent of preventing others from hurting my freedom. Law restrains violence and creates liberty. Without it, we would obviously sink back into anarchy and be at the mercy of anyone and everyone.

The older philosophers, in their justification for the state, contrast with the easy and quiet life of normal times the fury of unrestrained and individual feuds, such as, they supposed, preceded the creation of tribes with codes of law. They speak of that earlier stage of the history of the race as making life "nasty, brutish, short." Whether they were historical in the surmise does not, for the moment, interest us. But it is clear that, previously to law, there could have been no liberty.

Civil institutions, legislation, and so forth are valuable, therefore, just insofar as they enable the will to follow reason, and are harmful insofar as they make that following impossible. That is the supreme test. Antireligious legislation or the privilege legislation that is afforded to Catholics must be judged for its wisdom on this principle: How far does it permit a man to do his duty?

This, then, must be my ideal as a Catholic, this perception of law as safeguarding liberty, and this perception of liberty as being nothing else than the free opportunity for carrying out law. It is a state of soul, an attitude not an action, a being not a doing, for "the kingdom of God is withn you."[131] Within the stage of my soul is acted the whole drama of life. Then only am I really free when law itself becomes the spring of action. Then only have I understood what is meant by liberty, when I have identified myself absolutely with law, when my will is absolutely absorbed in the divine law, which is the divine will and the divine reason. Then only have I the "glorious liberty of the sons of God,"[132] when I am so strongly impregnated with submission to the will of God that I obey not out of fear, as a servant, but out of love, as a son.

The spirit of Christ is just that. He was the most free of all mankind, unhampered by evil habits, denouncing without fear what called out to Him for judgment. Yet with all His freedom, nay, because of it, He was absolutely obedient to the Father. "I come to do the will of Him that sent me"[133] comes almost monotonously from His lips. He was free because law-abiding.

By freedom, therefore, I must mean not indetermination or hesitancy, but a very real determination whereby all constraint to the divine will is removed and I become free because I am identified with it. Begun on earth, this freedom can be completed only in Heaven, where there is perfect freedom, where alone our sonship is finally achieved, where we shall be truly "born of God,"[134] one with Him, where alone is finally observed "the perfect law of liberty."

[131] Cf. Luke 10:9.
[132] Cf. Rom. 8:21.
[133] Cf. John 6:38.
[134] 1 John 3:9.

∞

You can profit from your mistakes

It is one of the signs of man's superiority over the animals that he can make mistakes, and, moreover, profit by them. An animal is guided by that queer faculty that we do not understand, but label "instinct" under the pleasurable, although inaccurate, impression that when we have given anything a name, we have at once explained it. But all that we really mean by the phrase is that they live, build their homes, choose their food, cross ocean or forest or huge tracts of territory, guided solely by means of this compass-like faculty that forever directs them. Hence, they very seldom go wrong. They know just when and how to act, and when and how to cease from acting.

Birds may teach their young to fly or to swim, and beasts may learn from their elders hints for hunting; but it is something very unlike (because apparently without any stupidity), the schooling through which every child of man has to pass. The animals are practically always right, because they have practically no choice. Instinct, to serve its purpose, must be sure.

Man, on the other hand, has been endowed with reason. He has, therefore, the fatal faculty of freedom, in the sense that he may argue, deduce, be persuaded, or prove only from experience (his own, or accepted authoritatively from others) what is useful or healthful to him, what is most or least conducive to his comfort. Unlike the beast, therefore, he can and has to make mistakes, although his reason also can profit by their making.

Mistakes are, therefore, the means by which man eventually achieves success. And the very same qualities of reason that are the causes of his mistakes are also the causes of his progress. It is the very fact of being able to argue, deduce, and so forth that gives him the power to learn from error. Our books on self-help, of which the English-speaking world has always a plentiful store, and the customary stories with a moral make us realize that failure should not be a signal for giving in, but merely a provocation for going on.

This is surely perfectly evident. It is only by mistakes that we shall probably learn anything at all — by making mistakes, noticing why we made mistakes, and thereby profiting from our mistakes. We must study our failures to see where and why we failed.

But there is something more that I can add and that is this: our own natural mistakes are the best for us, just because they are our own. When we listen to foolish advice, are overborne by it against our judgment, and follow it and fail, we shall probably not get the same benefit we would have gotten had we followed our own inclinations and failed. In other words, the mistake we made was not ours, but another's, and it is exceedingly difficult to learn from anybody else's mistakes. It is not seldom that we profit from another's success, but seldom from another's failure.

Hence, there is a great deal to be said for those who are determined to follow out their own line of life at their own risk; at least it is probable that nothing you may say will affect them. You may turn from them with irritation, remarking that only when they have come to grief will they understand and thank you, but that is an open confession that it is precisely their own mistake that alone can profit them. Of course they will fail, but it will be a failure entirely in accordance with their own character, and from it, therefore, they may well hope to "make good."

You can profit from your mistakes

To the advice of others I should always listen with great patience, but I should not act merely on what is told to me. I must weigh it carefully, consider the particular authority with which others speak and the better opportunities they have had of judging, the consensus of opinion, and so forth. But, finally, I must make up my own mind. If I choose at all, I shall in all probability choose well; but even if I come to grief, that should teach me more good than harm.

In war and peace, in art and science, and even in the spiritual life, it is probable that I gain more from defeat than from victory. It is my faculty of being able to make mistakes that enables me to make profit by them. "They say best men are molded out of faults"; "some rise by vice and some by virtues fall," is Shakespeare's comment upon life. It is the teaching, too, of the Gospel, where Magdalen achieves far higher praise than Martha. For to fail and gain profit out of failure is the peculiar glory of man in an imperfect world, unless he be preserved, as was the Queen of Saints, from the consequences of the Fall.

∞

True criticism recognizes the good in others

It is a jeer as cheap as any other to say that a critic is only an artist who has failed. It is, indeed, perfectly possible that plenty of criticisms that we hear are the result of jealousy and are merely expressed at the expense of a more successful rival. But it is utterly untrue to imagine that criticism can only be of such a nature, or even that remarks based entirely upon such petty personal spite can ever be really criticism that is worthy of the name.

Each soul, my own soul, has need of a distinctive and clear critical faculty, which it is part of my business in life to train. In an age that is alive and swarming with ideas (as every age must seem to the generation that inhabits it), no one, if he is content to accept everything and everybody at their own face value or at the price at which they esteem their own importance, can hope to walk unscathed. To be the dupe of every charlatan is not Christian, but criminal. On the contrary, Christianity is meant to give us such a philosophy of life, such a genius and feeling for the real and the true, that we can detect the fallacy, the blustering or cunning fallacy, of the spirits that move around us. It is part of the Faith to test and discern of these spirits whether they be of God.[135]

---

[135] 1 John 4:1.

True criticism recognizes the good in others

Yet even so, to detect the defects of people and systems is a very rudimentary — the very lowest — form of criticism. It must always be a function of criticism to discover error, and I must train myself to possess it, lest I follow, in blind hero-worship, some wayward but forceful leader.

But it is much more necessary for me to be able to detect beauty, half-hidden or ill-expressed. That is the highest, because it is the most creative, form of criticism and will be of most intense help to me in the spiritual life. For really, all through my days on earth, so much is coming into my view that is, for all intents and purposes, lost on me, just because I have no eyes to see it. One of our writers has put all this idea very clearly in the form of a deft paradox: "Experience," says he, "is a matter of intuition," by which, I suppose, he means that merely having existed for a long time need not teach us wisdom. For "the Bourbons learnt nothing and forgot nothing" — with all their tragedies and their failures, their incessant successes and defeats, they never seemed to consider wherein their failure lay, for it is an intuitive gift that can alone make profit out of experience.

In other words, we see only what our eyes have been trained to see, and not necessarily what is really there. A man who has disciplined himself to observe his surroundings, whose wit has been made nimble enough to notice and to deduce, can pass through the same place as a duller soul and find it alive with interests and principle and the lessons of life. Each finds what he has himself brought. Not sight, but insight, is man's chiefest need, the requisite faculty of discerning what is wasted on others. The critic in this sense is the most noble and magnanimous and helpful of men, for his gift of finding fault is balanced by his gift of finding value.

Now, to achieve this wonderful state of soul, of discovering signs of beauty beneath the rough and the unlovely, there is required an intense appreciation of the ways of others, an intense gift of sympathy. To understand them and to see their value, I must be able to put myself in their place, grasp the ideals possible to them in their circumstances, learn the pedigree of their thoughts and aspirations, and endeavor to find out the difficulties that they had to overcome. I must love them, in other words, before I can find out what there is to love in them. I must begin to expect beauty before I can hope to see it when it comes. Sudden appreciations of art or friendship are really the violent explosion of a fuse that has subconsciously been long alight.

I must, therefore, in my attitude toward life be ready to find good. In discussing people, I must be as much alive to their valuable qualities, however hidden, as to their worthless ways, however blatant: the latter will be noted by the obvious-minded, the former by true critics alone.

That is the true science of criticism, and its spiritual power is enormous. It enables me to pass by, as of no account, the petty gossip of the world. Any fool can see another's folly, but the wise alone can see another's wisdom. Just as the artist-critic can still discern gleams of beauty amid much roughness and lack of technique, can trace the hand of genius (even though untrained) in lines, unkempt, ill-drawn, and ill-focused, so should the true follower of Christ be able to discover, by the quick intuition of charity, very much of grandeur and nobility in character, that otherwise would be passed by as of little account. Indeed, the cynic is not even human. Let me not search the whole world for an honest man, but find in every man a whole world of honesty.

∞

Work provides you with many benefits

Labor is the law of life. Even before the Fall, action of some kind was necessary. The curse of God that followed upon sin only added the punishment of difficulty and weariness. Man must always work, but since the sin of Adam, it has become a burden as well as a necessity. That it is a necessity is apparent from the very facts of consciousness. It is the price we pay for existence. Life is incompatible with inactivity, for if we stagnate, we die. Will, fancy, conscience, reason, and every known power of man is subject to the same law of development — namely, to preserve a faculty, it must be exercised. Without such frequent recourse to activity, the power will become atrophied, will cease really to be of any value.

Labor, therefore, is the origin of all true greatness and dignity, the badge of intelligence. God on His throne is a principle of fuller life than ours, because of higher activity; and the infinite life of the blessed Three-in-One, the constant interchange of Power, Wisdom, and Love is the richest labor (although, of course, without difficulty or weariness) of which existence is capable. The development, then, of the faculties is essential to their preservation, is a condition of life, since life itself must be always dynamic — that is, moving, growing, changing — not static or hardened, or still, or wrought into a perfect shape without intensity. A language or a science is dead when it is no longer capable of being freshened to meet the ever-widening experience of life.

Labor of some kind (even if it brings with it no sense of toil) is a condition of human life. But since the Fall, there has been added a sense of weariness, the result of which is to act upon human nature and make it shun activity as inconvenient. The difficulties that labor itself now always universally implies tend to make the average man escape from labor when he can. It is possible, indeed, that I am so interested in my work or profession that it is a real pleasure to me to be engaged in it; and the very sense of weariness that overcomes me as the day closes may itself bring with it an added joy, as of duty done.

Yet, for all that, I know, and with increasing years am made daily conscious, that the very interest of the work adds to the exhaustion of the toil quite as much as though the whole of it were extremely distasteful to me. Whether I enjoy my profession or am out of all sympathy with it, it must certainly prove every year more exacting. Difficulties are assuredly not far off from me at any time; so that to earn the bread of mind or of body, I must first toil for it. While, therefore, I am assured that activity is the whole condition of life, I must also recognize the fact that this activity is bound to be full of toil in the continuance of human life. It is a toil, but not in itself a degradation. To work at certain trades may be degrading, but work in itself is a necessity for God and for man.

My attitude, therefore, toward all labor, whether my own or another's, must first be one of reverence, since, in so fulfilling the law of my being, I am made after the image and likeness of God; He, too, is a worker.

Both pagan and Christian thinkers have made it their definition of God that He is sheer activity, that there is nothing that He can do and, as far as He is concerned, has not done. There are no latent capacities in Him. His power and wisdom and love are active to the extent of infinity. So, besides simply accepting labor, whether of mind or heart or hand, as something sacrosanct, alone worthy to be exchanged for the material comforts of life, I must also remember that, by a divine betrothal, toil is married to labor, so that none may put them permanently asunder. No one should be exempt from either. All should work, and all should feel the weariness of work.

Moreover, of course I can see for myself how much I need the discipline of it, the actual strengthening, developing power it has on my character; and, correspondingly, the harm that is done me when I have no work. To be unemployed by man is to be dangerously near being employed by the Devil. I must be prepared for the difficulties that attend the exercise of my profession, nor should I seek to scamp my work in order to avoid the toil of it. "Work first and fee second" should be, therefore, the object of human industry. The fee is important, but work, to be well done, must be done for its own sake.

∞

God calls you to a unique vocation

We have each of us our vocation in life. Unfortunately the word *vocation* has become restricted to that particular form of life which includes only religious or priestly life; and, in consequence, the idea is not seldom to be found even among pious people that only those whom God has summoned to stand away from the cares and joys of normal existence have a calling from Him; all others are "in the world." This little phrase again suggests the same unjust belittling of the vocation of the layfolk, so that these are led not to realize the high importance of every profession of man or woman.

After all, the majority must marry and be given in marriage, must stay and help on the machinery of existence whereby the whole world goes round. It cannot be, then, only a minority whom God calls. Each of us has been placed here to do a certain work; each has his separate vocation, just as each, according to the scriptural expression, has been called by a separate name. In the Old Testament, this notion of a name whereby God knew us from all eternity is evidently only a way of expressing the particular office to which each of us is summoned in the economy of God.

How is it possible for me to know what my vocation is? There are certain obvious clues: my capacity for some particular form of life (whatever it may be that suggests itself), my desire for it, and the possibility for me to attempt it. All these are necessary; but perhaps my desire for the life is what most convinces me and least convinces others. We cannot explain, but are deeply conscious of, the appeal.

I must, therefore, make up my mind as regards my vocation. I must ask the advice of my confessor, my parents or guardians, and those who best know me. I have to consult my own inclinations, opportunities, and prospects. Then I have to pray for light and, finally, make up my own mind as to what profession in life it is to which God calls me.

But suppose I find out later that I ought to have been something else? That supposition is impossible if I have honestly made up my mind. Is it not possible for me to frustrate my vocation, to remain in the world when I should have entered the cloister? No, certainly not; so long as I honestly tried to make up my own mind. My conscience has judged as best it could, and God can ask no more from me. However, therefore, I eventually make my decision, so long as it is my conviction that God bids me do this or that, I must unfailingly, as far as may be, carry it through.

To stay and labor and marry requires, as much as does the priesthood, a separate and distinct call. Such a life is a holy and a sacred living. I must realize, therefore, that God has an interest in my life, and that should give a dignity to my whole view of my soul and its work here. What God has made, let no man call common or unclean. Whatever my line of life, I may be sure that I have received a divine calling to it.

Consequently, I must learn to be very patient with life. It is no use now longing for the peace of the cloister and wondering whether I was not called to that life. Every Catholic child feels, at one time in life, a desire for the religious state, but that fades with the many and continues in the few. But although all are not, cannot be, called to such a vocation, to each there is his own vocation.

God, indeed, has no need of any of us. Preacher, priest, worker, rich and poor, old and young may try to do their best; but all that they achieve their whole life through, God could have effected by the single act of His decree. Yet He has allowed me the high privilege of partaking with Him in the continuance of the world's history. He has allowed me to become a partner, a member of His firm, a helper in His voluntary aid society.

Perhaps I long to be this or that, feel powers within me that are clamorous for expression, yet find no opportunity to put them to their full advantage. I become miserable, discontented, perhaps bitter. Can I never learn that to wherever God calls me, the road must always lie open? If I cannot do what I would like, it is because what I like is not what He likes. There may be obstacles that I must endeavor to surmount, but do not let me become impatient of them. Perhaps my vocation is only to struggle, never to achieve. As a model husband, citizen, parishioner, nay, as a model Catholic, I have a vocation sacred and unique. I can imagine a higher vocation than I have, but, for myself, it is certain that there is not a holier one.

∞

Each person must follow his own path to God

I have my own pathway to God. I can find no one on earth with whom on every point I am in complete accord, and therefore I can find no other way to God than the way of my own being. Others may advise and help, but they can never know me really, for they have little else to go on for judgment except what I tell them myself, so that whatever they may say has to be modified and, as it were, edited before it can be of any use to me. Their counsel and directions are based upon their own experience, but of mine they know very little. After all, none other has had my life, my hereditary influences, my education at home and in school, my interests and hobbies and tastes and pleasures. In other words, I am myself different from anyone else, and, in the full sense of the word, unique.

It is for this reason that my prayers must be my own. No words of others, no books that others compose, can ever fitly represent the needs I have and the thanks I personally owe to the Creator, Redeemer, and Sanctifier. For the same reason also, I must continually remind myself that I have something to give God that He can get from none other. There are times when I cannot help wondering what use I am in the world to Him and how He could ever have sent me here at all. Then I have to realize that, however much I am a failure, stupid and sinful, yet because I am unique, I have a unique offering to make — that is, myself. God gets from me a peculiar glory that no other work of His hands can show, and therefore in me alone is some fragment of His splendor reflected. My own pathway to Him, however much it may resemble the ways of others, must be really my own, in the sense that it is, on the whole, different from every other.

Now, I have also to realize that as I am unique, so is everyone else. Just as my hereditary tendencies, my upbringing, my temperament, my mixture of faults and virtues, my ambitions, my hopes, my fears, my past, my present, and my future are entirely peculiar to myself, so also are to others their own tendencies and temperaments and tempers. All of them look out into the world from themselves as the central point; they are conscious of their own view of life as I am of mine. The universe is something my soul is aware of when it looks through the windows of the senses on the things and persons about it. As I am different from them, so are they also different from each other.

We are always repeating our wonder at the endless variety of nature, with every leaf and every flower and every sunset apart and alone and unique. We notice the monotony of life, yet have to confess that no day is really exactly like another; and although, to us, each sheep in a flock is exactly like the rest, yet, to the shepherd, each is absolutely distinct, with a character of its own. So God also tells us that He has called each of us by a name that from all eternity He has singled us out for Himself, that even the hairs of our head are numbered. So close an inventory has He made of our gifts, that our work is unique and alone. Each is a separate stone in the vast edifice that He is erecting to His own glory out of the sons of men.

As, therefore, on this account I claim for myself the right to go to God in my own way, accepting, of course, the truths and practices of the Church, so, precisely for that reason, must I also be willing to allow the same freedom to others. The rights I demand for myself are rights, not privileges; therefore, they must be conceded equally to all the world.

Therefore I must be tolerant. Each has his own way to God: I cannot pretend that I alone know the way in which He wishes to be served. I know, indeed, by faith that He has established His Church to be the sole teacher of truth, and therefore I try to bring all to this wonderful mistress of the ways of God. But, even so, I am certain that He does give the light of truth to all who serve Him, and if I find that what I say has no influence on my fellows, I can surely leave it to Him to guide them aright. If the need arises, He will send an angel from Heaven or a star to direct their feet.

And, again, within the Church the varieties of holiness are innumerable, the patterns of the saints endlessly diverse; to each, therefore, his own way, and I must be in no hurry to foist my own upon them. Nay, it is this very variety that produces the beauty of holiness in the world. Just as, in a garden, the loveliness of the effect is due to the shades of color, the diversity of form, and the contrast of flower with flower, so in the garden of God is it with the glowing differences of soul from soul.

Hence, it is noticeable in the lives of the saints that their own growing independence in life has effected an increasing tolerance. As they realized their own special calling (for to each living soul comes a distinct vocation), they came to recognize the sweet harmony that all these notes produced. "Such a man rejoices in everything. He does not make himself a judge of the servants of God nor of any rational creature; nay, he rejoices in every condition and every type he sees. . . . And he rejoices more in the different kinds of men he sees than he would do in seeing them all walk in the same way, for so he sees the greatness of God's goodness more manifest."[136]

[136] St. Catherine of Siena.

∽

Cheerfulness is good for your soul

Sin excepted, says St. Francis de Sales, that glad-hearted servant of God, there is nothing that does such harm as melancholy. St. Catherine of Siena goes even farther, for in one of her delightful letters to her friends, which are so alive with charm and banter, she writes to a young man who fancied that he had to be particularly gloomy because he wished to appear as a poet: "Is not sorrow the worst of all our sins?" It is true that this is merely a question, and therefore it may be said that she does not *say* that sorrow is so desperate a thing, but only asks whether it is or not. Yet even so for such a saint, with all a saint's horror of sin and her exquisite appreciation of the majesty of God, to declare melancholy worse than all other offenses or even to ask whether it is so or not, is a very large step to take, but it is one that it is perhaps of very great importance for us to take also.

St. Catherine is, indeed, famous for the exact theology of all her writings, so that we have no business to shrug our shoulders and put it all down to a woman's exaggeration. Nor need we go very far from our own hearts to find the precise meaning of this seemingly astonishing remark. We have only to watch ourselves when we are really at our worst, to understand the deep meaning of it and also to take comfort for ourselves in its lesson. Every priest who has had to deal with souls, anyone whose privilege it has been to share the secrets of another's experience, will repeat the same story. There is nothing that does us more harm than the feeling of melancholy or discouragement or hopelessness that too often comes over us when we have tried really hard and then fallen.

It is clear that neither St. Francis de Sales nor St. Catherine could ever really have meant that sorrow was, insofar as it is sinful, greater in gravity than any other sin. Obviously, all that they are referring to in sorrow are its effects on the soul, and here there is certainly reason in abundance for their saying. After all, it is not the fact that we have fallen that does us so much harm, but that discouragement makes us lie fallen. To have spurned God's love is indeed a terrible outrage on things human and divine, but to remain in the attitude of outrage — is not that worse still? To fall is bad enough, but why remain fallen?

Now, it is just this that discouragement produces in my soul. I try very hard to overcome some fault. Perhaps, by the kindness of God, to a certain extent I succeed. Then comes a catastrophe, and I find myself back again in all my old ways. The natural result of this is for me to say that there is no use in my going on trying. I have tried, and I have failed. Had I not better renounce any further attempts? But "is not sorrow the worst of all our sins?" Is it not far worse in its effects, for it reduces me to such a state of hopelessness that I despair of ever doing anything again?

It is worse, therefore, just in this: that it has a far more disastrous effect upon me. It numbs and paralyzes all effort. Has not the disheartenment that followed sin done me more harm than ever the sin did — driven me from God, or at least kept me at arm's length from God? When I examine my life, I am, in common honesty, obliged to confess that nothing has done me so much harm, injured my faith and hope and love half so much, as the state of depression into which I let myself fall.

Cheerfulness, then, and humor, are of very much need in the soul's life. The battle is half-won when you enter into it with a smile. To jog on through all the growing weariness of it, to stand the long hours under fire with few opportunities for doing anything, to bear with the dull and comfortless work of the trenches — all this requires a considerable amount of nerve, but it is achieved only through the inspiration of hope. Faced with the wear and tear of it, we shall surely fail unless we can keep our courage alive.

Notice how children smile bravely through their tears, pretending they are not in pain, when they know that their pain will make others sad, will even make the pain itself harder to bear. Of course, this means and entails a good deal of self-effacement. When self-love is hurt, it longs to air its grievances, it longs to tell everyone else of the troubles through which it has passed; nor can it listen in patience to the grumbles of others without wishing at once to answer them with its own tale of suffering.

Oh yes, it is not easy to put out of our minds every selfish notice of how others treat us, remembering all that they have done against us, and to be patient with the petty ways in which they snub us. Yet all the while, we have to carry our trouble patiently and bravely, not letting everyone enter into the secrets of the King.[137]

Because I have a headache, does everyone else in the house need to know about it? Why should I have a consuming desire to tell every person I meet all about my aches and pains? Do I not find it boring when others so pester me? Why, then, should I inflict mine on them? Or, again, my spiritual failings or the progress of my soul — are not these my affairs only, mine and God's?

All the world's a stage, and I am but a simple actor who must enter smiling, and leave that smile upon the faces of the audience.

[137] Cf. Tob. 12:7.

∞

Holiness means heroically facing life's difficulties, big and small

A saint, in the meaning of the Church, is not a mere ordinary Christian who at last has managed to enter the gates of Heaven, but is essentially a heroic soul. When the process of canonization is set in motion, the judges are not content with everyday goodness, with piety or charity or a quiet life of peace, such as could be discovered in almost any good Catholic house in all Christendom. They are on the lookout for something a great deal more vigorous than this. They are searching for such a love of God as shall be expressed in energetic and forcible ways, such a love as will do heroic things, raised above normal standards; often a scandal to some, who suppose it to be too tolerant or too intolerant according as their own measures are under- or oversized.

The phrase, indeed, in which this is expressed is "heroic sanctity." A saint, then, in this sense, is a hero — a man, woman, or child, with a genius for morality. Of course, everyone has in him or her some love of God, some goodness, just as everyone has some power of expressing himself in language; but as there are people whom we recognize at once as possessed of a special fluency and distinction of style, and whom we therefore regard as masters of literature, standing head and shoulders above the crowd, so also there are those whose very goodness has a distinction and a fluency that puts them in a category apart. They are God's heroes, the "arm-fellows of God," the saints. They are possessed of "heroic sanctity"; that is to say, they have expressed their love of God in a heroic degree.

When, then, I say to myself that God sent me here to love Him, that He has called me to Him and that, from time to time, I do feel that He wishes me to be a great deal closer to Him than I actually am, I am surely criticizing very severely my present way of life.

Is there, of a truth, much heroism in my method of carrying out the gospel? My hours of rising are regulated by my work; are they ever regulated by my piety? Weekday Mass persistently followed may be a difficulty, but it is certainly at least an occasional possibility. How many times do I assist on a weekday at that which I profess by Faith is the very Sacrifice of Calvary? It would be very hard to go regularly: precisely, it would be heroic — an outward and visible sign of an inward invisible love that passed the love of ordinary souls.

Nor is it merely in relation to God's worship that this heroism is to be shown. There is the monotonous grind of daily life. My charity, my patience, my tolerance, my truthfulness, my love of justice — are they not rather carelessly interpreted and put into practice? Is there much heroism in the way I manifest them? Perhaps I am very often repeating to myself that it is easy to be heroic; easy to die for one's Faith, but hard to live for it; easy to bear in patience the great sorrows of life, but difficult to put up with daily and hourly annoyances. But the heroic is precisely that which is most difficult; the word means no more than that. If, consequently, to live for one's Faith is harder than to die for it, then, of the two, to live for one's Faith is the more heroic. Perhaps, for certain souls, to bear quietly the breakup of a friendship (it is difficult to imagine anything more terrible in life) is not so trying as to refrain from impatience when, in a moment of hurry, a shoelace is broken. This last for them would be the true test of sanctity.

Now, have I not to confess that these true tests of holiness would find me, indeed, very far from success? Have I not avoided too often any way that seems to be rather out of the ordinary? I do not mind doing good, whereas it is of far greater importance to *be* good. For me, kindness, generosity even, may be cloaks of malice and excuses for not loving God. It is no use my being kind or philanthropic or prayerful unless God's love burns within me. If I have no charity, the rest profits me nothing. Just as it is possible that I may make fasting an excuse for omitting the weightier things of the law, so it may well be that I sweat my employees and build a hospital, am impatient at home and go out to console the sick. I am avoiding the heroic things and not in reality showing holiness.

Heroism consists in being heroic, and just as it is easier to do gentlemanly things than to be in one's soul a gentleman, so it is much easier to feed a starving foe, or to tend to him when he is wounded, or succor him when he is drowning, than to forgive, love, and pray for him when he is boastful and full of success. Yet this last is just what a saint and only a saint would do. It is heroism, or the love of God expressed in a heroic degree.

I must, then, realize my dignity as a Christian and see that in my vocation to follow Christ, it is just the difficult things that I must try to do, simply because I have first made my soul instinctively apprehend the spirit of Christ.

∞

Live your Faith generously,
not merely for rewards

There is but one thing incompatible with sanctity, and that is meanness. Sin may be found in the saints. In nearly every biography, we find the writer hard pressed in his attempts to defend some one action or other of his hero, and we prefer, perhaps, to skip the whole episode by admitting that no doubt the saints may have done wrong. They were human children of Adam, heirs to an imperfect nature, at best unprofitable servants.

Some, we are persuaded as we read their letters or their books, had a very quick temper, nor do they seem even at the end to have brought this wholly under control. Some, from what we can make out, must have been extremely difficult to get along with, disagreeable and meddlesome by nature and not wholly to have overcome this defect by grace. Some, again, had lapses from discretion and provoked evils they had steadily endeavored to avoid. But in none do we ever notice any real meanness. For a saint is one who loves God heroically; and a hero has no place for littleness in his soul.

People are sometimes known to be pious and good yet incredibly mean, with petty jealousies and narrow suspicions, and an intolerant attitude toward sinners. Indeed, piety, in its least pleasant sense, flourishes at times in those souls who are incapable of any-thing great and for whom the sanctity and the sin of the Magdalen are alike impossible. But these are not the saints, who are God's chosen ones; they have not that characteristic of heroism which is altogether inseparable from real saints. We can quite easily sup-pose the saints to be sinners (indeed, they were saints only because they had realized themselves as sinners). We cannot at all imagine the saints to have been mean.

Now, this generosity that we associate with holiness is not an act so much as a state, an attitude toward life, or rather, the values of life. It bases itself upon the very simple principle that the more a thing costs, the more it is appreciated. When people say to you that they cannot see the good of religion, you can be sure that reli-gion has certainly never cost them anything; nay, there is no rea-son for me to go outside my own heart, for I can be sure that, in my spiritual life, what I least value has cost me least. At times, I find myself saying that I would be willing, eager, to sacrifice a good deal for God if I could only taste and see His sweetness; that I would gladly spend more time in prayer and meditation and the thought of divine things, but that I get no good out of them, and find my-self no better; that I would willingly suffer if I could only obtain that peace of soul which alone makes suffering bearable.

What really do I mean by all this? Simply that I will not work except for a reward. Surely it is precisely this that so many of our non-Christian friends are always telling us: that Christianity is not at all self-sacrificing, but is really incredibly selfish, only it is self-ish for rewards that do not happen to appeal to most people. Surely my life does in some sort justify this taunt. I do find myself building upon foundations other than Christ laid down; for it is His way al-ways first to give freely, and from the very freedom of the gift to find the recompense. Never surely did His soul overflow so fiercely with the joy of the spirit as when, after death, He passed out into peace; never surely, if it may be said with reverence, did He love

453

the human race so well as when He died for it. Just as we can see how valuable we must be to Him to have cost Him His life, may we not almost say that it was when dying to save us that He saw the greatest possibility of goodness in us?

A generous soul, therefore, throws over all those ideas and principles that are really at heart selfish. I must first pay the cost if I would obtain the benefit. It is no use my saying that I will put off going to daily Mass until such a time as I can really get good out of it, for that will never be until I have actually practiced going. I must first attend at some personal inconvenience to myself before I can hope for my dryness to be softened by the falling of God's gentle dew upon it. To buy cheaply is to lose the value of a thing. "Easy come, easy go" we say of certain ways of acquiring wealth: the money has come without effort; with as little effort will it be spent. But to the man who has stinted himself to save enough to buy some cherished thing — a book, a work of art, or a seat at the opera — the high privilege he has won is a privilege indeed. The child the mother most loves is the one who has cost her most dear.

We wonder sometimes why those we have loaded with favors are so ungrateful; they are ungrateful for what we have done, just because they had everything given to them. Had they obtained these things at a cost to themselves, they would have held them dear. So, in my life, the sacrifice must come first; it is prayers said with difficulty that in the end will be of most avail. To enjoy life, I must lose it; to love the world, I must be crucified for it; to love God, I must have sacrificed to Him not the worn-out end of my days, but my noblest, highest, and best.

Christ is an example of politeness

Politeness often seems the most charming of natural virtues, but it is almost the least common of supernatural virtues. It is really astonishing to notice the large number of pious people who have absolutely no appearance of politeness, and who exhibit extreme difficulty in trying to be polite. Perhaps this may be due in part to an intense desire to speak and act truly, and a feeling that this is incompatible with politeness.

How is it possible for me to be courteous if I really show my genuine opinion and feeling on every occasion? If my life is really honest in deed and word, shall I not be obliged to act in a manner extremely disagreeable to my fellows? They will continuously be demanding praise when I can only blame. Surely, then, it is argued, it would be better to give up all this conventional and artificial politeness and revert to that better attitude of truth.

Sometimes it is obvious that the real trouble is not an endeavor to achieve truth, but carelessness, thoughtlessness of the feelings of others. Even people whose lives are in many ways edifying have this startling omission: they neglect to consider their fellows.

But a further excuse is sometimes brought forward — namely, that the character of our Lord warrants such a disregard of these conventions. His figure is outlined to us as that of a puritan, whose speech was "Yea, yea," and "Nay, nay,"[138] and who never spoke at all unless there was direct and serious need. They picture Him to us without charm or gracefulness, a Baptist with the rugged ways of a prophet, whose business it was to denounce perpetually whatever pleased mankind. In their attempt to excuse their own want of tenderness and their awkwardness of mind and manner, they endeavor to make our Lord after their own image and likeness.

Of course, in reality, our blessed Lord is the very opposite of what they would make Him out to be. The strong and denunciatory side of His life is only one aspect of a character that was divinely complex. It was certainly the side that least appeared to His contemporaries; for them, there was contrast rather than comparison between Christ and the Baptist. Our Lord consorted with publicans and sinners, did not teach His disciples to fast, and was so far removed from the sternness and ruggedness of the desert-preacher that the accusation leveled against Him was that He was a glutton and a wine-bibber.[139]

The miracles that He wrought were evidence of His wonderful tenderness and showed, as the Evangelists intended that they should, that He had compassion upon the people. Moreover, they were performed with a gracefulness that doubled the value of His kindness. He "wrought all kind of service with a noble ease / That graced the lowliest act in doing it."[140] On one occasion, He feeds four thousand in the desert, but He carefully selects for this a spot where "there was much grass in the place,"[141] thus choosing to make His miracle all the more welcome. His very generosity was done politely, thoughtfully. His rebukes have the same charm, unless they happen to be launched against hypocrisy, which can be

[138] Cf. Matt. 5:37.
[139] Cf. Matt. 11:19.
[140] Alfred Lord Tennyson, "Idylls of the King."
[141] John 6:10.

cured only by being broken. Notice His delicate treatment of the woman taken in adultery, the polite tenderness: "Has no man condemned thee? . . . Neither will I condemn thee. Go thou and sin no more."[142] In that last phrase is His only recognition of her fault.

I must make careful examination of my own ways of acting. How far are my acts of kindness spoiled by the manner in which they are done? Perhaps I go out of my way to help people, but perhaps also my very attempts to help them are done in so thoughtless a way that I succeed only in crossing their tempers and irritating them. There are people I meet in life who, in conferring a favor on me, seem to impress me with the fact that it is I who am doing them a favor. Am I like that, or are my favors plainly favors? Do I ever take the trouble to hide from the people I benefit the fact that it is a sacrifice to me? May not my generosity be more intolerable than my meanness, not in its matter, but in its manner?

Or do I follow the gentle spirit of Christ and look upon politeness as a necessary condition of all true charity? The titter of laughter at a social mistake, the hardness of speech that is brutal in its frankness, and the scorn lavished on all attempts at making repentance easy to the sinner are surely not as we have learned from Christ. It is possible, indeed, that I do not realize how rude I am, for each of us is immoderately quick to claim always a sense of humor, an experience with the deepest suffering, an instinctive tact, whereas all these three great gifts are the privilege of only rare souls. Politeness means thoughtfulness, and is due especially to the poor, to all in discomfort, to the old, to the afflicted, and to children. It is frequently neglected by me because I happen to be in a hurry, and if I am one of those people who are always in a hurry, I can take it for granted that I shall always be neglecting opportunities of politeness.

Let me be very attentive to other people, have a remembrance of their troubles, and never be eager to announce to them my own.

[142] John 8:10-11.

∞

The Christian life calls for obedience

Obedience is an essential of the religious life, but it is no less essentially the virtue of the Christian life; it is an essential for all those who would follow Christ.

The gospel story, indeed, reads in that sense like a Greek tragedy, for there is a persistent insistence upon the idea of necessity working its way throughout. When watching the tragic plays of the great poets, we feel that the characters are like puppets in the hands of some higher power. Struggle as they may against the fatal end, they are driven resistlessly to the divine purpose; the human will is forced to accept the divine.

Of course, as Christians, we know this to be untrue, because the will is free; yet, for all that, we are assured that the plan of God is never disarranged. "I come to do the will of Him that sent me"[143] is a refrain that comes repeatedly in the fourth Gospel; and as a counterpoint, we have His relief when all is ended: "I have finished the work Thou gavest me to do."[144] It was this, too, that His last conscious breath confessed: "It is consummated."[145]

[143] John 5:30; 6:38.
[144] John 17:4.
[145] John 19:30.

Even in the Synoptic Gospels (as the first three Gospels are called), where the dramatic side of Christ's life is obscured, or at least not brought out in full detail, we read of His saying to the protesting Apostles, "It is necessary that the Son of Man should die."[146] His life, then, for Him was planned along simple lines: it meant that He came into the world to do a certain definite work, and that He was straitened until it should be accomplished.[147] His idea of goodness consisted almost wholly in this immediate subjection to His Father. His model prayer contained it; His own prayer in the Garden meant little else; His chosen ones were not those who said "Lord, Lord" but those who did the will of the Father.[148]

What, then, became a dominant principle in our Lord's life must become equally the dominant principle of mine: obedience. It helps to make life so much simpler, and the good life a thing of practical clearness.

First of all, I have to get pretty clearly into my head what it is that God requires of me, and this itself means a good deal. I find myself a child in a family, a citizen in a state, a worker under some employer, a Catholic member of a church. Here, then, straight-away I am subject to four separate authorities and have to discover the rules and requirements of each. I have to find out for myself what orders these four authorities lay upon me and the limits of the obedience they may claim. There will be a great easing of my troubles when I have become convinced of these things. It shows me at least some of my pathway and prevents, to a certain extent, my stumbling. I must, therefore, discover these four leading sources of governance, their actual and binding commands, and then fulfill them to the best of my ability.

[146] Cf. Luke 24:7.
[147] Cf. Luke 12:50.
[148] Matt. 7:21.

Secondly, it will be of importance for me to find out further to what vocation God calls me, for I am convinced that there is a certain work in the world that God has created me to perform for Him. Each has his vocation, and each has his capacities for that vocation. God wants me for some purpose. What is that purpose? Unless I can find it out, I can never say, "I have finished the work Thou gavest me to do." This vocation will be disclosed to me in different ways, and it will be added to indifferently throughout life by countless opportunities for doing good that will be continually opening to me. I must obey in lawful command those lawfully set above me, and must follow the calling marked out for me by God.

Obedience is indeed a law in all finite things, for the Infinite can obey nothing but Itself. But in the grades of finite creation, "we may observe that exactly in proportion to the majesty of things in the scale of being is the completeness of their obedience to the laws that are set over them. Gravitation is less quietly, less instantly, obeyed by a grain of dust than it is by sun and moon; and the ocean falls and flows under influences which the lake and river do not recognize." Ruskin's physics may, in this example, be not entirely accurate, but they form an allegory, for it is certainly true that the higher in the scale of being, the more exacting the commands.

Obedience, therefore, does not debase, but rather exalts mankind. It is the sign of the nearness of our approach to Christ, and in Christ it is the sign of the complete union between His will and intelligence and the will and intelligence of God the Father. The superman, whom our generation has been taught to honor by prophets of Prussia and the philosophers of our own press, is placed above all law, unrestrained by morality or any other hampering influence. Yet when I analyze what it all means, I find that even the superman rests upon obedience — that is, the obedience of others. And if this obedience is good for their characters, then it is justified as being beneficial; but if it spoils them, then the superman stands self-condemned. And if he himself, above all law, is to govern by his whim or fancy, then reason itself is overthrown and all the arguments in favor of his supremacy have lost their value.

The gospel of anarchy is a contradiction, for it teaches the law that there is no law, but I, although the child "of an age that knows not how to obey," must endeavor to copy in my life the obedience of Christ.

∞

Be yourself in your spiritual life

To be original by effort is to destroy the whole purpose of originality, for it is the sole justification of exceptional conduct that it
should be natural and spontaneous. Now, by striving to be original, I am obviously striving for effect, am obviously unnatural, and
shall be found as a result to be merely aping another's ways. It is evident, indeed, that nearly all rules have to be broken through; for
it is certain that, under stress of great passion or unusual enthusiasm, the ordinary vehicles will be too hopelessly slow-footed to
reach so immediate a goal. The language, or the forms of art, or the
material out of which the masterpiece is to be manufactured can
never be so facile as to represent the swiftly changing emotions of
a man who is charged with the vehemence of life.

It is this which is the only valid justification of originality. It
means, in other words, that, by violating ordinary rules and traditions, some emotion or truth can be expressed that can be expressed in no other way and is, further, worth expressing.

Here, then, it is clear that we are in no way straining ourselves
to be other than we are; we ape no fashions of another that appeal
to our fancy or attract attention. In faith, originality can be shown
by looking at things in a fresh way, but not by any fantastic interpretation that robs truth of half its meaning or magnifies to excess

the restrained truth that it enshrines. In life, originality is seen in those who adapt themselves wisely to the ideas of the new generation and swiftly seize on those modern things which prove the living value of humanity. Originality is justified when a man is driven by the inadequacy of material or form to employ the means at his disposal in a new way.

Originality consists, then, rather in the way a thing is done, either by the employment of old material in a new mode, or by boldly seizing a new material for the old purpose. In either case, the material or form must be inadequate, and are momentarily to be set aside so as better to express something that, in their customary manner, they would be unable to do.

It may, indeed, be made a matter of most interesting discussion as to which is really the higher type of mind: the man who can take over everything as it was before his time and without violating any traditions, and so transform the old with the freshness of his own spirit as to give it the appearance of something entirely new; or the man who finds everything of his own period so hampering and confining that, to fulfill his purpose, he is driven to break all laws and evolve for himself new rules and new traditions. These will, no doubt, in time become as classical as those he overthrew, and the new rebel will, when old, become a master. But, for the time, he has had too much originality to stay within the fold. Surely the greater mind is precisely that which bears the stamp of originality most easily and naturally.

The type that we should, above all others, idealize is that which dispenses with materials and rules so inevitably that it will be impossible, after the event, to devise any other way in which the same idea could be so well expressed. Here is the very essence of the problem. Originality must spring from the nature of the man, must well up from the individuality of his thoughts. Once an effort to break away from tradition is introduced, the strain is obvious to all. A man who toils with pain will be with equal pain welcomed.

Now, this is true of all human life, for it is in his own life that each of us is a real artist, and out of it he must carve his masterpiece to be presented to God. It is no use for me to form the fashion of my own life even on the model of a saint's life, for the result will certainly not adequately represent my own capabilities. I am an individual soul, and I have to get to Heaven in my individual way. I have the example of the saints, who are as different from each other as are the flowers in a garden. The examples are various, at times contradictory, but in no single case can I find a saint, living or dead, who completely realizes my ideal.

I must, therefore, see always that, as far as may be, I follow the lines of my own nature. I must ape nobody else, but must see my own gifts and use them in my own way, or else will my soul be cramped where it should have been given full play, and enlarged where it was not rich enough for expansion.

By being myself quite simply, I am original and give to God what no one else can give Him. When I imitate others, God is getting only secondhand offerings; when I am myself, He receives a unique testimony. Every system will fail at last. For the moment, stiff arrangements of prayer, meditation, and life may bring about success, but at the cost of my individuality; and my soul will suffer the torments of a tortured conscience. Faith and morals are laid down for me by the Church; and these principles are enough, because they are divine. The rest — the examples of saints, the fashions of prayer, the systems of meditation — if I am to be myself, can never satisfy until I have made them my own. Christ alone, God as well as man, infinite as well as finite, can supply a model capable of imitation without the destruction of individuality.

∞

The absence of religious feelings
is good for your spiritual life

Consider the immense power that feelings have over us! Our whole attitude toward life, our efforts at improvement, or the ceasing of all effort, are unfortunately very largely affected by our feelings. Prayers are often taken up and then dropped simply because we do not feel in the mood. We seem to think that God is pleased, not by our prayers, but by how we feel during our prayers, and suppose ourselves to be saints when we feel saints, and sinners when we feel sinners; while probably the very opposite is true. For, on the whole, we may be certain that we are never nearer to God than when we feel furthest away from Him.

I find myself distressed when my thanksgivings after Communion are dull and cold, when I do not experience any of those waves of emotion with which, I fondly imagine, everyone else is thrilled. Perhaps if I looked into every other soul in the church, I would find them very much as mine, and if I looked into the heart of God, I would find that He was content.

But first I have to impress upon myself the fact that I have very little command over my feelings; indeed, I suppose that is really my very complaint, whereas it should be my excuse. I would like to feel the sweetness of His presence, and I do not feel it. Is that my fault? Not at all! For evidently I *want* to feel it; therefore, as far as I am concerned, I should be experiencing the very raptures of the blessed. The reason, then, that prevents me is evidently beyond my control. Instead of losing heart, therefore, let me *take* heart, for the cause of the trouble is not mine to remedy. It is probably some external thing — weather, health, digestion — that adds or takes away my feelings in my prayers.

If, then, I cannot produce at will the several emotions proper to the occasion, the fault evidently does not lie with me, is in fact no fault at all. I cannot be held responsible for lacking what is not, indeed cannot be, under my control. Inability, therefore, to feel devout, to enjoy one's prayers, to find pleasure in visits to the Blessed Sacrament, to taste the sweetness of Holy Communion, to discover sensible sorrow for my weekly or monthly tale of sins, to thirst for the rewards of Heaven or even to understand that they are rewards at all, to appreciate with proper devotion the pageant of the Mass, and so forth is not sinful, since it is not willful or deliberate.

Try as I may, I cannot command these feelings. The speaker whose kindling words rouse my enthusiasm and work me up to a pitch of emotional frenzy has more command over my feelings than I have myself. In fact, I might almost make it out as a principle of psychology that others have always more control or more effective influence over my emotions than I have myself. They are more likely to compel me to weep, to love, and to laugh than I can force myself to do.

But then I must deliberately realize that religion cannot be built up out of such frail and uncertain material. The city of God rests upon foundations surer than these that ebb and flow; it is upon the reason and the will that the whole fabric must be reared. As long as my will is turned to God and endeavors to keep hold of Him, to follow His teaching, to obey His law, I am doing the best I can, and He can expect no more of me than that.

Can I not really go one step further? Not only can I not control my feelings, and not only, therefore, does their absence prove no sin to me, but is it not very much better for me that these should rather be against me than with me? Are not my prayers really more valuable just because they have no such accompanying thrills of pleasure? For consider that the object of the Christian life is union with God, and that this union is, for the Christian, achieved by self-surrender, which is itself stimulated by the example of Christ and by His merits, communicated through the sacraments.

Now, to obtain self-surrender, I must above all else be unselfish, and therefore probably shall have to battle against all the instincts of my nature. My talks with God, my prayers, sacraments, and so forth must be supernaturalized, deliberate. But if these pious exercises brought with them such torrents of delights, would there not be a danger of my taking them up, not because they were a duty but because they were a pleasure, not because I wished to be unselfish but because I thought only of myself?

But actually I have no such temptations. If I persevere in my prayers, then my efforts are certainly supernatural, for there are no natural motives for continuing them. I get no delight, no repayment; of my good works it cannot be said, as once it was to the Pharisee, that I have already had my reward,[149] for so far I have found no reward. To go through all my exercises of piety is, moreover, my only way of love — not that sensible love which keeps me alive and active in my human friendships, but a deeper love that follows upon duty done, a love that hastens after its Lover, not for the consolations that He gives, but for Himself.

---

[149] Matt. 6:2.

∞

Sentiment has a place in the Christian life

I cannot control my emotions, cannot command my sentiments or feelings. Well, then, let me beware lest I undervalue them, for their influence upon life is enormous.

Stop and think how much of the day is arranged for by mere sentiment. My hours of rising, of business, are regulated by little else; or at least by custom, which is largely sentiment crystallized. For I can soon notice that different nations have their different hours when the streets are busy or silent, and the variety is based not merely on climate, but on that vague and uncertain principle "We have always done so."

Again, the arrangement of my room, the knick-knacks upon the mantelpiece, the pictures on the walls, the photographs, indeed the very idea of having photographs at all — are not all these things due entirely to sentiment? My day, my work, my pleasure, the things with which I surround myself, my calling in life, my prayers, my home — are they not one and all steeped in emotions, dominated by emotions, ruled and regulated by emotions?

I say that I cannot control my emotions. Can I say as truly that they do not control me?

Before answering that question, let me be clear upon this point: emotions are not necessarily unreasonable. Occasionally something is dismissed as being "mere sentiment"; now, the fact of anything being merely sentimental does not degrade it at all, for in some ways and at some moments our emotions are the finest things we have. Men are, in given instances, at their best when they obey instinctively the call of emotion; and what puts reasoning beings at their best cannot fairly be called unreasonable.

I must, therefore, start with the idea that very much of my life, and of the life of the race, is governed by reasons of sentiment. There is no contradiction in this phrase, since sentiment in man can be reasonable. Now, when I have faced that fact deliberately and begun to realize its meaning, I can then go on to consider sentiments and so forth in relation to religion. I find that, in dealing with my fellows, and in dealing with myself, sentiment plays a considerable part, and that it does so (when under proper safeguards) without any harm either to them or to myself; in fact, the world would be harder and poorer if sentiment was barred out.

Hence, I expect to find the same in my relationship to God — namely, that sentiment should have its place in the united and harmonious worship that my whole being renders to its Maker. A religion, therefore, that neglects, ignores, or denounces whatever is sentimental simply because it is sentimental, stands itself condemned, for it is the religion not of man, but of only a part of him. It is inhuman; it can have effect only upon a starved and stunted portion of mankind, and then only for a time. My worship of God, and therefore my religion, must appeal to the whole man; it must induce me to put into His hands the whole offering of myself. Puritanism may work wonders of good when it follows upon a period of laxity and disorder, but it cannot last. It holds the seeds of its own decay, since it scorns a part of nature and makes Christianity not a fulfilling but a distinction of the law. My dealings with my fellows, my dealings with myself, and my dealings with God will all be considerably affected by sentiment. And if religion is to rule me all the day, it must rule all of me.

I should, therefore, be very careful that my attitude toward sacred things does not become harsh, gloomy, unnatural, or inhuman. It is one thing to say that I cannot control my feelings, and quite another to say that I should ignore them. It is one thing to say that my prayers are likely to become more deliberately supernatural if they are untouched by feeling of pleasure, and quite another to say that, therefore, we must abolish feelings. I cannot repose on feelings, but that is no reason for expelling them.

St. Gregory wrote to St. Augustine, in England, not to destroy, but to hallow to divine service the heathen temples of our Saxon forefathers.[150] Let me, too, consecrate to God that buoyancy and gladness of soul which is all too frequently supposed to be a sign of the pagan joy of life. It is not pagan, but human and, like the rest of man's nature, needs to be baptized unto Christ. If my devotions tend to cast out love, to sneer at the poetic side of religion, to crush enthusiasm or gracefulness or youthfulness, then I must be on my guard at once, for such devotions cannot last. My faith should not be uncouth, rigid, stilted, or repulsive, but glad, easy, and natural. Devotion to the comeliest of the sons of men, the thought of His beautiful boyhood, of the firm majesty of His splendid manhood, will keep supple the sinews of love. The ideal of God's maiden Mother, pure, yet womanly, the Mother of fair love, will prevent my emotions from becoming divorced from religion and growing befouled.

---

[150] St. Gregory I (d. 604), Pope from 590, writer, and Doctor; St. Augustine of Canterbury (d. c. 605), Bishop.

∞

Live your Faith thoroughly

Somehow or other, although it is bewailed by many who describe themselves as having lost it, fervor has about it a rather unpleasant sound. It seems to suggest an individual with an extreme love of singularity, who carries his or her head slightly on one side, adopting this quaint posture in times of public service or generally in church, and is endowed with a bustling activity that meddles with everybody and everything. With sublime superciliousness we look on fervor as an unpleasant gift, the particular attribute of the Latin races, the Celts, and a large proportion of girls. It would be possible to take the ordinary notion of a fervent Catholic and define him to be an interfering person with much pretension to piety, but of such a kind as varies from season to season.

Now, of course, this is not fervor at all. The critical busybody probably has no conception of what fervor means; for people of this type owe their characteristics very largely to temperament, and depend not unfrequently for their restless and disturbing influence far more on the color of their hair than on any spirit of God. Such supposed fervor, frequently inspired by the best heart in the world, is supposed, by those who indulge in it, to be of the very essence of the Faith, whereas it does an immense amount of harm to the Faith by making people to suppose that Catholicism means chiefly a burning desire to set right everyone but oneself. And exaggerated postures at prayer do much to disgust others with religion and bring in a notion that talking to God is unnatural, stilted, unmanly, and conducted chiefly for the benefit of spectators.

All this, then, shows us what fervor is not, but when we turn to discover what exactly it is, we shall find it extremely difficult to define it in its spiritual significance. Feelings, we say as Catholics, have no lot or part in supernatural religion in the sense that we do not deepen our holiness by them. My feeling good is no guarantee that I *am* good; because I feel devout in my prayers, I have no right to suppose my prayers to be in consequence any more pleasing to God. Whether our feelings are present or absent does not in itself affect our fervor one way or the other. We must exclude, therefore, the emotional side from our notion of what is meant by it.

But if it is at all possible in one single word to sum up what we conceive fervor of soul to signify, perhaps it would be better to say that it stands for thoroughness in religion. A fervent Catholic is a Catholic who is absolutely thorough in his Faith. He performs all, and more than all, his duties with a promptness, a regularity, and a cheerfulness, extending to every detail of a complicated existence. Nothing escapes the principles or application of his Faith.

But perhaps it will be suggested that thoroughness is not so much fervor itself as an effect of it; and this may indeed be a more accurate description of the process. Yet for all practical purposes, we may test our fervor, not by our feeling but by our thoroughness. It is the slipshod way of gabbling prayers, dodging or deferring duties, or sheltering our laziness under the excuse of ill-health that betrays its absence.

Praxiteles, the Greek sculptor who carved even the backs of the statues on the frieze of the Parthenon, because although men did not see, the gods did, was a fervent, because thorough, artist.

I must, therefore, see whether in my spiritual life I am so poor a workman as to scamp my work. I probably find myself denouncing laboring folk and commercial people generally for doing as little as they can in their contract work. Now just let me realize that I, too, am a laborer. I am given my life so that I may build up something out of it to be, as well as I can make it, worthy of God. I am a spiritual bricklayer. How is my work done? Do I take an interest in the thing growing under my hands? Is each brick carefully placed and steadily fixed in position? Is the full time given to my work — none of it idled away? Is my choice of material exercised with a view to the bettering of the thing done, or do I merely seize on the nearest things to hand, broken ends, or rubble, or bricks that I see are flawed?

This may seem fantastic and too metaphorical. Well, then, let me take my own profession. Is it a pride to me that all that is turned out from my business is as good as any other firm can do it? Should I, then, be ashamed if my professional life was as hastily rushed through, as foolishly left incomplete, as is the spiritual life by which, in the abstract, I set such store? A firm that makes its boast that no inferior goods leave its factories or its business houses has what may be called commercial fervor; but when it begins to give up its high standard of work, we note that it is near its fall. People will soon lose confidence in it. Its pride in its work has gone, and the loss of pride precedes a fall.

Such honest pride, too, I must take in my soul. I must be an industrious apprentice, a worthy journeyman, a willing and competent laborer, a painstaking artist. In all the work of my soul I must be, above all things, thorough, and I shall then be fervent.

ornamental flourish

Form your life after Christ's

Our power of influencing matter is limited to the form. We can affect only the transitory, for the rest endures. If I am given a piece of wood, I can carve it or burn it or destroy it utterly; but that does not mean more than that I can change its form, for even when I appear to destroy it, all that I am really doing is resolving it into other chemical elements. "Matter," scientists say, "is indestructible," and they undoubtedly declare a fact. A candle burning until it is extinguished has ceased to exist as a candle, but that of which it was originally composed yet remains constant. It has changed its form, but the matter still persists and, through each successive crisis, remains unchanged, save for the mere method of its existence.

Thus also, industrial perfection can do nothing more than transform raw material into a finished article or, by the mere process of traffic, shift an object of exchange from a glutted market to one where a demand in effective force exists for it. We are dealing, in the phrase of John Stuart Mill, with "form-values."

To the form of a thing, therefore, are all our energies limited; the matter lies beyond us. Of course, herein lies a deep difference between us and God, for it is open to His power to create and annihilate — that is, to call the substance itself out of nothingness and to reduce it to nothingness again. This is a divine attribute that cannot be communicated to creatures. To God alone is it possible to produce such an effect, for to Him alone is the material itself in its existence and in its essence obedient in all that goes to make it up and in the very fact that it exists. To Him the matter and the form, to us the form alone.

Yet this need not be considered really much of a limitation, since the form, transitory though it be, is of much greater importance to us than the material that endures. It is the form that gives value to the whole. Things are governed by their form in their movement, activity, and speed. It is the shape of the falling body, as St. Thomas most accurately notices, that accelerates or retards its progress, although the weight, too, has to be considered.

Again, in so delicate a thing as an instrument of music, it is surprising what an effect the very shape (apparently so accidental) has upon the sound. And in matters connected with precious stones, it is obvious also how enormously their value is enhanced or depreciated by their being well or ill cut.

Form, which seems so trifling, means so much. It dominates matter, and it does an even more wonderful thing: it dominates the soul. St. Paul, it is noticeable, always speaks of life in terms of movement, and describes Christ as taking the form of a servant and as being the figure of God's substance. He seems, that is, to lay special emphasis on the fact that it is the nature of man and the nature of God, the resemblance to both, that made the Hypostatic Union (the union of these two natures in one Divine Person) the explanation of the Incarnation. And as of Christ, the form of man and God was of such ineffable consequence, so also of the human soul; although the matter (so to say) of it is beyond our control, the form of it, in the language of St. Paul, is of practical importance, for that we can mold as we will. "Be not conformed to this world, but be reformed in the newness of your mind."[151]

[151] Cf. Rom. 12:2.

Here, in this phrase, we are taught as a conclusion that the soul, of itself, chameleon-like, tends to adopt the appearance of its environment. The form of it, which governs its movement, its value, and its purpose is of such importance that with it alone lies the power of human energy.

But St. Paul teaches more than that, for in the very structure of the sentence he lets us see the difficulties of our life. To "conform" is the word he uses as regards our attitude to the world, and to conform is the easy way of suiting myself to what is done around me; I do as others do, I follow the flowing tide, I take the line of least resistance. But to "reform" is to react with deliberate effort against the tendency of my nature and of all surrounding influences. By reforming, I take the line of greatest resistance.

I cannot create my soul, nor can I annihilate it, for thus to act is the high and incommunicable privilege of God; but as I have been given my soul, I have a power of forming it after what fashion I will. I am limited, indeed, to this single act; but this is only just such a limitation as can give a definiteness to my work that would otherwise be wanting. If we could annihilate ourselves at will, how impetuously would the impetuous rush upon their ruin and the scrupulous hover doubtingly over their self-slaughter.

It is the form, then, that I can influence, and therein I find work enough, for it is the form that molds the action of the soul. Here it is good for me to consider that, unless I take deliberate care, I shall simply copy the life around me. I shall conform to the spirit of the world in which I am immersed. But to achieve that newness of mind whereby I am formed after the fashion of Christ, I must make careful scrutiny of myself, and, contrasting myself with that Divine Model, reform my soul gradually to that perfect pattern.

Bede Jarrett, O.P.
(1881-1934)

Born in England in 1881, Cyril Jarrett received the name Br. Bede when he took the Dominican habit in 1898 at Lancashire. He studied at Oxford and at Louvain, where he received an additional degree in theology. After his ordination to the priesthood in 1904, he was stationed at St. Dominic's Priory in London. At the age of 33, he was named Prior there and, just two years later, was elected Provincial — an office he would hold for the rest of his life, being re-elected an unprecedented four times.

In addition to attending to his duties as Provincial, which included opening a new church and priory in London, he undertook a demanding schedule of preaching and lecture engagements in England and abroad, and he established an ongoing series of Thomistic lectures in London. Among his scholarly contributions were several historical studies, as well as a lively biography of St. Dominic.

Fr. Jarrett looked upon life as a great adventure, and this joyful spirit pervades and characterizes his writings, which combine a solid foundation in Church doctrine with a down-to-earth insight applicable to everyday living. Reflecting his great understanding of human nature and the mercy and love of God, Fr. Jarrett's works continue to inspire people in all walks of life.